THEIR DARKEST DAY

THE TRAGEDY OF PAN AM 103
AND ITS LEGACY OF HOPE

Matthew Cox
AND **Tom Foster**

GROVE WEIDENFELD

New York

Published by Grove Weidenfeld
A division of Grove Press, Inc.
841 Broadway
New York, NY 10003-4793

Published in Canada by General Publishing Company, Ltd.

Library of Congress Cataloging-in-Publication Data

Cox, Matthew.
   Their darkest day : the tragedy of Pan Am 103 and its legacy of
hope / by Matthew Cox and Tom Foster.—1st ed.
      p.   cm.
   Includes bibliographical references.
   ISBN 0-8021-1382-6 (acid-free paper)
   1. Pan Am Flight Bombing Incident, 1988.   2. Victims of terrorism
—Case studies.   I. Foster, Tom.   II. Title.
HV6431.C695   1992
363.12'465'0941483—dc20   91-33079
                                                     CIP

Manufactured in the United States of America

Printed on acid-free paper

Designed by Irving Perkins Associates

First Edition 1992

10   9   8   7   6   5   4   3   2   1

To the 270 people murdered in Lockerbie

For my wife, Anne, and for the twins, Clara and Molly
M. C.

For Anne, Kelly, my parents, and M. B. Payne
T. F.

ACKNOWLEDGMENTS

MANY PEOPLE helped with this book. The authors are especially grateful to Eric Harper for his research assistance and for his foreign-language translations.

For their support, guidance, counsel, and assistance, the authors also wish to express their thanks to the following:

Jan-Olof Bengtsson, Jane Dystel, Anne, Ava, Howard, and Kelly Foster, Jussi Karlgren, Adrienne Kantz, Honorable Mr. Justice B. N. Kirpal, Clara Knowles, John Lammers, Linda Mack, Randy McMullen, Anne Moore-Cox, Bryan Oettel, Pat Robinson, Frank Ryan, Maurice Smith, Pat Trainham, and Isaac Yeffet.

We also wish to recognize the management and our colleagues at the *Post-Standard*, particularly Stephanie Gibbs and Jonathan Salant, whose thorough and sensitive coverage accounts for portions of this book.

Others in the United States, Great Britain, and Germany who provided information on security procedures, intelligence, and the criminal investigation cannot be acknowledged by name, but their assistance is no less appreciated.

Above all, this work would not have been possible without the cooperation and time extended by so many of the relatives and friends of the victims. To this extraordinary group of people, the authors owe their deepest gratitude.

CONTENTS

PREFACE

THE NEWS arrived in a wire service bulletin and made its way through our newsroom in Syracuse, New York, like the chilling December winds outside. A Pan Am jumbo jet filled with holiday travelers had crashed in Lockerbie, Scotland, on its way from London to New York. There appeared to be no survivors.

We were both reporters for the *Post-Standard*, the city's morning newspaper, and we soon learned that two hundred and seventy people had been killed, including thirty-five students enrolled in a Syracuse University overseas study program. Normally the week before Christmas is one of the slowest of the year for us, but on December 21, 1988, the newsroom was awash in activity. As people turned off their Christmas lights and Syracuse grew darker, reporters for the paper began the most difficult work of their careers. Within hours, one of us was at John F. Kennedy International Airport in New York, where Pan Am Flight 103 had been scheduled to land. The other stayed in Syracuse, talking by phone to people who knew some of the flight's passengers. By early morning we had spoken with a few of the victims' relatives.

More than three years later, that dialogue with the relatives is continuing. We watched them organize into a lobbying group that pushed for aviation security reforms. We listened to their angry attacks on government officials and Pan Am. And we saw the ways in which a terrorist bomb shredded their personal lives. At times, the stories of family tragedy we heard overwhelmed us. But early on, a couple who had lost their only child told us something that wouldn't leave our minds. During an emotional two-hour interview, one of us offered our condolences. The overture was politely rebuffed. The man and woman didn't need or want sympathy. They wanted to know who had killed their daughter and why it had been allowed to happen. "Just do your job," they said.

xiii

Our research led us to Lockerbie, London, and West Germany. In Washington, D.C., we pored through thousands of pages of government documents, including notes of interviews with the Pan Am employees who were the last people to see the passengers alive and with the baggage handlers who had put the suitcase bomb on board.

We have been with the families of the flight's victims in their moments of triumph and their times of frustration. We saw them evolve from a chaotic mass of confused strangers into two highly efficient groups capable of shaping public opinion worldwide. We also saw a less inspiring side, as personality disputes mushroomed out of control in the emotion-charged atmosphere of their gatherings. And yet these were, after all, just ordinary people thrust together by catastrophic circumstances; despite the bickering, that commonness was their strength.

It was the relatives' anger that caught our attention initially, because a significant portion of it was directed not only at the terrorist bombers but also at the United States government. Many of the relatives said that when their loved ones died, so did a faith in their government. They felt betrayed by the Federal Aviation Administration, which failed to enforce the security rules that would have prevented the bombing, and by the State Department, which responded with insensitivity to their early inquiries about the identification and return of bodies. Then late in 1991, when prosecutors in the United States and Great Britain announced an indictment charging two Libyans with carrying out the attack, many relatives saw this as yet another betrayal. They said President Bush was conveniently ignoring evidence that implicated Syria, a nation with which his administration was trying to build closer ties.

The relatives' campaign to discover how and why the bombing occurred, and to improve aviation security, is an integral part of the Lockerbie story. Just as they felt compelled to learn as much as they could about the bombing, so have we felt compelled to continue telling their story, long after other reporters have moved on to something else. The victims' families have come to believe that it is their right to have everything about the bombing revealed, for their sake and for the benefit of anyone who boards a commercial airplane. We agree.

CHAPTER 1

AT HEATHROW

As THE sun went down and the overcast December afternoon turned to evening at London's Heathrow Airport, members of the ground crew wondered if Pan American World Airways Flight 103 would leave on time.

The men in the cockpit were confident that it would. At a preflight briefing Captain James B. MacQuarrie told the Pan Am employee in charge of ground security he believed he could get the plane to depart on schedule. MacQuarrie and First Officer Raymond Wagner made the same assertion to the Pan Am duty manager.

The Boeing 747 MacQuarrie was scheduled to fly from London to New York on December 21, 1988, was the second leg of Flight 103. Today getting off on time was a questionable proposition because the flight's first leg—a Boeing 727 flying from Frankfurt to London—was running late. That was not unusual; nor was it unusual for air and ground crews to discuss departure times. At a major airport like Heathrow just a short delay could force passengers to miss connecting flights, and keeping on schedule was a major concern, even for the security workers whose job it was to keep weapons and explosives from getting on board.

It was the ground security coordinator's responsibility to ensure that the flight met all the security requirements mandated by the Air Carrier Standard Security Program of the Federal Aviation Administration (FAA). When it came time for Flight 103 to close its doors, though, it was the duty manager Christopher Price who went to the boarding gate to decide if the plane was ready to leave. Pan Am had designated Price an alternate ground security coordinator for Flight 103, which meant he had assumed some of the responsibilities for ensuring that the airline complied with FAA security standards. But Price had never been trained for the job of ground security chief; he was to admit later that he saw his primary responsibility as making sure the plane got off on time.

Pan Am's security procedures required passengers reporting in for the flight to be screened by guards from Pan Am's security subsidiary, Alert Management Systems, Inc. The guards were supposed to examine passports and tickets, then ask each passenger six questions to determine if he or she should be singled out as a selectee for further questioning. If a passenger was labeled a selectee, the Alert employee was supposed to place an X on the passenger's ticket coupon. Everyone else's coupon was supposed to receive a check mark. But on this day the tickets of thirty-eight passengers who were boarding Flight 103 in London had no security markings at all, making it impossible to tell if they had been screened. Although Pan Am's boarding agents were supposed to refuse unmarked boarding coupons at the gate, they allowed these passengers to board the plane.

That was not the only flaw in the airline's security program. No one at Pan Am searched the 747's cargo hold before luggage was loaded. The airline used hand-held metal detectors to examine carry-on luggage, violating FAA rules requiring X rays or hand searches. And no one bothered to tell the captain his plane was carrying luggage that didn't belong to any of the passengers.

After clearing security, passengers boarding the flight in London waited inside Heathrow's Terminal 3 to begin the eight-hour trip over the Atlantic. One of them was Christopher Andrew Jones, a twenty-year-old Syracuse University student who was returning home from a semester of study in London. Christopher Jones was a handsome, scruffy-looking young man who stood six feet one inch tall and weighed about 190 pounds. His favorite attire was sneakers, a T-shirt, and cut-off army fatigues.

For Jones, Flight 103 offered the promise of one more chance to party. The next day at 8:45 A.M. he was scheduled to report to work at a bookstore near his hometown of Claverack in New York State's Hudson River valley. Many of his friends were on this flight, so it represented his last chance to see them before the monthlong vacation. Jones's girlfriend, Erica Elefant, had been scheduled to travel with him, but a couple of weeks earlier she had turned in her Flight 103 ticket and made arrangements to travel to Paris; she and some friends wanted to visit France before returning to the United States. Jones had gone with Elefant the day she went to the Pan Am office in London to trade in her Flight 103 ticket. He tried to talk her out of changing her plans by predicting it would be a "real party flight."

Jones checked in for the flight without his girlfriend and was assigned 52K, a window seat five rows from the rear of the plane.

Also boarding the flight at Heathrow was Melina Kristina Hudson, a sixteen-year-old high school student from Albany, New York, who was going home from an exchange program at Exeter School in England. Hudson, an attractive girl with flowing dark blond hair, was leaving Europe earlier than she and her family had anticipated. When she arrived at Exeter in August 1988, she had planned to stay through the fall and spring, until the school year ended. But she was the only American in the exchange program and grew homesick. After her mother had visited her in England in November, Melina Hudson decided she would come home for Christmas and finish the school year at Albany Academy for Girls.

As she waited to board Flight 103, she had a lot to be excited about. Her mother had promised to teach her to drive a car. And then there was the upcoming prom. Hudson was in her junior year of high school, and she was hoping to be invited to the spring formal dance at Albany Academy, a private boys' school across the street from the girls' academy. She had even purchased a dress for the occasion in England. The dress was neatly packed inside one of her suitcases.

Hudson originally had planned to fly home on Pan Am on December 22. She had telephoned her father on December 20 to give him her arrival time, and Paul Hudson had scribbled the information on a napkin. But for some reason her plans changed; she told her mother in a subsequent telephone conversation she would come home one day earlier. Hudson was disappointed because it meant she would have to miss a disco party in England. Her mother, Eleanor, was puzzled by the change but figured it was no big deal. "A day less or one day more—it wouldn't matter," her mother said.

Hudson's ticket was stamped with seat assignment 29A, which placed her above the 747's left wing.

Charles Dennis McKee was on his way home for the holidays, too. McKee was a six-foot five-inch, 270-pound army major who was beginning to go bald. He liked to travel casually, dressed in jeans and a T-shirt, and he never carried his military identification papers. "Tiny," as his army colleagues called him, was returning home from the U.S. Embassy in Beirut, where he worked for the army's Intelligence and Security Command. Recently, however, he had been temporarily assigned to the Defense Intelligence Agency as assistant attaché for military affairs to the U.S. Embassy in Lebanon. In simple terms, Chuck McKee was a spy.

McKee didn't tell his mother he was going to fly home until the day before he left. The call reached Beulah McKee at her home in Trafford, Pennsylvania, catching her by surprise.

"Is that you?" she had asked. The connection was clear as a bell.

"Yes, it's me. I'm coming home for Christmas."

"Well, where are you?"

Her son, who had recently turned forty, laughed. "I'm still over here." He would not say where "here" was. Anytime family members wanted to write him letters, they had to address them to a post office box in Virginia.

The family knew very little about his work. "We never knew what he was doing, where he was, or where he was going back to," his mother said. "I'd say to him, 'I worry about you.' He'd just laugh it off and say, 'You don't have anything to worry about.' "

McKee had a reservation at the front of the 747, in the spacious Clipper Class compartment. His seat number was 15F.

Syracuse University junior Karen Lee Hunt, a twenty-year-old English major, had seat number 31K, next to a window over the right wing. She and Christopher Jones were two of the thirty-five students on the plane who had been enrolled in a Syracuse University overseas study program. Hunt had almond-shaped brown eyes, milk white skin, light freckles, and a long neck. Her friends said she looked like a cat.

Hunt had taken the bus from her London apartment and arrived at the airport carrying about all she could handle. In the days preceding her flight home to suburban Rochester, New York, she had gone Christmas shopping in London. It had taken her hours to figure out a way to fit everything into her luggage. She had purchased ski socks and a pair of boxer shorts for her boyfriend, Mark Esposito, a T-shirt from a London pub and an expensive teddy bear for her ten-month-old cousin, Tyler, a tie for her father, and cosmetics, liqueur-filled chocolates, and a teapot for her mother. She had a special gift for her thirteen-year-old sister, Robyn: a Guns N' Roses album not available in the United States. She laughed when she told a friend in London how much trouble she was having packing the album for her sister. Hunt really didn't even like the hard rock band.

Robyn and Karen Hunt were close. On the day her older sister went away to college, Robyn clung to Karen and refused to let go. The night before Karen left for London, Robyn had been crying in her own bedroom. Karen tried to cheer her up by lying beside her on the bed and goofing around with a cassette tape recorder.

"We started recording and stuff, and I said, 'No, Karen, I don't want to record on this,' " Robyn said.

"And she said, 'Why not?'

" 'Because I'll be sad when you leave if I listen to it.' And I go, 'Well, what if your plane crashes?' Just like that. I didn't really think anything of it."

Karen ignored the remark and pretended she was a radio reporter broadcasting a story from London. Then she rewound the tape and changed its speed so her voice sounded high-pitched, like a munchkin's. Finally Robyn laughed.

In late October Karen Hunt's mother, Peggy, had taken an overnight British Airways flight to Heathrow so she could spend nine days in Europe with her older daughter. At first Mrs. Hunt had been unsure she would be able to make the trip because she had not earned much vacation time at her new office job. But when she thought how fast Karen was growing up, she decided she would regret passing up the opportunity.

"I had thought this would be the last time we would have to do something this special together," she said. "I guess it was because she was getting out of college, and she probably was going to be married. Normally I don't think the mother and daughter go off on too many trips after the daughter gets married."

Hunt was an attractive girl who liked to wear loose, outdoorsy clothes. She did not particularly care for jewelry. About the only piece she wore regularly was the anklet her sister had made for her at summer camp. Hunt had changed a lot since going to Syracuse University. Her boyfriend, Mark Esposito, said that when he first met her in her freshman year, she seemed to lack confidence. By the time she went to London as a college junior, she had matured into a young woman who could not get enough of the world. Her decision to travel to London was based in part on her desire to be exposed to a different culture. Every day Hunt wrote about her experiences in a journal.

During Mrs. Hunt's stay the two women toured London and traveled to Paris. One night at her London flat Karen prepared dinner for her mother, who thought: *My little girl is growing up.* On another night the two women lay awake in their beds, lost in discussion.

"We got into a deep conversation about a personal relationship that I once had with a male friend, and she was relating that to her present circumstances in her life," Peggy Hunt said. "I remember that I told her some things that we never really talked about. She was really interested, and we must have said some funny things." One of Karen's roommates walked into the flat and found the mother and daughter on their beds, laughing like schoolgirls.

Glenn John Bouckley, a twenty-seven-year-old native of Great Britain, was returning home to upstate New York with his American wife, Paula, twenty-nine. The couple, who had seats in row 39, checked in for Flight 103 after parking their rental car in London and returning the keys. Bouckley was a slightly built man who stood an inch shorter than his wife. She had reddish brown hair and expressive hazel eyes.

They were returning from an eight-day vacation in Britain, where Bouckley had been best man at his brother's wedding. Like Karen Hunt, the Bouckleys were bringing home a lot of luggage. They had celebrated Christmas early with his family and had been given many gifts. They also were bringing home some household items that had been in storage for most of the past two years.

The two had met through the mail after one of them saw the other's name in a newsletter for fans of the rock group Queen. They exchanged letters, and seven years later, on a windy fall day in 1986, they were married in St. Peter's Church in Sowerby Bridge. The Bouckleys had lived the first seventeen months of their married life in Great Britain but moved to Paula's hometown, near Syracuse, in March 1988, hoping to find better jobs. She found work as a supermarket cashier, while he worked in an electrical parts store.

This was the Bouckleys' first trip to England since they had moved to the United States nine months earlier. Bouckley had been the best man at his brother Christopher's wedding on December 17. The two brothers were the youngest in a family of six children, and they had been best friends. Ever since childhood they had planned to be best man at each other's wedding.

The day after the wedding the Bouckleys began touring Scotland in their rental car. Scotland was one of Paula Bouckley's favorite places. She loved the lush green landscape and the castles. They drove for three days, passing through the countryside east of a village called Lockerbie. They shared dinner in Edinburgh on December 19 with Christopher Bouckley and his bride, who were spending their honeymoon in Scotland. When they returned to England, Glenn Bouckley refused his mother's invitation to stay through the Christmas holiday. They already had tickets to return home on Pan Am Flight 103, he explained, and he had to be back at work in Syracuse on December 22.

Thomas Joseph Ammerman, an executive for a Saudi Arabian shipping firm, was another passenger waiting to board Flight 103. He was returning to Old Tappan, New Jersey, after completing a three-week business trip to the Middle East. He was anxious to be home for Christmas with his wife, Carolyn, and two daughters, Casey and Jill, who were six and four. But when his company asked him to attend an unscheduled meeting that would make him miss the noon flight and put him on Pan Am 103, he agreed.

Ammerman had just gotten a big promotion at work and was beginning to feel able to provide his own family with the kinds of things his parents had given him. Tom, one of five children, had grown up in Haworth, New Jersey, a small town in the shadow of New York City. His father, Herb, had been an Exxon executive and the embodiment of civic responsibility: the mayor of Haworth, a leader in his church, the president of the high school booster club. His parents were devout Catholics.

Tom Ammerman had been graduated from Villanova University in 1974 with a degree in history and had expected to go into teaching, but jobs in that field were scarce, so he took a job with the Farrell Lines as a loading dock supervisor. He immediately fell in love with the shipping business. After rising through the ranks and taking an office job, he left Farrell for another firm, Waterman Steamship Corporation. Later still he was hired by the firm in Saudi Arabia.

Before leaving for the Middle East in early December 1988, Ammerman had told his mother he was anxious to complete the business trip and return home to his family, most of whom still lived in New Jersey. Christmas had always meant a big family gathering for the Ammermans, but this year everyone planned to make an extra effort to be together. Herb Ammerman had died in August, and his children wanted more than ever to spend the holiday with their mother.

Tom Ammerman's seat assignment on Flight 103 was 16E, one row behind Chuck McKee in the Clipper Class section.

The 727 that flew Flight 103's first leg touched down at Heathrow at 5:40 P.M. local time, nearly two hours after leaving the gate in Frankfurt. The plane parked at stand K-16, Terminal 3, next to the larger 747 that would take over the flight designation for the trip to New York City.

Among the forty-nine passengers transferring from the 727 to the 747 was George Watterson Williams, a twenty-four-year-old army first lieutenant stationed in West Germany. Williams was serving at an airfield in Bad Kreuznach, southwest of Frankfurt, where he was an airborne scout on board one of the army's sophisticated OH-58D helicopters.

Geordie—everyone called him that—was going home to see his parents in Maryland. Some high school friends who had moved to California were going home to Maryland, too, and they were planning a New Year's Eve celebration with Geordie.

Williams ended up on Flight 103 by accident. Originally he had planned to take Pan Am Flight 61, which left Frankfurt earlier in the day and would have taken him directly to Dulles International Airport near Washington, D.C., without layovers in London and New York City. But he had arrived at the airport late and had missed his flight. Williams had spent the night of December 20 with his girlfriend, Lisa Moffatt, whom he had been dating since late October. It had been their last chance to be together before Christmas, and Williams had been reluctant to say good-bye. When he finally got out the door on the morning of December 21, he was behind schedule. He had to pack and go to the bank, and then he got caught in a traffic jam. He missed the 1:20 P.M. flight. Pan Am's Frankfurt ticket agents helped him get a seat on Flight 103. When he transferred onto the 747, he was assigned seat 33K.

Another transferring passenger was three-year-old Suruchi Rattan. She was supposed to have taken Flight 67 out of Frankfurt earlier that day with four members of her family, but the group—representing three generations—had missed the flight. Suruchi and her relatives were returning to the United States from New Delhi, where they had just attended the wedding of Suruchi's uncle.

Suruchi was traveling with her brother Anmol, two, her mother, Garima, a twenty-nine-year-old computer programmer, and her grandparents, Om and Shanti Dixit. (Her father and her uncle, both doctors, had flown home ahead of the family to return to jobs in the United States.) Suruchi's grandfather Om Dixit, fifty-four, was a slightly built, gray-haired professor of earth science at Central State College in Ohio. In 1964 he had immigrated to the United States, where his wife, Shanti, fifty-four, joined him nine years later. On the day of the flight Shanti Dixit wore traditional Indian jewelry, including a silver chain around her neck.

In India three-year-old Suruchi had endeared herself to her new aunt, Sandhya. After the wedding ceremony the elder woman had applied a moist red powder called sindoor to her forehead to indicate her status as a married woman. Then she had turned and caught a glimpse of her niece smearing the red sindoor all over her own face.

"You should get married," Sandhya Dixit said with a laugh.

"OK," Suruchi had replied.

Suruchi liked red so much that for the trip home she had chosen to wear her bright red kurta and salwar—a knee-length tunic and matching pants.

During her short visit to India Suruchi had taken to calling Sandhya Dixit *Mami*, which means "auntie" in Hindi. When it came time to go home, Suruchi became unnerved when she realized her aunt was not getting on the plane with her. (Her aunt had to remain behind in India to arrange her immigration to the United States.) But everyone reassured her that the separation would be brief.

Flight 67's route was New Delhi to New York, with a refueling stop in

Frankfurt. During the layover in Frankfurt Anmol began to have trouble breathing. The little boy had no history of breathing difficulties, but on the family's visit to India he had developed a fever that required antibiotics and a brief hospital stay. The purser on Flight 67 contacted the ground crew, which summoned a medical worker who boarded the plane and examined the sick child. After the examination the plane left the gate with Suruchi and her family on board. After the plane had pulled away, the pilot told the tower that the child was still ill. He took the highly unusual step of bringing the plane back to the gate. All five members of Suruchi's family got off. Garima Rattan took Anmol to an airport clinic, and a Pan Am ground security coordinator, Harold Hoffman, allowed Flight 67 to leave with the family's unaccompanied baggage on board. Pan Am service agent Angelina Jadran recalled later that there was some hope the child could receive medical attention in time for the family to catch Flight 73, which was scheduled to leave Frankfurt in the early afternoon, but it took longer than anyone expected to find a doctor. The family missed Flight 73 and had to be rebooked on the later departure, Flight 103. On the 747 from London to New York the five members of the family had seats in rows 23 and 24.

Also on board the Frankfurt to London leg of Flight 103 was Khalid Nazir Jaafar, a muscular twenty-year-old man with sandy reddish hair and blue eyes. He wore a brown leather jacket and black denim jeans. Jaafar was going home to Detroit after a trip that had taken him to Beirut, Lebanon, and Dortmund, West Germany; he had been traveling in Europe and the Middle East before enrolling in an automotive school in the United States.

Jaafar was on Flight 103 because after shopping around, he had concluded it offered the cheapest fare. He was an experienced traveler, and his father said he was coming home with only a soft-sided carry-on bag and a duffel bag.

On a previous return trip from Lebanon, Jaafar had been stopped by customs officials in Detroit and questioned about a package of dried Lebanese soup mix they found in his luggage. The authorities held him for several hours, suspecting the powdered substance might be a drug. The experience was enough to prompt Jaafar to remark to his father that he wouldn't be carrying goods home from Lebanon anymore.

Jaafar had spoken with his father by telephone the day before boarding the Pan Am flight and told him he would arrive at the Detroit airport shortly after midnight. He reminded his father to be there to meet him. His seat assignment was 53K, directly behind Christopher Jones.

In all, 259 passengers and crew from twenty-one different countries made their way on to the second leg of Flight 103. A passenger service agent remarked later that everybody who checked in—the Frankfurt passengers and those beginning their travels in London—seemed to be in the holiday spirit.

Shortly after the arrival of the 727 from Frankfurt duty manager Christopher Price left a central service control area and walked to the Flight 103 boarding gate. He watched as passengers from the 727 walked down the boarding ramp, through the terminal, and up another boarding ramp into the larger plane. He spoke briefly with workers supervising the baggage and cargo loading; they said everything was going smoothly. Price also made small talk with a security officer, before turning his attention to the departing plane.

Only a few minutes remained before Flight 103 was supposed to push away from the gate. Price walked over to Nicola Milne, the Pan Am gate supervisor, and asked her if everyone had boarded. No, she said, two passengers were missing. Moments later a Pan Am employee stepped out of the 747 and said one of the missing passengers, a woman, had been located on board. But the other was nowhere to be found. Price checked the passenger list and saw that the missing passenger was named Jaswant Basuta. The Pan Am computer showed Basuta had checked two bags, which were now deep inside the belly of the 747. Pan Am's records also showed that Basuta had come to London earlier in the month from New York and that he was returning on a round-trip ticket. Price concluded Basuta's unaccompanied bags did not pose a security threat to the flight and decided not to pull them off. He also decided not to say anything to the captain about the missing passenger. Price saw his main responsibility as "schedule integrity": making sure the plane lifted off on schedule. At 6:00 P.M. Price told the ramp coordinator to close the door. The 747 had been opened up to accept cargo and passengers for only forty minutes. Price told Milne to continue looking for Basuta in the lounge. Then the duty manager began walking away from the boarding area.

Jaswant Basuta was a middle-aged bearded auto mechanic who had immigrated to the United States in 1974. A practicing Sikh, he wore a white turban on his head. He and his wife, Surinder, a hospital technician, lived in a modest apartment complex in Tarrytown, New York, with their daughter, Jatinder, eighteen, and their son, Rony, fourteen. Basuta had come to Europe earlier in the month to attend his brother-in-law's wedding in Belfast, Northern Ireland. After the wedding he visited other relatives in the London area. The night before he was scheduled to return to the United States he stayed with relatives who lived about half an hour from Heathrow

Airport. Nonetheless, he instructed a brother-in-law who had agreed to drive him to the flight to pick him up at 3:00 P.M., even though the flight didn't leave until 6:00 P.M. He thought that he would rather spend hours sitting in the terminal than take the chance of missing the flight.

Basuta had compelling reasons to be on time for the flight. He was due to report for work at a new job at an auto dealership at 8:00 A.M. the next day; if he missed Flight 103, he would probably miss his first day of work. Also, Basuta had missed or nearly missed overseas flights twice before. Within the family his reputation in this respect was mildly embarrassing to him.

At 3:00 P.M. Basuta had his bags packed and was waiting for Atma Singh Banwaitt, the brother-in-law who had agreed to take him to the airport. But Banwaitt was late; he had taken time to pick up his grandson from school and did not arrive for another hour. It was 5:15 P.M. by the time Basuta and a group of relatives who had come to see him off reached Heathrow. Basuta got his luggage X-rayed and was standing in the economy-class check-in line when Barbara Marsh, a Pan Am service agent working the first-class line, cleared the last passenger in front of her. She called to Basuta and said she would take him in her line. She accepted his bags, looked at his ticket, and directed him to Gate 14.

Basuta was about to head for his flight when another of his brothers-in-law, Maghar Singh Sidhu, offered to buy him a drink. As a Sikh Basuta is not supposed to drink, but he ordered a scotch. His brother in law Maghar Sidhu broke into laughter. "In England we only drink beer," he said, and ordered Basuta a bottle of Carlsberg Special Brew. Basuta moved away to buy some soda and candy for the nephews and nieces who had come to see him off; when he returned, he quickly drank the beer. Maghar refilled his glass, Basuta drank it, and the process was repeated several more times. Atma Banwaitt, the brother-in-law responsible for the group's late arrival, nudged Basuta and reminded him of the time.

"You're going to miss the flight," Banwaitt said.

"Don't worry," Basuta replied. "When the passenger is not seen, they call you over the loudspeaker. There's no way the plane can leave without me. They always start calling over the phones first."

Finally Basuta decided it was time to say good-bye. He hugged and kissed his relatives, shouldered his carry-on bag, and walked toward the boarding gate. Many of his relatives followed, stopping when they reached the sign that said "Passengers Only." Basuta waved to them, turned around, and began to jog. Then, noticing that there were few other passengers in the hallway, he broke into a sprint.

At a station for passport examinations Basuta held his passport in the air.

He kept running, and the woman at the desk waved him on. He came to the end of the long corridor and turned left. After another turn he entered another long corridor. On one side was a moving walkway. He hopped on the conveyor and set down his shoulder bag to catch his breath. A man wearing a suit approached from the opposite direction, walking along the hallway that ran parallel to the conveyor.

"What flight are you catching?" the man asked.

"Flight 103."

"You're not going to make it that way."

Shouldering his bag again, Basuta vaulted the conveyor's side rail and resumed his sprint down the hallway. At the sign for Gate 14 he turned left. After another turn he was there. As he looked around at the nearly empty boarding area, a familiar, sinking feeling began to wash over him. He had done it again. The gate to the plane was closed, and the only people in the boarding area were a handful of Pan Am employees, including duty manager Christopher Price. Basuta turned to the group, told them his bags had already been loaded, and pleaded to be allowed to board the plane. Through the window at the gate Basuta could see the humpbacked outline of the 747 on Heathrow's lighted tarmac.

"It's a matter of my job," he said. "If I miss my flight, I may lose my job."

Price, who had just ordered the plane closed, told Basuta that he was too late, that Flight 103 had pulled away. "If the plane is gone, where is my luggage?" Basuta asked. An Alert security guard who witnessed the exchange said Basuta appeared to be slightly drunk. Price called the passenger control desk to say Basuta had been found, then went to finish some paperwork. Basuta turned around and began walking away from the gate.

The 747 that Basuta was so desperate to board was named *Clipper Maid of the Seas*, which was emblazoned on the side of the fuselage in bright blue letters. The jumbo jet had arrived in London at seven minutes after noon from San Francisco and been parked at stand K-14, where its cargo and passengers had been unloaded. From 2:00 to 4:00 P.M. an Alert security officer had stood watch over the plane.

The *Maid of the Seas* was a relatively old jumbo jet. It was the fifteenth 747 built by Boeing, and it had been delivered to the airline in February 1970, only a month after the world's first Boeing 747 had begun service. The aircraft recently had received extensive modifications as part of the U.S. Air Force's Civil Reserve Air Fleet program. Under the program, airlines are paid to agree to make available to the military jetliners that can be used to transport troops or supplies in war or during national emergencies. During the three months the plane was undergoing a government-funded overhaul in Wichita, Kansas, workers had reinforced the cabin floor and made other structural changes. Typically a plane that goes through the CRAF renovation program is expected to gain an additional twelve years of life expectancy, so *Clipper Maid of the Seas*—with eighteen years of service behind it—still had many years of life ahead. The previous week the plane had received an extensive mechanical review in San Francisco.

In the 747's cockpit Captain MacQuarrie and First Officer Wagner ran through a series of equipment checks by rote, then pulled out a list as a backup to make sure nothing had been overlooked. Flight Engineer Jerry Avritt, who had just supervised a security search of the cabin, checked the distribution of fuel for the 3,469-mile journey across the Atlantic Ocean. Heathrow's controllers gave the Pan Am crew permission to start the engines, and the whining of the four Pratt & Whitney JT9D-7A turbofans muffled conversation inside the fuselage. At 6:04 P.M. the aircraft was cleared to taxi. Pan Am 103 was pushed back from the gate. In addition to the luggage of the 243 passengers and 16 crew members, the plane carried about twenty tons of cargo, including forty-three bags of military mail and more than a hundred bags of commercial courier mail. After being warned of construction on an outer taxiway, the crew steered the plane on an inner taxiway to the main east west runway and awaited clearance for takeoff. After about a fifteen-minute delay the engines began their crescendo. MacQuarrie pulled the plane onto runway 27L and accelerated due west.

As the 747 picked up speed, the invisible force of air rushing past the aircraft's wings began to take hold. Wings have a special shape, called camber, that is curved on the upper surface and comparatively flat on the bottom. This shape causes air passing over the top to travel farther, and therefore faster, than the air rushing beneath the wing. The faster air moves, the less pressure it exerts on the wing. As the plane increased its speed, the pressure on top of its wings became increasingly lower than the pressure below the wings, creating lift. The flaps on the trailing edge of each wing enhanced the effect by deflecting air downward. Before the 747 reached the end of the runway, the airfoil created by the 196-foot wingspan produced enough lift to hoist the 713,002 pounds of aircraft, passengers, and cargo into the air. Pan Am 103 took off at 6:25 P.M.

MacQuarrie immediately steered the craft in a northwest route known as a Daventry departure, one of about six preset courses out of Heathrow listed in a guide stowed in the plane's cockpit. After clearing Heathrow's congested airspace, the 747 headed almost due north, over Burnham, an aviation landmark consisting of a tower about ten feet high that emits a constant high-frequency signal pilots use for navigation. Because of the curvature of the earth, the shortest route between London and New York is not due west over the ocean, but north. When it passed over Burnham, Pan Am 103 was at six thousand feet, a level that allowed it to fly below incoming planes circling one another in a waiting area north of Heathrow called the Bovingdon stack. As the 747 headed north over Coventry and Derby in England's Midlands, it gradually rose to twelve thousand feet. Flight 103 continued its slow climb until 6:56 P.M., when it was about twenty-five miles north of Manchester. Then the crew leveled it off at thirty-one thousand feet—nearly six miles high—and made preparations to head over the Atlantic. MacQuarrie cut the engine thrust, "dragging" the engines back to cruising speed. For seven minutes Pan Am 103 flew level and straight, closing in on Scottish airspace.

Earlier in the day, while the plane's occupants had gone about their business, a celestial event had unfolded silently in the heavens above them. At precisely 3:28 P.M. Greenwich mean time, the sun dipped to 23° 27' south latitude—the Tropic of Capricorn. As the sun reached the solstice, winter began in the Northern Hemisphere.

It was the darkest day of the year.

CHAPTER 2

TROUBLE IN THE MIDDLE EAST

MORE THAN two years before Flight 103 lifted off from Heathrow, President Ronald Reagan, saying he wanted to make the world safer for Americans, dispensed some quick and vengeful justice in the middle of an April night. Air Force and Navy bombers attacked five targets in Libya, damaging what the White House referred to as Colonel Muammar Qaddafi's "terrorist infrastructure." At one of the targets, a military barracks that served as Qaddafi's headquarters, the Libyan leader's adopted infant daughter was killed and two of his sons were seriously wounded.

The National Security Agency (NSA), the supersecret arm of U.S. intelligence that operates a worldwide network of electronic listening posts, had provided Reagan with what he called conclusive proof that Libya had carried out a terrorist attack on a West Berlin nightclub eleven days earlier. The April 5, 1986, bombing of the German nightclub had killed an American serviceman, Sergeant Kenneth Ford, and a Turkish woman, and wounded two hundred thirty others.

The NSA had intercepted messages sent from Tripoli to the Libyan people's bureau in East Berlin calling for an attack that would inflict "maximum and indiscriminate casualties" on Americans, Reagan said in an address televised to the nation. The NSA was also eavesdropping on the Libyan people's bureau when it reported the success of the nightclub mission to operatives in Tripoli.

Armed with that evidence, Reagan ordered the air strike, which he described as an action of self-defense against Qaddafi's terrorists.

The U.S. attack was denounced by most nations, but the president's popularity soared at home. Confidence in his handling of foreign policy surged to a record high of 76 percent in a *New York Times*/CBS News poll. While Americans abroad braced for a new terrorist onslaught, Libya seemed unwilling or unable to stage an organized response. Other terrorists in sympathy with Qaddafi tried to strike back, but no Libyan-orchestrated attacks materialized. Americans began to believe they had delivered the kind of message the Libyan leader understood.

"We believe that this preemptive action against his terrorist installations will not only diminish Colonel Qaddafi's capacity to export terror, it will provide him with incentives and reasons to alter his criminal behavior," Reagan said.

The president was half right. Qaddafi's behavior had changed, but his ability to launch terrorist strikes remained intact. Prior to the raid, Qaddafi had issued highly visible, almost boastful denunciations of the United States. After the April 1986 bombing he maintained a low profile. Behind the silence, however, was a new cunning.

By the summer of 1988 many terrorism analysts in Washington, D.C., had incorrectly interpreted Libya's silence as a newfound fear of U.S. reprisals. But a sinister series of preparations for new terrorist attacks already had begun. On the tiny island nation of Malta in the Mediterranean Sea, a representative of Libyan Arab Airlines had begun using his office at Luqa Airport to store plastic explosives supplied by the Libyan intelligence service, Jamahirya Security Organization (JSO).

The man storing the explosives, Lamen Khalifa Fhimah, claimed to be a representative of Libya's national airline, but in fact he was an operative for his government's intelligence service. According to U.S. authorities, JSO was in the business of carrying out terrorist attacks around the world. By placing agents like Fhimah in jobs with Libyan Arab Airlines, the JSO had access to baggage loading areas and a tremendous advantage in planning and carrying out aviation bombings.

U.S. officials knew nothing of this activity in the summer of 1988. They continued to believe that the threat posed by the African nation of about four million people had been greatly diminished. And after a tumultuous Independence Day weekend in the Persian Gulf, Americans thought they had far more reason to fear terrorist attacks sponsored by Iran.

On July 3, 1988, the crew of the USS *Vincennes* was patrolling the Gulf as part of a peacekeeping force in the Iran-Iraq War when it mistakenly identified a civilian airliner as a hostile F-14 military fighter plane and shot it down with two surface-to-air missiles. The plane, Iran Air Flight 655, was carrying Muslims making their pilgrimage to Mecca at the zenith of the Islamic holy year. All 290 people on board were killed. The civilian aircraft was squarely within its flight path and barely five hundred feet shy of its assigned cruising altitude of fourteen thousand feet. It had been in the air only seven minutes. The United States called the shootdown an unfortunate miscalculation in a war zone. Iran called it an act of war.

Iran observed a national day of mourning on July 4, and as the bodies of Flight 655's passengers came home to be buried, the funerals turned into large anti-American demonstrations. At a July 7 funeral for dozens of victims, a crowd estimated at ten thousand chanted, "Death to America." In front of a speakers' podium, a spear with an Iranian flag attached to it had been thrust through an American flag and presidential seal. Iranian President Ali Khamenei called on the United States to remove its fleet from the Persian Gulf and reiterated his call for vengeance: "The Iranian nation and officials assert that they reserve the right to take revenge in any manner and at any place, and, God willing, they will exact revenge with force."

Four days after the destruction of Flight 655 a warning appeared on a U.S. State Department computer bulletin board used to disseminate warnings about terrorist attacks to American businesses with overseas operations:

Country: Iran
Date of Incident: 07/03/1988
Subject: Iran Airbus Shot Down
Date of Entry: 07/07/88

Teheran

The Military Airlift Command (MAC) issued the following message on July 5, 1988: In response to the U.S. shootdown of an Iranian airliner on July 3, 1988, we believe the threat to U.S. interests worldwide has significantly increased. We have seen no specific reporting of terrorist plans to retaliate, but we believe Iran will strike back in a tit-for-tat fashion—mass casualties for mass casualties. Smaller pro-Iranian groups may stage their own attacks to show their support, but Iran may stage a large-scale terrorist bombing against the United States. Targets could include aircraft, airports, USOs or restaurants. . . . We believe Europe is a likely target for a retaliatory attack. This is due primarily to the large concentration of Americans and the established terrorist infrastructures in place throughout Europe.

Within days of the Airbus incident Iran's plan for retaliation seemed to be taking shape. U.S. intelligence officials received information that Ahmad Jibril, leader of a terrorist group known as the Popular Front for the Liberation of Palestine—General Command (PLFP—GC), had paid a visit to government officials in Teheran. Other evidence—such as bank transactions and communications intercepted by the United States' massive intelligence-gathering apparatus—seemed to indicate a developing relationship between Jibril and Iran. It appeared that Jibril might be offering his services for a retaliatory strike.

WHILE U.S. intelligence monitored the PFLP—GC's courtship of Iran, a European cell of the terrorist group was attracting some attention of its own in Germany. Within fifteen weeks of the Flight 655 shootdown West German authorities were closely watching the activities of a PFLP—GC cell that appeared to be gearing up for some sort of attack. The surveillance was being conducted by West Germany's domestic intelligence service, Bundesamt für Verfassungsschutz (BfV). Its officers followed the movements of the terrorists and used electronic eavesdropping devices, hoping to discover the group's intentions. They had already learned that the PFLP—GC cell was headed by Hafez Kassem Dalkamouni, an aide to Jibril who had recently arrived in the country.

Dalkamouni was first sighted in Germany in 1988 by Israeli intelligence agents, who extensively monitor suspected terrorist activity in Europe. They saw him in the city of Neuss; they informed German authorities of Dalkamouni's presence in Germany in September. They also reported that the PFLP—GC had begun moving weapons and explosives into a network of safe houses around Europe.

Initially no one knew what kind of attack the group was plotting. But before long Israeli intelligence uncovered startling evidence that the PFLP—GC planned a barbaric assault on Jewish children in West Germany. Mossad, the Israeli intelligence agency, intercepted a parcel mailed from Munich to an address in Lebanon that intelligence agents had previously linked to the PFLP—GC. The package contained photographs and diagrams of the guarded, barbed wire-fenced Jewish kindergarten building in Munich. Word of the intercepted parcel was relayed to German police. That attack never materialized, but the PFLP—GC could be expected to strike against multiple targets.

The threat of an attack was especially high as a result of PLO leader Yasir Arafat's initiative to open talks with the United States. In the preceding twenty years, whenever a peace initiative had emerged in the Middle East, the chance of an offensive by a rival group that wanted to disrupt talks had increased significantly. In the fall of 1988 the time was right for such an attack by extremist Palestinian forces. The trick for intelligence agencies was to determine what form the assault would take. The effort to solve that riddle revolved around Dalkamouni, the most important operative intelligence services had identified. The code name for the surveillance of Dalkamouni and his group was Herbstlaub (Autumn Leaves). By early October the BfV was trying to piece together the meaning of a series of visits and telephone calls.

Dalkamouni was living with his sister and brother-in-law, Hashem Abassi, at 16 Isarstrasse in Neuss. Soon Ahmed Abassi, the younger brother of Dalkamouni's brother-in-law, surfaced in Germany also, having traveled from Sweden. Ahmed spoke German and English; the German agents thought he might have been called in to act as Dalkamouni's translator.

On October 14 the BfV noticed a white Volvo with Swedish license plates pull up to the Abassi apartment in Neuss. Three men, all of whom appeared to be Arabs, got out and unloaded packages.

The same week an even more interesting visitor arrived at Abassi's apartment. Marwan Khreesat, a television repair shop owner from Amman, Jordan, showed up at Dalkamouni's doorstep in Neuss with his wife and with two bronze-colored Samsonite suitcases, one of which contained a Toshiba BomBeat 453 radio-cassette recorder. Khreesat's ties to Ahmad Jibril went back nearly twenty years. Khreesat is believed to have fashioned the PFLP—GC bomb that brought down Swissair Flight 330 on February 21, 1970—the first attack on an aircraft using a barometric triggering device. He also has been linked to the bombing, on the same day, of an Austrian Airlines flight from Frankfurt to Vienna that managed to land after an explosion blew a hole in the fuselage. And Italian authorities say that two years later Khreesat's work appeared again, this time in the form of a bomb concealed inside a record player given to two young Englishwomen who had been duped by Arab men they had met in Rome. The two women escaped injury after the bomb they had unwittingly carried aboard an El Al flight from Rome to Tel Aviv exploded in midair.

In West Germany Khreesat went right to work. On October 14, 1988, police followed Dalkamouni and Khreesat as the two men traveled around Neuss, purchasing items that seemed to be the components of a bomb. At the Huma department store the two men bought alarm clocks. They also went to Kaufhalle, a shopping mall in Neuss, where they purchased switches and batteries. Over the next several days police followed the men as they made several trips to Frankfurt, where they visited a second-floor apartment near the city's zoo. German police had never heard of the man who had rented the apartment, and at first they had no idea how he might fit into Dalkamouni's terrorist network.

Back at Abassi's apartment Khreesat sat down at a table in his bedroom, opened the back of the Toshiba radio-cassette recorder, and, using a screwdriver and pair of pliers, began assembling what authorities believe was a bomb. Dalkamouni brought him packages wrapped in aluminum foil and secured with black tape. For two days, according to an account in the *Sunday Times* of London, Khreesat toiled in his bedroom. West German police later found traces of explosive on the table where he worked. Telephone taps at the apartment, meanwhile, picked up a series of incriminating calls. One was a conversation between Dalkamouni and a man in Damascus who called himself Abed. "Everything would be ready" in a few days, Dalkamouni told him. Khreesat, calling himself Safi, got on the line and reported: "I've made some changes to the medication. It's better and stronger than before." Abed responded, "Things are under way." Another call monitored by police indicated other operatives were about to arrive in Germany. Dalkamouni called a takeout restaurant in Nicosia, Cyprus, where a man answering the phone said he had obtained a visa and was ready to come to Germany. Finally, in the last week of October, West German police intercepted a call from a man named Abu Hassan in Damascus. "Things are almost ready," Dalkamouni, speaking from the apartment, told the caller. "I'll be with you on Friday."

By this time surveillance teams in five West German cities had identified and in some cases photographed sixteen people who were believed to be working with Dalkamouni or somehow aiding his operation. A member of the federal police agency Bundeskriminalamt (BKA) placed an entry in the police operations log that noted that the PFLP—GC cell's activities were becoming increasingly unclear and uncontrollable. Manfred Klink, the BKA's highest-ranking counterterrorism officer, decided it was time to move.

Early in the day on Wednesday, October 26, police began a sweep of twelve apartments and four businesses in Frankfurt, Berlin, the Hamburg area, and Neuss. Dalkamouni and Khreesat were arrested outside the Kaufhalle mall in Neuss, where they had driven to make a call from a public telephone. In their green Ford sedan agents found blank passports, 2.2 pounds of explosives, a number of detonators, and a Toshiba BomBeat Model 453 radio-cassette player that had been rigged with explosives and a barometric detonator. It was an altitude-sensitive bomb, built to destroy an aircraft.

At the apartment near Frankfurt's zoo, meanwhile, police made another startling find, uncovering what one security official later described as enough weapons to "arm an army." They seized an antitank grenade launcher, thirty hand grenades, six submachine guns, a carbine, and a pistol with a silencer. Along with the weapons, police found battery-powered delayed-action detonators, fourteen seven-ounce tablets of TNT, and eleven pounds of Semtex—enough plastic explosive for fifteen bombs like the one found in Dalkamouni's car. At other locations police found sticks of explosives, bars of TNT, silencers, detonators, and a police radio scanner. It was the largest terrorist weapons stockpile ever seized in West Germany. In the Frankfurt apartment alone, police had captured the raw materials for dozens of attacks. Police arrested the apartment's occupant, still unsure of his identity despite the weeks of surveillance. He was later identified as Abdel Fattah Ghadanfar, a Palestinian in his late forties who has been known to police in several countries by various aliases.

By the time the raids were over police had arrested fourteen suspects in Neuss, Frankfurt, Hamburg, Mannheim, and Berlin. All had met or spoken with Dalkamouni during the Autumn Leaves operation. It looked as if German police had effectively rolled up a terrorist network. But one day after the arrests the German effort mysteriously began to unravel. In a Düsseldorf courtroom Judge Christian Rinne, citing a lack of evidence, quickly released almost all the suspects. Courts in Germany operate under the Napoleonic Code, not under the common law system used in Great Britain and the United States, and according to the German system, within twenty-four hours of an arrest a magistrate or law officer must decide if there is enough proof of a crime to continue holding the suspect. In this case Judge Rinne concluded the German government had not produced enough evidence to continue detaining the men.

Among those released was Ramzi Diab. Police had documented several meetings between Dalkamouni and Diab over several weeks. When he was arrested, however, Diab told investigators he had met Dalkamouni only ten days earlier, at a local hamburger stand. Diab told police he thought Dalkamouni was a used-car dealer, not a terrorist. Inexplicably police failed to take Diab's fingerprints while he was in custody. They also failed to take action against him for traveling on a false passport.

Diab, who was born in 1959 in Palestine, is also known as Qweik Salah Solman Taiz. Israeli authorities once arrested him on a terrorism-related charge. They released Diab in a 1985 prisoner exchange that had been arranged by Dalkamouni. The police who picked him up in Frankfurt became suspicious of Diab's identity and called BKA headquarters in Wiesbaden to verify the passport data, but the BKA failed to respond to the call.

Had the BKA agents checked their computer files, they would have learned from Interpol that the passport Diab was carrying had been stolen in 1985. "If the guys at the BKA headquarters at the Interpol relay station had done their work, this wouldn't have happened," one intelligence source in Germany said. "We are talking here of pure bureaucratic failures, people not doing their jobs. The German handling of this thing, it is not so much intentional mistakes but just guys, you know, not doing their jobs."

After two weeks only Dalkamouni, Khreesat, and Ghadanfar remained in West German jails. Soon Khreesat was released as well, even though he had been arrested with a bomb in his possession, was the subject of an outstanding international warrant stemming from a 1972 El Al airline bombing, had been traveling on false identification papers, had made trips to buy materials for bomb timing mechanisms, and had been overheard in telephone calls implicating him as a bomb maker. His sudden freedom was particularly strange because the investigating judge and federal attorney general had written of Khreesat in an investigative report, "His assignment was to manufacture explosives." Moreover, Dalkamouni had admitted in a sworn statement that Khreesat was a bomb expert who had been imported from Jordan for his skills.

Judge Rinne's statement explaining the release of Khreesat said, "According to the facts known so far, the accused is certainly suspected of the alleged charge. The strong suspicion of crime necessary for a warrant of arrest is, however, lacking." A spokesman for the federal attorney's office, Dr. Hans-Jürgen Förster, explained the release this way: "The investigating judge canceled the arrest warrant because, in his opinion, it didn't present a compelling case."

Even though most of the suspects were released, the Autumn Leaves operation seemed to have averted a bloodbath. But the object of all the firepower was initially unclear, leading to some nervous speculation. The PFLP—GC apparently had been preparing to slip a radio-cassette player bomb on Iberia Flight 888 from Madrid via Barcelona to Tel Aviv on October 29. The terrorist cell also may have planned attacks on an El Al flight bound for Tel Aviv and on a Frankfurt bar frequented by American soldiers, the West Germans concluded.

Although they could not say with certainty exactly what they had prevented, the German police were visibly proud when they displayed the haul of weapons for news photographers.

"We can conclude that we are dealing with an organization," the chief federal prosecutor, Kurt Rebmann, said. "We can conclude that they were planning the most serious crimes, including murder, but where, when, against whom, and with what motives is still totally unclear."

THE BOMB West German police seized from the trunk of Dalkamouni's green Ford was exceptionally well made. The Toshiba radio-cassette recorder that housed the device was ten inches wide, seven inches high, and two inches deep. Inside the recorder was a 10.5-ounce block of the Czech-made plastic explosive Semtex, which had been wrapped in white paper that bore the Toshiba name in red ink. A set of wires connected the Semtex to four 1.5-volt penlight batteries, which had nothing to do with the operation of the radio or cassette player. The Semtex and extra batteries rattled around inside the device because they were not secured.

The radio-cassette bomb was triggered by two devices: a two-inch pressure-sensitive barometric switch, which turned to the on position when an airplane reached an altitude of about three thousand feet, and an electronic timer, which was set for forty-five minutes and was activated when the barometric switch was turned on. The device was arranged so that if the plane descended below three thousand feet, the barometric switch would return to the off position and the timer would reset itself to forty-five minutes. This feature was characteristic of bombs built for use against the Israeli airline El Al, which routinely places luggage in pressure chambers to trigger barometric timers that otherwise would detonate in mid-flight. Had the bomb seized in Neuss been placed in such a pressure chamber, it would have foiled a test of less than forty-five minutes.

The bomb was primed when a small plug was placed in an external antenna socket. When the plug was out of the socket, the bomb would not go off. The process of detonation would begin when the timer closed the circuit, allowing an electrical current to travel to a detonator, which was encased in aluminum and embedded in the plastic explosive. The detonator was about an inch long and as thick as a pencil. The small explosion it created would generate enough heat and shock to ignite the surrounding Semtex.

Modern planes fly at such high altitudes that their cabins and cargo holds must be pressurized. When a jumbo jet is at cruising altitude, the pressure inside typically is kept at the equivalent of about eight thousand feet above sea level. That means that when a jet takes off and begins climbing to thirty thousand feet, air pressure inside the cabin changes with the pressure outside the skin of the aircraft until the jet reaches eight thousand feet. At that point the plane's equipment prevents the pressure from dropping further. The barometric device inside the bomb found with Dalkamouni and Khreesat would have worked on any commercial airliner flying virtually any route, and the timer would have started within minutes of takeoff when the plane reached three thousand feet.

"The detonating mechanism . . . is suited to detonate explosives automatically in an aircraft," a BKA report on the bomb said. "When the necessary operating height has been reached the fall in pressure connected with it will start the timing mechanism, and when the delay period has lapsed the detonator will be activated."

The suitcase bomb seized in Neuss was the descendant of sophisticated explosive devices developed by terrorists in the early 1980s. Unlike older airplane bombs, which used bulky, easier-to-detect dynamite, the more modern suitcase bombs get their power from plastic explosives.

Plastic explosives are so named because they are easily shaped or formed, not because they are made with plastic, although some are. The main ingredient in most plastic explosives is RDX, scientifically referred to as cyclotrimethylenetrinitramine. The Germans call it Hexogen. The bomb found in Dalkamouni's car was made from Semtex, the Czechoslovakian-made explosive that is orange-yellow in color.

Semtex-H, one variety of the plastic explosive manufactured by Czechoslovakia, contains RDX, a crystalline substance that looks like table salt, and another explosive ingredient called PETN, or pentaerythrite tetranitrate. These ingredients, highly explosive on their own, are heat- and impact-sensitive, but when combined with vegetable oils, waxes, or other binders, they become stable. Semtex is malleable because of its vegetable oil base, which gives it an oily texture in warm weather. The mixture is virtually odor-free.

Semtex is produced at a manufacturing complex in western Czechoslovakia near the small village of Semtin. The government-run facility has produced about a hundred tons of plastic explosives a year for the past twenty years. The government of Czechoslovakia sold Semtex-H to the Communist government of North Vietnam during the Vietnam War. After the war ended, Czechoslovakia began supplying it to Libya.

The damage caused by a Semtex explosion occurs when the material is converted from a solid to a gas, all in a matter of milliseconds. The laws of physics do the rest. Since the gas must occupy ten thousand times the volume of space that the solid mass did, the detonation causes a violent outward movement known as a pressure wave. The speed of the outrushing gases is more than 4.7 miles per second. By comparison, the velocity of a dynamite explosion can be as slow as 1.5 miles per second. It is this supersonic pressure wave that allows even a cigarette pack-size chunk of plastic explosive to blow the roof and doors off a car.

The advantages over dynamite are many, and terrorists like plastic explosives for the same reason the military does. Ounce for ounce they are many times more powerful than dynamite, and they can be rolled wafer-thin and easily concealed, jostled, and banged—all without danger of explosion. Most important for terrorists, they cannot be detected by conventional X-ray machines that airlines rely on for keeping bombs off planes.

The sophistication of the bomb's detonating mechanism was a trademark of Marwan Khreesat, who had nearly two decades of experience building explosive devices designed to destroy aircraft, dating back to the bomb that exploded aboard Swissair Flight 330, en route from Zurich to Tel Aviv on February 21, 1970. The bomb, stowed in the plane's rear cargo hold, was detonated by a barometric device that was triggered as the plane reached an altitude of fourteen thousand feet. Smoke from the blast obscured the pilot's view as he tried to make an emergency landing, and the plane crashed in northern Switzerland. Forty-seven people died.

Over the years Jibril's group has received support from both Syria and Libya and earned a reputation for ruthlessness. The PFLP—GC, one of the most effective and enduring terrorist organizations the world has ever known, is distinguished neither by religious fervor nor political clout. Rather, it is respected for its military effectiveness and its emphasis on tactics. Since its formation in 1968, the PFLP—GC has seen the war to evict the Israelis from Palestine in terms of what it could do militarily, and its leaders have constantly refined their methods for guerrilla attacks and bombings.

Israeli intelligence seized on an opportunity to strike back at Jibril and other Palestinian terrorist groups in February 1986. Sources told Israel's intelligence agents that a Libyan executive jet carrying terrorists participating in a sort of terrorist conference was about to travel from Tripoli to Damascus. Among those scheduled to make the trip were Abu Nidal, leader of a group once labeled by U.S. officials "the most dangerous terrorist organization in existence"; George Habash of the PFLP; Naif Hawatmeh of the Democratic Front for the Liberation of Palestine; and Jibril. Four F-16 Israeli fighters forced the plane to land at a military airport in northern Israel, but none of the terrorist leaders was on the jet. That was not the worst news for Israel. Abdullah Ahmar, the assistant secretary general of Syria's Ba'ath party and the second most important political figure in his country, was one of the flight's passengers. No sooner did the Israelis release the aircraft than threats of reprisals began to surface in the Syrian press.

Ahmad Jibril issued his own call for revenge at a February 1986 press conference in Tripoli, home of his ally Colonel Muammar Qaddafi.

"There will be no safety," Jibril said, "for any traveler on an Israeli or U.S. airliner."

CHAPTER 3

AN AMERICAN IN LONDON

CHRISTOPHER JONES was oblivious to the murky world of international terrorism in the summer of 1988. He spent his time working as a clerk in a CVS drugstore in South Yarmouth, on Cape Cod. He lived with several friends in an apartment and was trying to save money to help pay his tuition at Syracuse University.

Christopher Jones had grown up in Massachusetts and was a fan of Boston's baseball and basketball teams, the Red Sox and Celtics. And he loved toys. He kept a basketful of them in his room at his mother's house in Claverack, New York. During the summer he went to Toys "Я" Us and bought a large pink Fred Flintstone inflatable punching bag. He told his mother he planned to take it to Europe with him in the fall, but no matter how many times he tried packing it, it wouldn't fit into his suitcase. Before he left for England, he inflated the bag and placed it in the family room of his mother's house. It was a child's punching bag, the kind with sand in the bottom so it would right itself anytime it was knocked over.

Jones kept himself well supplied with squirt guns and plastic insects and, often when visiting a bar, would slip a plastic bug into someone's drink. His love of toys reflected the part of him that seemed to want to put off growing up. When he was eleven years old, his only sibling, Jennifer, got a job baby-sitting for a child next door. Jennifer was ten, and the job paid fifty cents an hour. Jones's mother asked him if he might consider getting a paper route, so he could begin putting aside money for college.

"Oh, no. It's OK for Jen to work but not me," Jones said.

29

"How do you figure that?" his mother inquired.

"Well, it's obvious. When Jennifer grows up, she'll have choices in her life. She can marry some rich guy and never have to work again in her life. Now when I grow up, I'm going to have to work until I die. So I'm going to take it easy now."

Jennifer Jones died before she had the chance to fall in love and get married. In January 1988, while participating in an American Field Service exchange program in Ecuador, she developed juvenile diabetes. Within a week she was dead.

Christopher Jones once told a born-again Christian he didn't believe in God because God never would have allowed his sister to die so young. But he also told his girlfriend, in a separate conversation, that he hoped he was wrong because if there was a God, there was a heaven, where he would be able to see Jennifer again.

In college Jones was an English major minoring in political science, though he wasn't quite sure what he would do when he graduated. During high school he told his friends that his goals in life were to become a sportswriter for the *Boston Globe*, to marry upon retirement, and to spend the last days of his life at the Boston Garden watching the Celtics win the National Basketball Association championship.

Jones's parents were divorced. His father lived in Massachusetts. His mother, Georgia Nucci, was a real estate agent in Columbia County, outside Albany in upstate New York. Jones moved out of his mother's house when he left for college in the fall of 1986. It was an especially difficult day for Jennifer, who realized this was the last time she and her brother would be living under the same roof. Every time he left the house carrying a load of his belongings to the car, she burst into tears. Jones's friends were helping him move, and they teased his sister by taking out handkerchiefs and dabbing at their eyes.

Jones left home, and the following March his sister left for Ecuador. The last time she talked with her brother was in October, three months before her death. She was eighteen, and he was nineteen. She became ill on December 29 and died on January 3. Her mother and stepfather, who had flown to Ecuador aboard a commercial flight, brought her body home the day she died.

At first Jones was not sure he wanted to study in England. It had nothing to do with his sister's death. His reservations had to do with being in unfamiliar surroundings. His girlfriend at college, Erica Elefant, had applied to the London program, and he decided to do the same, but when the acceptance notice came, he was ambivalent. His mother, who had traveled to Europe when she was at college, recalls that Christopher did not think he would enjoy traveling.

"Up until he went away, Christopher had an absolutely provincial attitude about things, no knowledge of the variety of experiences in the world," she said. "Before he went, I said, 'Why don't you get a student ID?' and he said, 'Well, why would I want to do that?'

" 'Well, that way you can get cheap transportation and stay at youth hostels.'

" 'Well, what do I want to travel for? I'm not going to travel. I'm not going to go to other countries. I'll stay home and study.'

"And I said, 'Chris, don't be a nerd. You're going to want to travel.' "

In September 1988 Jones and the other students in the Syracuse program flew out of New York's JFK Airport on two commercial flights. Jones had a seat on the second of the two planes. His mother and stepfather took him to the airport, and they got there several hours early. Part of the reason for the early arrival was that Jones's mother and her husband were extremely slow drivers. They often left hours ahead of schedule, just to be sure they would not arrive late. And part of the reason was Jones. He was eager to get going. When Jones arrived at JFK with his mother and stepfather, they took seats in a lounge and tried to fill the time.

Jones was dressed in shorts, dirty high-top sneakers, and a T-shirt. He couldn't sit still. He would stand up and pace, then return to his seat. "He was like a cat on a hot tin roof," his mother said. "He wanted to talk to the other kids, he wanted to stay with us, he didn't know what he wanted to do. . . . I finally said, 'Would you feel better if we left, and left you here to just talk with these other kids who are going and get on with it?' and he said, 'Yeah. . . . Why don't you go?' " When he hugged his mother, he saw that her eyes were beginning to grow moist; he told her not to cry. She said she wouldn't, and she kept her promise.

In London Jones rented an inexpensive apartment with three other students. The four young men shared a single bedroom, sleeping barracks-style. Jones liked the apartment because it had a large living room, which was perfect for parties. About once a month he and his roommates held a bash to which they invited as many of the university students as possible. Sometimes they placed signs in the school's London center, advertising the events. They were bring-your-own gatherings, and the students who attended them drank beer and spirits into the early morning. Jones and his friends took photographs of the parties. Many of the people in the pictures have bright smiles and glazed eyes.

"He always tried to meet as many people as he could, to try to become close to them," said his girlfriend, Erica. "He was fun-loving. He was always ready to go out and to drag people out with him."

It turned out Jones's mom was right about traveling. He loved it. He took frequent weekend trips through Europe, often sending his mother postcards that he signed, "Your favorite son, Christopher." He was her only son. In one postcard he bought during a trip to Dover Castle, he wrote, "This is one of the most fun days I've had here. I felt like a kid, climbing around. So much fun! I don't want to grow up, mommy." He called home every week, sometimes asking for money, always filling her in on his thoughts.

There was a reason for his faithful correspondence. "Christopher and I talked about the possibility—what if you go away and die?" his mother said. "I mean, you had to talk about it. If you didn't, that wasn't very honest because that was the thing that was hanging over us. And one time he said to me, 'I hope you don't mind my calling every week, but you know, if I should die while I'm over here, I wouldn't want you to not know what was going on.' "

Jones's return flight in December had been chosen months in advance. Students participating in the Syracuse University program had a choice of three flights home, and they were asked to indicate their selection before leaving the United States. The three flights were on December 19, 20, and 21. Some students, eager to do more traveling in Europe before returning home, elected not to take any of the flights and to make their own arrangements. Jones chose the December 21 flight because he wanted to make his time in Europe last as long as possible without staying in England over the holidays.

As Jones was partying with friends and seeing the sights of Europe, the pink Fred Flintstone punching bag he had been so reluctant to leave behind was still sitting in his mother's family room. One day in the fall, as she looked at the bag, Georgia Nucci remembered that her son's breath was inside. She also noticed that the bag was slowly deflating.

SIXTEEN-YEAR-OLD Melina Hudson was enjoying her summer vacation. She was between her sophomore and junior years of high school, and she had a lot to look forward to. Some days she walked with a girlfriend to Albany's Washington Park, where the friend had rehearsals for an outdoor play in which she had been cast. Other days Hudson walked to her father's downtown real estate office, where she worked part-time. With her three brothers, her parents, and an Italian exchange student who lived with the family, she took a short vacation to Gloucester, Massachusetts, where the family went on a whale-watching expedition. She also enrolled in a six-week accelerated mathematics course at Albany Academy, hoping to prepare herself for the fall term at Exeter School in England.

Hudson was excited about going to England, and she spent a good part of her summer preparing for the trip. Like her father, Paul, Melina Hudson was a careful planner. She drew up lists of what to bring with her, and she kept refining her choices.

It was largely because of her mother's hospitality that Hudson wound up attending Exeter. In May 1988 a group of students and faculty from Exeter came to Albany to establish an exchange program between their school and Albany Academy. Shortly before they arrived, the wife of the academy headmaster called Eleanor Hudson and asked her to provide rooms for several of the visitors, including Exeter's assistant headmaster and the school's secretary. The administration of the academy knew the Hudsons through their oldest son, Stephen, who was graduating from Albany Academy that summer. Eleanor Hudson agreed to host some of the visiting group, and during their three-week stay Melina became friendly with her family's guests. In fact, she grew so friendly with them that she decided to enroll herself in the exchange program.

The Hudsons were strong proponents of overseas study. Their son Stephen had been an exchange student in Italy, and they had always hoped their daughter would decide to study overseas, too. England was a natural choice for Melina Hudson. She had been fascinated for years by British society. As a young girl she sometimes clipped photographs of Princess Diana out of magazines.

Hudson was bright and had a strong, determined personality. In the eighth grade she underwent surgery to correct scoliosis, a severe curvature of the spine. Part of the procedure involved placing metal rods in her back. After leaving the hospital, she developed a painful infection that had to be dressed every day. She attacked the ordeal head-on, boiling the instruments before the nurse came to the family's house to change the dressing.

Melina Hudson loved ballet. Before her back operation she was a devoted ballet student who had, on occasion, performed with the Berkshire Ballet Company. She hung her pink ballet slippers on a nail on the wall of her bedroom. On another wall, above the headboard of her bed, she had hung a poster of a girl in leotards, putting on her ballet slippers. The poster's caption said, "Trust Your Dreams to God."

After school and on weekends Hudson sometimes did community work.

She was a volunteer tour guide at Albany's City Hall and worked at a local soup kitchen for the homeless. She also worked part-time as a page at the city library.

Hudson's family gave her a going-away party in August, and it was a celebration that filled the family's brownstone house with friends and relatives. Melina's maternal grandparents, Italian immigrants now living in Cleveland, Ohio, drove to Albany just to attend the party. She was especially close to her grandmother, for whom she had been named. As a going-away present her brother Stephen gave her a copy of Billy Joel's album *The Stranger.* One of her best friends wrote a message on the album's cover: "Melina—I don't really know what to write. Have a great time. I hope you get your Oxford man. This isn't too mushy—sorry." Hudson took the album with her when she left for England. She also took a gold ring that her parents had given her. Paul Hudson had given the ring to his wife years earlier; before turning it over to their daughter, they placed a small sapphire in its center, flanked by two diamonds, and inscribed Melina's name on the inside of the band.

IN THE summer of 1988 George and Judy Williams flew to Germany to visit their son, Geordie, an army first lieutenant. On the way, they were joined by Mrs. Williams's cousin from Ireland, Maurice McIlmail, and his wife, Margaret. The four toured the small airfield at Bad Kreuznach, southwest of Frankfurt, where Williams's helicopter unit—Company G, Fourth Aviation Regiment, Fourth Brigade, Eighth Infantry Division (Mechanized)—was stationed.

Geordie Williams was not a pilot, but he had one of the most challenging jobs in army aviation. He sat in the left seat of the OH-58D, the army's newest scout helicopter, serving as an aerial observer and a fire support officer. His job was to find enemy targets and assign them to attack helicopters, artillery, or fighters.

Williams enjoyed the challenge of his job and loved being in the air. He had been trained to fly the helicopter in case the pilot got hit, and he took the controls whenever he could. Thanks to his friendship with his pilots, he took over more often than he was supposed to, both in training at Fort Rucker, Alabama, and in Germany. He had started talking to his folks about switching to the air force so he could fly jets, or enlisting in the Air National Guard when he got out of the army.

During their visit to Germany the Williamses listened to their son describe his life in Germany. His missions frequently involved flying east to the border with East Germany. He told his parents that on these trips he waved at the East German guards in the towers. "They never did wave back," he said. "I guess they had orders not to."

When he was sixteen, Geordie Williams had decided he would become a soldier. He said at the time that every young man owed his country at least two years of his life.

He had been given the same first name as his father, grandfather, and great-grandfather. But his family called him Geordie, an Old World derivative of the name that helped distinguish him from the rest of the Georges in the family. His birth on May 17, 1964, was an event his parents had awaited for ten years. His mother had had two miscarriages, and after Geordie was born, she had no other children.

At Joppatowne Senior High School Williams ran track and cross-country, competing in the same event that his father had run, the quarter mile. He was not a star, and he never was able to beat his dad's best time, but he was part of a team that took the state indoor championship in Maryland. A tough competitor, he also displayed tenacity. In his junior year in college, after his grades had begun to slip at Western Maryland University, officials threatened to take away his ROTC scholarship. Though he had been raised to respect authority, his parents had also taught him not to be intimidated by anyone, so he traveled to Virginia to plead his case to the top officials in charge of the ROTC program. In the end they agreed to let him keep his scholarship.

The Williamses enjoyed the visit in West Germany so much that before leaving, they made arrangements to reunite with their son and the McIlmails for another vacation the following year. The next trip, they decided, would be to Scotland.

THE SUMMER of 1988 was no vacation for the balding spy called Tiny McKee, a large, muscular man who had served eighteen years in the military. He was working for his government in the volatile environment of the Middle East, performing what his army intelligence superiors referred to as an "extremely sensitive mission."

McKee's mother, who lives twelve miles east of Pittsburgh in Trafford, Pennsylvania, never knew for sure where her son was stationed. She believed he had been someplace in the Middle East for about four years. "He didn't talk, he didn't say where," she said. "I guess he felt that the less he said, the better and safer it would be for everyone." So secretive was McKee's work that his family was kept in the dark about some of his achievements. Although he had been graduated at the top of his class in five military schools, his relatives were unaware he had even attended two of them. McKee seldom discussed his work, even with such friends as Lieutenant Colonel Scott Tolman of the Army Intelligence Service.

In Beirut McKee officially was on temporary assignment to the Defense Intelligence Agency. He also was working for the Central Intelligence Agency. There is speculation that McKee boarded Flight 103 carrying photographs and videotapes indicating the American hostages captured by radical groups were being held in the Bekaa Valley of Lebanon.

McKee was an exceptional officer, one of the best and brightest in the United States military. In job evaluations, in which superiors had the option of assigning him scores on a scale of 0 to 70, he consistently received a perfect 70. He had served in two elite commando units, the Green Berets and the Army Rangers. He was fluent in Arabic, having completed a nine-month intensive course of study in that language at the Defense Language Institute in Monterey, California. "He told me that learning the language was more than learning words, that it was much more," said James Bock, McKee's close friend and former brother-in-law. "For instance, when somebody said, 'No,' it could mean, 'Not yet,' 'Maybe,' or 'I would like to say yes, but the organization that I represent wouldn't let me.' "

McKee was a strong man who played basketball in high school and lifted weights as an adult. He also enjoyed photography. He had pursued it as a hobby for about ten years and was the official photographer at his nephew's wedding. He carried his cameras, and a Bible, almost everywhere he traveled.

McKee enlisted in the army shortly after graduating from Penn State in 1970 with a bachelor's degree in police science. He received a draft notice the day of his college graduation and, rather than be drafted, decided to enlist. After investigating several branches of the military, he chose the army because he wanted to work in intelligence.

McKee had been married briefly and had a daughter, Aimee, who was born in 1971. McKee and his wife were divorced when Aimee was four, and now she lived with her mother in Florida.

McKee's work for the military took him around the world, including posts in Germany and Saudi Arabia. In 1975, when McKee was a second lieutenant, an army colonel filled out one of the young officer's first performance ratings. "Of all the newly commissioned officers whom I have known in the course of my career, Lieutenant McKee clearly falls in the top one percent," Colonel Alexander L. Galli wrote. He urged that his colleagues "closely monitor this officer's career development; he has a great deal to offer the Army." Within a year of that review McKee was fulfilling Galli's prophecy. His records say he was stationed in Munich, West Germany, and participating in a "sensitive intelligence operation." An evaluator wrote in a 1976 job rating that McKee had shown "outstanding ability" in developing and managing an intelligence operation that revolved around "a highly placed, valuable information asset capable of fulfilling national level intelligence requirements." The same report noted that McKee showed "moral strength, honesty and courage in defending beliefs and opinions." McKee's rank rose steadily, to first lieutenant in 1977, to captain in 1979, and to major in 1986.

McKee's security clearance was upgraded to "secret" in June 1979, and he was ordered to begin studying Arabic at the Defense Department language school in California. He completed the course in 1980 and five years later was working in the Middle East as a regional desk officer. His duties included coordinating army security in the region.

"For more than six months, Chuck McKee was the only Mid-East desk officer working the highly volatile and always complex issues of Lebanon, Jordan, Saudi Arabia, Kuwait, United Arab Emirates and Israel," Army Colonel Billy C. Brown wrote in a June 1985 job rating. Brown said McKee had shown himself capable of handling "intelligence related issues," and he recommended McKee be promoted immediately. "CPT McKee wants and needs the toughest and most challenging duties in military intelligence."

He soon received that tough and challenging assignment. In all his job reviews after June 1985, McKee is evaluated by "special operations officers" whose names have been deleted from the service records released by the army. In July 1986 McKee was working as a desk officer responsible for "special operations." By 1987 he had successfully completed a mission that involved his deployment in "an extremely hostile environment." McKee's last formal job review, written on July 29, 1988, indicates that from January 26 to July 7 he was engaged in "an extremely sensitive mission" in a "highly volatile environment."

"Maj. McKee continues to perform one of the most hazardous and demanding jobs in the United States Army in an exceptional manner," the 1988 job evaluation says. "He is recognized as the most knowledgeable individual on the operating environment in the country and is relied upon for his advice and assistance in the conduct of all in-country operations. . . . He spent the entire rating period in a highly volatile environment on an extended tour of duty, often working 18–20 hours per day to accomplish his project-related and other official duties."

McKee had done everything the army had asked of him. Yet by 1988 he told James Bock that he was thinking of retiring from the military in two years to begin studying international law. McKee also discussed his future with his mother, telling her he hoped to complete his military career with a short-term posting in the Washington, D.C., area.

A careful planner, McKee was meticulous about his finances. He owned investment properties in the United States, including houses in California and North Carolina. His will was prepared and filed, and he had purchased several insurance policies, naming his mother as beneficiary.

McKee's work in the military involved danger and intrigue, but there was a gentler side to his personality. He collected dinner plates, which he kept in a china cabinet, and he was fascinated by sand roses, formations that harden into delicate shapes in the desert. McKee gave sand roses away to friends and relatives and kept three baskets of them in the basement of his mother's home.

After his daughter was born in 1971, McKee brought a philodendron to his wife's bedside. When the couple divorced and McKee's wife said she didn't want the plant, McKee took it back. He kept it in his barracks at Fort Bragg while he was undergoing airborne training, and every time he was reassigned, the plant went with him. The rigors of long-distance travel took their toll on the plant, and at one point it looked like a dry brown stick, but McKee refused to throw it away. About five years before he boarded Flight 103, an army friend asked McKee why he kept hauling the plant around since it was nearly dead.

"This plant," McKee responded, "will never die."

CHAPTER 4

FLAWS IN THE
SAFETY NET

THE DAY after West German authorities found the radio-cassette bomb in the trunk of Dalkamouni's green Ford, German authorities prepared a warning about terrorist strikes and sent it to Interpol, the international police agency. It was clear that the radio-cassette bomb was intended for an attack against an airliner, and it was possible that similar bombs made by the PFLP—GC had escaped detection.

The aviation security system that was supposed to protect passengers like those on Flight 103 was not so much designed to thwart bombs as it was a response to a hijacking that had taken place three years before. On June 14, 1985, two terrorist followers of Hizballah, also known as Islamic Jihad, hijacked a TWA flight en route from Athens to Rome. For more than two weeks the hijackers terrorized the passengers and crew, killing one passenger, U.S. Navy diver Robert Stethem, and holding another thirty-nine U.S. citizens hostage.

It appeared that the Reagan administration was being dragged into the same type of drawn-out hostage ordeal that had plagued the presidency of Jimmy Carter. And then the standoff ended. On June 30 the hostages were released by their Shiite captors, driven to Damascus under the protection of the Red Cross, and flown to West Germany. Syrian President Hafez al-Assad played an important role in the resolution of the crisis, agreeing to accept the hostages from the Shiites before releasing them to West Germany.

The extended drama of the Flight 847 hostage crisis, covered in graphic detail by American newspapers and television crews, had a dramatic impact on the public's confidence in aviation security. The FAA responded to the public's concern by imposing stricter standards, known as extraordinary security procedures, at airports where the risk of terrorist attack was greatest. Both Heathrow and Frankfurt airports were covered under the tougher standards, one component of which prohibited an airline from transporting an unaccompanied bag without first physically inspecting it to be sure it did not contain weapons or a bomb.

Airlines incorporated these new procedures into their existing security programs and submitted them to the FAA for approval. In Pan Am's case the new rules came under Section 508 of the airline's security manual. On April 16, 1986, the FAA certified that Pan Am's manual satisfied the new requirements.

After making the new rules part of its corporate security program, Pan Am boosted one-way ticket prices by five dollars on all international flights, saying the new revenues would offset the increased security costs it was incurring. Pan Am also began using the new procedures as a marketing tool. One year after the Flight 847 hijacking, the airline began an advertising campaign to introduce what it called "one of the most far-reaching security programs in our industry." Pan Am's advertisements said the new system "would screen passengers, employees, airport facilities, baggage and aircraft with unrelenting thoroughness." In a television commercial that began airing at about the same time, Pan Am chairman C. Edward Acker said, "We at Pan Am are determined to provide a secure environment for our passengers." To heighten the visibility of the airline's new system, Pan Am's security subsidiary, Alert Management, stationed a team of dogs and their handlers in front of the airline's gates at JFK.

Behind the scenes there were indications that Pan Am's new security was little more than window dressing. The dogs, for instance, were not trained to sniff bombs at all, according to Fred Ford, Alert's first president. "They were your well-behaved German shepherds," he said. "They leased them from a kennel on Long Island."

Flaws in Pan Am's antiterrorist program were made explicitly clear in a report that the airline itself commissioned. To evaluate its system, Pan Am hired a well-regarded security consulting firm headed by Isaac Yeffet, former security director for the Israeli airline El Al. The firm, Ktalav Promotion and Investment Ltd., produced a document that became known as the KPI report. Yeffet was well qualified to conduct the evaluation because of his experience with El Al, which has developed the most effective security methods in the world as a result of decades of threats from Palestinian terrorists. Yeffet concluded, in a confidential report submitted to Pan Am in September 1986, that the airline's claims of effective security were a sham: "The striking discordance between the actual security level and the security as advertised by the corporation (and for which passengers pay a surcharge) may sooner or later become a cause of harmful publicity. In the event of casualties or damage resulting from terrorist action, the question of fraudulent advertisement would assume even graver significance."

On the front lines the security workers who screened passengers needed better and more extensive training, the report said. They worked in a system that relied too heavily on machines, and they were not particularly skilled in using that technology. KPI reported that people who operated Pan Am's X-ray machines often did a poor job, allowing bags to pass through even when it was clear that X rays had failed to reveal all of a suitcase's contents. And Pan Am failed to use decompression chambers to screen baggage at any of the nine sites surveyed by the consultants—including Heathrow and Frankfurt. Decompression chambers are designed to activate pressure-sensitive detonators on bombs before they are put on airplanes.

"There is virtually no training program for the security staff, not even at the senior officer level. The few hours of training which they get do not afford the elementary training expertise required for detecting explosive charges," the report added. "At some stations there are staff members who have not had any training whatsoever. Most security officers have never seen explosive devices, whether real or dummy, nor have they handled explosives." Airport security supervisors also lacked the contact they needed with local police and intelligence agencies to make them more aware of terrorist activity, according to the report.

"We cannot but conclude that under the presently operating security system Pan Am is highly vulnerable to most forms of terrorist attack," KPI said. "The system, even if it operated everywhere according to the standards it has set for itself, cannot afford adequate protection to its passengers, its aircraft or its personnel. It must be regarded as good fortune that, for the time being, no disastrous act of terrorism has struck the corporation."

The consultants also criticized Pan Am for failing to emphasize to its workers the need to understand the methods used by terrorists. Before passengers boarded a flight, Pan Am workers were supposed to ask them six questions designed to identify those travelers who should be screened more carefully. But the KPI report found that many passengers were asked only some of the questions or none at all. Furthermore, the report stated, "From the way the questions are put, it is clear that the questioners do not understand the importance of the questions, nor do the passengers." Terrorists have frequently gotten bombs on planes by disguising them as gifts and giving them to unsuspecting passengers. Yet Pan Am's security workers were making only halfhearted efforts to identify travelers who were carrying gifts. "Our experience is that by asking the questions in a proper way, one gets completely different and much better responses," the report said.

Security needed to be put on equal footing with other aspects of the airline's operations, the firm concluded. Under Pan Am's system, security procedures were sometimes suspended if they jeopardized the timely departure of a flight. At Dulles International, outside Washington, D.C., the consultant found that a busload of late passengers and their luggage had been taken directly to a plane without security screening, over the objections of the security officer on duty. "This insecure state of affairs is a result of many causes, most of which stem from the fact that the corporation does not regard the security issue as a professional service," KPI said. "Local managements tend to treat security matters with low priority, and at more than one station the attitude toward security activities and security personnel is condescending." The consultants said Pan Am needed to rethink its entire security framework if it intended to live up to the claims of its advertising. "Under the present security system, Pan Am is highly vulnerable to most forms of terrorist attack," the report reiterated. "The fact that no major disaster has occurred to date is merely providential."

The findings of the consultants were never presented to the airline's board of directors or to individual managers. Pan Am's top executives were skeptical of KPI's recommendations, which they suspected were part of an effort by KPI to obtain a lucrative ongoing security consulting contract.

The airline later claimed that it had implemented some of the consultants' recommendations, but there is clear evidence that many of the problems the firm had highlighted went unaddressed. For example, according to the 1986 consultants' report, Pan Am failed to screen its security employees' backgrounds adequately. All too often, KPI stated, Pan Am hired security workers who had "unsuitable personality profiles" or whose backgrounds had not been sufficiently scrutinized. Some Pan Am security officers even had criminal records, the report said. Two years after the KPI report was delivered to Pan Am, the airline's entire security operation at Frankfurt was headed by a man with several criminal arrests. Ulrich F. X. Weber had been arrested at least five times in Illinois on charges of writing bad checks in 1981 and 1982. Charges were dismissed in four cases; in the fifth case he was ordered to pay restitution and serve a year's probation. In addition, Weber had been fired from his job with Rockford Alarm in Illinois in 1982 after he had been accused of stealing property. He had received an "other than honorable" discharge from the Illinois National Guard for unexcused absences that same year. And in 1986 he was absent without leave from the U.S. Army while serving in West Germany. He was later court-martialed. In a well-run security operation Weber's background would have precluded him from engaging in even the lowest level of security work. In Pan Am's operation he was supervising security at one of Europe's most dangerous airports.

As KPI was compiling its list of Pan Am security flaws, the federal government was raising some concerns of its own. On October 7 and 8, 1986, the FAA convened a special meeting with Pan Am representatives at the agency's European headquarters in Brussels. The FAA called the session because of what it described as Pan Am's "apparent widespread failure" to implement the tougher security measures the government required following the 1985 TWA hijacking. The FAA looked as though it might be cracking down on Pan Am, but in fact, the agency was willing to look the other way when the airline violated security rules. For example, the new standards required airlines to apply security procedures to workers who clean and restock supplies on aircraft. Yet Pan Am dropped that screening at Frankfurt in April 1986 even though its own security manual required that it be conducted. The airline took that action, Pan Am security chief Daniel Sonesen said, as part of "a working agreement" with the FAA. The agency never cited Pan Am for this violation.

Pan Am sought a similar understanding with the FAA on another vital security procedure it found troublesome: screening passengers and luggage from the connecting flights of other airlines. At Frankfurt this was a particularly troublesome requirement because the airport was the busiest on the Continent. Screening bags and people took time, and at a busy airport like Frankfurt delays of even a few minutes would disrupt a flight schedule. Also, Pan Am security agents sometimes failed to identify a passenger for further screening until after his or her bags had been loaded onto the plane. To abide by the FAA rules, the passenger's bags would have had to be retrieved from the cargo hold and subjected to new scrutiny, causing additional delays. Pan Am, seeking to avoid delays, bought extra machines and began X-raying every checked bag from a passenger connecting from another airline, regardless of whether the bag's owner was deemed suspicious by the security staff. This solution kept the airline from having to retrieve bags from the hold. And it appeared to go beyond the

FAA requirements by ensuring that all bags—not just some of them—would be X-rayed. But the procedure was fundamentally flawed. Pan Am was now relying on the X-ray machines to find bombs, ignoring the equipment's inability to detect plastic explosives. The procedure also destroyed the airline's ability to match each piece of luggage in the hold to a passenger on the plane.

THE ARREST of the PFLP—GC members in West Germany and the discovery of the radio-cassette bomb in Dalkamouni's car prompted the FAA to send out a November 2 alert similar to the warning the Germans had issued. The Germans followed up by displaying the seized radio-cassette device at a November 15 press conference. Two days after that the FAA issued another security bulletin. This one described the bomb and reminded airlines to be especially diligent about complying with one of the most fundamental security requirements for international flights: Match each bag on a plane to a passenger on board. Pan Am received the memo the same day it was sent out but did not change its procedures.

The British Ministry of Transport sent out two warnings of its own about the Toshiba radio-cassette player bomb seized in West Germany. The first, a bulletin sent by telex on November 22, said airline security staffs should be told about the bomb discovery "in order that they may be aware for the discovery of similar devices, particularly when dealing with high-risk operations or passengers who attract suspicion for other reasons." Pan Am claimed it never received the telex. The same day security officials at Heathrow Airport in London were shown a model of the Neuss radio-cassette bomb. The second Ministry of Transport warning—a detailed alert—was drafted on December 19, although it was not distributed for nearly a month. British officials delayed sending the memo because they wanted to include a color photograph of the device, and the photo was not immediately available. When the alert finally was distributed, it went out by mail, not telex. Pan Am did not receive it until January 17.

The notice warned that a bomb like the one found in West Germany "will be very difficult to discover" and offered the following observations about the Toshiba device: Neither the radio nor the cassette player would operate; the device's aerial jack plug was taped to the side of the radio (inserting the plug was the way to arm the bomb); an X ray of the radio-cassette player would show more wiring than normal; and finally, the device would rattle if shaken because the explosive and a second set of batteries powering the detonator were not secured.

The memorandum stopped short of advising that suspicious devices not be allowed on planes. Instead, it made a curious and very dangerous recommendation: "Any item about which a searcher is unable to satisfy himself-herself must, if it is to be carried in the aircraft, be consigned to the aircraft hold." The memo was suggesting that a suspected bomb not be kept off the plane but rather stowed in the plane's belly.

Events in Finland, meanwhile, had prompted a second set of warnings involving a terrorist threat, this time specifically mentioning Pan Am and Frankfurt. On December 5 a man speaking with an Arabic accent telephoned the U.S. Embassy in Helsinki. He said a bomb would be planted by a Finnish woman on a Pan Am flight originating in Frankfurt sometime in the next two weeks. The threat was taken seriously. On December 7 the State Department cabled the warning to scores of embassies and diplomatic posts. The FAA, on the same day, sent the warning to U.S. air carriers, including Pan Am.

On December 13 the warning was posted on bulletin boards in all sections of the U.S. Embassy in Moscow. It read:

ADMINISTRATIVE NOTICE
American Embassy, Moscow
December 13, 1988

To: All Embassy Employees
Subject: Threat to Civil Aviation

Post has been notified by the Federal Aviation Administration that on December 5, 1988, an unidentified individual telephoned a U.S. diplomatic facility in Europe and stated that sometime within the next two weeks there would be a bombing attempt against a Pan American aircraft flying from Frankfurt to the United States.

The FAA reports that the reliability of the information cannot be assessed at this point, but the appropriate police authorities have been notified and are pursuing the matter. Pan Am also has been notified.

In view of the lack of confirmation of this information, post leaves to the discretion of individual travelers any decisions on altering personal travel plans or changing to another American carrier. This does not absolve the traveler from flying an American carrier.

(signed) William C. Kelly,
Administrative Counselor

The notice was distributed to the entire American community in Moscow, including journalists, businesspeople, and students. Nancy Bort, a civilian embassy employee, made dozens of photocopies and placed them in embassy mailboxes used by American businesspeople. Pat Mears, the embassy's community liaison officer, made sure copies were received by the Anglo-American School.

U.S. officials later stressed that police had dismissed the Helsinki threat as a hoax. Hoax or not, the warnings to the airlines were never withdrawn. Pan Am's security manager in Great Britain, who was responsible for security in Helsinki, called his counterpart in Frankfurt to be sure he had received the warning, then traveled to Helsinki to set up procedures for screening selected passengers. Identical procedures were said to be in place in Frankfurt, where security staff members were supposed to "dump search" the bags of any Finnish traveler who fitted the profile described by the Helsinki caller.

Two years earlier one of KPI's criticisms had addressed the way Pan Am handled such warnings. Even when an airport received a warning, some members of the local security staff never saw it, the consulting firm said. At JFK and Miami airports a warning about explosives being smuggled inside a doll had gone out in early June of that year, but most security officers still knew nothing about it when KPI spoke to them in mid-July. KPI found similar problems at Pan Am's operations in Paris and Frankfurt.

Two years had passed since Pan Am received the KPI report, but little had changed at Frankfurt. Neither the warning about the radio bomb nor the Helsinki threat had filtered down to all the screeners checking Pan Am passengers and bags. At a time when Pan Am should have been taking extra precautions against unaccompanied bags and radio-cassette players— especially in Frankfurt—no special measures were in place.

Although some of Pan Am's security workers were ignorant of the threats, at least two passengers booked on Flight 103 found out about the Helsinki warning. Two college students, Karen Noonan and Patricia Coyle, had just ended a semester of studies through an exchange program in Vienna. On December 20 they attended a party at the marine barracks at the U.S. Embassy in Vienna. During the gathering Noonan and Coyle found themselves in a group of about half a dozen guests, including Coyle's boyfriend, Sergeant Curt M. Olsen, a marine guard at the embassy.

The conversation turned to the bomb threat that had been phoned in to the Helsinki embassy in early December. Someone said the caller had promised a Pan Am flight out of Frankfurt would be destroyed in the weeks before Christmas. One member of the group was worried about flying with the American carrier.

Olsen knew of the threat but was not greatly concerned. Before his transfer to Vienna he had spent an eighteen-month tour in El Salvador. In Central America he and the other marines had lived under constant threats of violence. Compared with those threats, the Helsinki warning seemed vague. When Noonan and Coyle asked him for his opinion, Olsen said he thought the other party guests were overreacting.

Noonan did not seem particularly worried either. To those at the party she appeared more occupied with thoughts of returning home to Potomac, Maryland.

Noonan and Coyle planned to leave Europe on December 21. Months before, they had booked seats on Pan Am Flight 39, which would have taken them directly from Vienna to JFK in New York City. But while they were in Austria, Pan Am had changed its schedules. Now Flight 39 would not leave until December 22. Rather than wait another day, the two women booked a flight that would allow them to leave Vienna on December 21. Their new route was less direct and required them to change planes in Frankfurt, where they were to board Pan Am Flight 103 to cross the Atlantic.

Many people within the aviation industry and at Pan Am realized the importance of the FAA rule requiring a passenger-baggage match. But some of them considered the task too enormous to be feasible. If a bag made a connection and the passenger did not, the missing traveler became a no-show, and his or her bags had to be removed from the connecting plane before it could depart. The only case in which an unaccompanied bag could be placed on a flight—clearly there needed to be a way for an airline to reunite separated passengers and bags—was if the airline opened and hand-searched each bag belonging to a passenger who had failed to board. In the chaos of the baggage transfers at major airports such as Frankfurt, this created a significant problem for busy airlines, such as Pan Am, because passengers who fail to board do not become no-shows until the last possible minute. Delays caused by retrieving the luggage of no-show passengers have ramifications for air traffic control, raising havoc with the timing of several flights.

The aviation industry resisted the bag-to-passenger match rule but was forced to accept it in the wake of the TWA Flight 847 hijacking, which placed pressure on governments to take tougher precautions against air terrorists. The International Civil Aviation Organization (ICAO) quickly adopted the bag-to-passenger match as a recommended policy after the 1985 hijacking. The United States soon followed suit. "It got into a situation of who could outsecurity the other and who could do more from a publicity basis," said David C. Leach, special assistant to the director of the FAA's Office of Civil Aviation Security. "It was a motherhood–apple pie situation. It was who could get out in front the fastest. So it was passed as a standard. At that point it was recognized by many of the major aviation countries of the world that there was simply no possibility of doing this immediately. It was just an impossibility with the number of transfer flights and so forth."

While Pan Am continued ignoring the FAA bag-to-passenger match requirements, there were some within the airline who questioned the decision. Alan James Berwick, Pan Am's chief of security in Great Britain and Europe, had been told by the head of Pan Am security at Heathrow that X-raying was an acceptable substitute for matching bags to passengers. In a 1988 memorandum to Pan Am's corporate headquarters in New York Berwick sought clarification of the policy and pointed out that "total reliance on X-ray itself was not necessarily a good thing." His memo went on: "I am very much aware of the limitations of the X-ray equipment and more important, those persons who operate it." Daniel Sonesen, in charge of Pan Am's corporate security worldwide, wrote back that Pan Am had negotiated another working agreement with the FAA that made the practice permissible. He said Raymond Salazar, the FAA's security chief, had personally approved X-raying as an alternative. Sonesen's telex said the policy was clear: If an interline passenger failed to show up for a Pan Am flight and if his or her bag was already on the plane, "we go!!!!!"

Salazar later denied that he had approved Pan Am's system. Yet during two FAA inspections of Pan Am's Frankfurt security operations in April and October 1988, the agency failed to cite the airline for circumventing the bag-to-passenger match rule, even though its agents observed the violation. Martin Huebner, the Pan Am security chief for West German operations, wrote in an October memorandum to FAA headquarters that "since Frankfurt introduced the X-ray of all transit baggage there is no longer reconciliation of the number of transit baggage made." And FAA Inspector Tommy Dome, in a report following his October 12 inspection of Pan Am operations at Frankfurt, wrote that Pan Am had "no verifiable tracking system" for bags transferred from other airlines.

Although it did not recommend penalizing Pan Am, Dome's Frankfurt inspection report included some generally critical findings that echoed the KPI report. In particular, it cited a problem with the airline's procedures for tracking passengers selected for further security checks. "The system, trying adequately to control approximately 4,500 passengers and 28 flights per day, is being held together only by a very labor intensive operation and the tenuous threads of luck," Dome said.

The FAA's strongest action against Pan Am regarding the deficiencies it had observed at Frankfurt came in an October 28, 1988, letter in which the agency asked the airline to document its passenger-screening procedures at Frankfurt. The FAA asked Pan Am to respond within thirty days. Huebner was not surprised by the FAA request. In a memorandum to his boss Huebner explained that many of the issues that concerned the FAA had been raised before internally at Pan Am but that nothing had been done. "I have discussed these items in the past with [Pan Am] station management at Frankfurt," Huebner wrote. "It has been pointed out to me that for financial reasons the security staff has to be kept to a minimum." Pan Am took nearly two months to provide the documentation requested by the FAA. The material, sent to the FAA's regional office in Brussels, arrived on December 21, 1988.

CHAPTER 5

THE DEADLY
CARGO

AT ABOUT 3:20 P.M. local time on December 21 at Frankfurt's airport, baggage handler Kilins Aslan Tuzcu picked up the first suitcase destined for Pan American World Airways Flight 103. Tuzcu, a native of Turkey, had been employed as a Pan Am baggage loader for seven years and was one of about forty-eight thousand people who worked at the Frankfurt airport. On this day he worked alone, organizing the bags that were brought to his work station on conveyor belts.

Tuzcu's job was to separate the Flight 103 luggage into three piles. On one cart Tuzcu placed the bags headed for London; after the Boeing 727 had landed in Heathrow, they would be taken directly into the terminal. On another cart he threw the bags bound for New York; in London those bags would be transferred directly to the Boeing 747 that continued the Flight 103 route. On a third truck Tuzcu placed the interline bags, which belonged to passengers boarding at Frankfurt from other airlines. As a security precaution, the interline bags had to be X-rayed before they were loaded onto the 727. By 4:20 P.M. 111 bags had been processed for the Frankfurt to London leg of Flight 103.

On the cart containing the interline luggage, Tuzcu loaded what he remembered later as twelve bags, a total backed up by baggage claim records maintained by Pan Am. Tuzcu recalled that there were four or five hard-sided suitcases, several soft-sided bags, and one or two pieces of luggage with tags indicating they were "rush" bags—bags that had been separated from their owners and were being rushed to catch up with them. About fifteen or twenty minutes before Flight 103's scheduled departure

51

from Frankfurt, Tuzcu drove the cart containing the interline bags to a mobile X-ray station.

The employee who was operating the X-ray station, Kurt Maier, had been working for Alert Management at Frankfurt for only two months. Maier's training had been minimal; it consisted of two sessions, one lasting half a day and another lasting a few hours. Since starting his job as a Pan Am security guard, Maier had been assigned to operate the mobile X-ray unit thirty-seven times, during which he had examined an estimated thirty-four hundred bags. In the course of those assignments there had been only six to ten occasions when he became suspicious enough about a bag's contents to take a look inside. On this day Maier worked a 9:00 A.M. to 5:00 P.M. shift. In a log he kept of his work, Maier noted that he checked ten suitcases, two garment bags, and a cardboard carton that appeared to contain wine bottles—a total of thirteen containers. This conflicted with the twelve-bag total recalled by Tuzcu and with the twelve bags accounted for by baggage claim records. At the time, however, no one noticed the appearance of this thirteenth bag.

At Maier's X-ray station Tuzcu took the interline bags off the luggage truck and placed them on a belt leading to the X-ray chamber. Maier looked at the screen as the bags filed through the chamber, but he saw nothing unusual and allowed all the luggage to pass. Tuzcu retrieved the bags as they came out of the X-ray machine and placed them back on the cart. Then he drove the cart to the waiting 727. Maier wrote in his log that he completed his examination of Flight 103's luggage at 4:25 P.M.

Inside the terminal Geordie Williams, Khalid Jaafar, Suruchi Rattan and her family, and other passengers on the first leg of Flight 103 passed through a German government screening point, where their carry-on bags were X-rayed and their bodies were scanned with a hand-held metal detector. The passengers then approached Gate 44, where Pan Am agent Wolfgang Manner ripped the boarding passes off their tickets and entered their seat assignments into a Pan Am computer. The purpose of the computer entry was to be sure all Flight 103 passengers were accounted for, but the computer might also have helped Pan Am perform its required security checks. The airline was supposed to make sure every passenger who checked a bag actually boarded the flight, to guard against an unac-companied bag getting on board. But on December 21 there was no such reconciliation of bags to passengers. Agents at the boarding gate had no communication with the ramp workers who had handled the luggage.

Monika Diegmuller was acting as Pan Am's ground security coordinator for Flight 103 at Frankfurt. Normally she worked as the terminal services supervisor, but that day she was supervising the preflight screening of passenger and carry-on luggage. When she checked with Alert and was told there were no security problems with the flight, Flight 103 received its "flight finalized" designation from departure control. Diegmuller told Flight 103's captain that the plane was ready to depart. At 4:54 P.M. local time the 727, carrying 128 passengers, was pushed away from the gate. As the first leg of Flight 103 lifted off for London, its cargo load sheet carried the notation that there had been "no known security exceptions."

AT HEATHROW the first suitcases destined for the 747 that was to fly the second leg of Flight 103 arrived late in the morning of December 21. They were interline bags—suitcases entering Pan Am's system from connecting flights operated by other airlines. They were directed to a baggage transfer shed, a point of intersection for luggage from five or six airlines. Inside the shed the bags were met by John W. Bedford, a Pan Am loader-driver who had been employed by the airline for fifteen years. Bedford worked alongside two Alert security guards, Sulkash Kumar Kamboj and Harjot Singh Parmar. It was the guards' job to operate an X-ray machine that examined the interline suitcases as they passed through the baggage transfer shed.

It was a busy day at Heathrow, as passengers scrambled to make it home for the Christmas holiday. The early bags for Flight 103, however, were coming in slowly. The flight was scheduled to leave at 6:00 P.M., but by midafternoon only four suitcases had arrived. As each bag came to the transfer shed, Bedford lifted it up and placed it on a conveyor belt leading to the X-ray machine. One of the guards examined the bag as it passed through the X-ray machine. At the other end of the belt the second guard placed tape on the bag to indicate it had been screened. Kamboj and Parmar took turns examining the early bags for Flight 103. Neither saw anything unusual.

As the taped suitcases came down the machine's conveyor belt, Bedford lifted them up and placed them inside a standard metal-sided luggage container that sat ten to fifteen feet away from the X-ray machine. The container was essentially a five-foot cube, one side of which was open to admit luggage. The opening was equipped with a sliding curtain. Ten such containers could fit into the forward cargo hold of one of the mammoth Boeing 747 jets. The container Bedford was using was labeled "AVE 4041 PA." The numbers had caught his attention earlier in the day, when he towed the container into the baggage shed, because Bedford had been born in 1940 and his wife in 1941.

Bedford placed the four bags, handles up, in a neat row along the back of the luggage container. Then at 4:15 P.M., as his shift drew to a close, he left the shed to visit another location known as the buildup area, where the bags from the first leg of Flight 103 would be unloaded. Bedford wanted to find out how many bags from Frankfurt were scheduled to continue on to New York City because those bags would have to be piled on top of the four bags now inside container AVE 4041 PA. But when Bedford reached the buildup area, a supervisor told him the bags from Frankfurt hadn't arrived yet. The incoming 727 from Frankfurt was running late. The supervisor told Bedford to bring the sparsely loaded luggage container to the buildup area, then punch out on the time clock and go home.

Bedford returned to the baggage shed at about 4:45 P.M. When he looked inside luggage container AVE 4041 PA, he noticed that two bags had been added to the four suitcases he had loaded earlier. These two bags had been transferred to Flight 103 from British Airways Flight 701 from Vienna. They were lying on their sides against the floor of the container, just in front of the row of bags at the back. The six bags now inside the container covered its floor completely. Bedford towed container AVE 4041 PA to the buildup area, just outside Pan Am's offices. Then he punched out and went home. The curtain to the luggage container was left open, awaiting the addition of the bags from Frankfurt.

The 727 from Frankfurt finally arrived at Heathrow at 5:40 P.M. Five minutes later Pan Am loader-driver Amarjit Singh Sidhu was sent to retrieve luggage container AVE 4041 PA, and he found it where Bedford had left it more than thirty minutes earlier: outside Pan Am's office, in the luggage buildup area. Sidhu closed the curtain and towed the luggage container to the side of the 727. Then he pulled back the curtain and looked inside. The bags were just as Bedford had left them. There was still a neat row of four bags lined up along the back, and two bags lying on their sides in front of them.

The next step was to fill container AVE 4041 PA with New York-bound luggage from the 727. There were three luggage handlers inside the 727's belly, and they worked quickly so the 747 bound for New York could get off on time. They placed the bags from Frankfurt on a belt that carried them out of the plane and to the handlers waiting on the ground. Sidhu and Pan Am's head loader at Heathrow, Darshan Singh Sandhu, took turns lifting the bags off the discharge belt and throwing them randomly inside container AVE 4041 PA. The first bags off the 727 ended up at the rear of the container. Those off-loaded later wound up at the front, near the curtain. The container filled quickly. Sidhu closed the curtain and drove the container to adjacent stand K-14, where the 747 was waiting. He left the container beside the larger plane and took another vehicle back to the 727. Container AVE 4041 PA, now fully loaded with luggage, was placed inside the forward cargo bay of the 747 along with nine similar containers. The containers were loaded two abreast, five against the left side of the fuselage and five against the right side.

As Flight 103 lifted off from Heathrow at 6:25 P.M. and headed for New York City, container AVE 4041 PA rested against the left wall, four containers back from the front of the plane. Its position put it slightly in front of the 747's left wing. A bomb made of Semtex and hidden in a radio-cassette recorder was inside a suitcase that had been transferred from Frankfurt and placed in the lower corner of the luggage container, on top of other suitcases near the container's outside edge. Most of the luggage in the container was piled above it, toward the center of the plane. As the minutes ticked off and the 747 gained altitude, a circuit closed and the bomb came to life.

ALAN TOPP saw it first. The air traffic controller at Scotland's Prestwick Airport was tracking Flight 103 as it crossed over the border between England and Scotland. The plane appeared as a small green box with a cross in its center and a code—0357 310 68566.9—by its side. The green box represented the plane. The coding was the aircraft's squawk, a signal transmitted by the plane. Flight 103's squawk indicated that the plane was flying at thirty-one thousand feet. The six digits at the end of the coding gave the elapsed time in seconds for that day. It was 46.9 seconds past 7:02 P.M. on December 21, 1988.

Topp, a controller with twenty-four years of experience, closely watched the progress of the Boeing 747 jumbo jet. Several other aircraft in the region flying low-altitude shuttle runs from London to Glasgow and Edinburgh had been granted permission to climb to higher elevations. Topp was making sure these smaller 737s and 707s steered clear of Flight 103's airspace.

Only a few minutes before he was scheduled to be relieved for a coffee break, Topp noticed the first change. Flight 103's coding and the cross in the middle of the box had vanished. Eight seconds later Topp saw another change. The little green box, an image created by ground radar that bounced off the skin of the plane, had broken into four smaller boxes. These smaller boxes were fanning out and now covered an area that represented about a mile of airspace. Topp thought he must be seeing some sort of false image.

Topp's work station had a bank of four radar screens, each covering a different region of Scottish airspace. He knew Flight 103 was flying near a radar aerial at a place called Lowther Hill, and he thought the flight's location might explain the two changes he had observed. Sometimes a flight passing directly over an aerial will enter an area of dead space, known as a zone of silence, in which it is momentarily invisible to radar. If Flight 103 was passing over the Lowther Hill aerial, that might explain the multiple images. Topp waited, but the small boxes didn't go away. They were continuing to fan out.

Topp reached for his radio telephone and tried to contact the plane's crew, with whom he had spoken minutes before. There was no response. He tried to reach them several more times, each time getting no reply.

In another office at Prestwick Airport air traffic control assistant Tom Fraser also was beginning to sense a problem. Fraser was working in the oceanic clearance office. Moments earlier he had been talking by radio to Flight 103 copilot Raymond Wagner, who had contacted the tower and asked to be assigned a track over the Atlantic Ocean. Because the ocean is so vast, no radar screen encompasses the whole area. Each airplane leaving the Continent is assigned an altitude and course and told to stay within it, to avoid collisions with other aircraft. A plane's track assignment is considered such a vital piece of information that before the crew can acknowledge receiving it, two crew members must be sure they have heard it. But Flight 103's crew never acknowledged the track assignment Fraser had given them. Frequency 123.95 MHz was silent.

"Clipper 103, do you read?" Fraser asked. He repeated the question several times. He radioed other aircraft in the area, asking them to call Flight 103, but they, too, were unable to reach the 747. Then Fraser's phone rang. It was Alan Topp from air traffic control, wanting to know if Fraser had lost radio contact with Flight 103. It was clear to both men that something was terribly wrong.

Moments before calling Fraser, Topp had come to a sobering realization. The image he was watching on his radar screen—the one he thought was generated by the radar aerial at Lowther Hill—was in fact being generated by another aerial at Tiree, a remote Scottish island on the Sea of the Hebrides, about two hundred miles to the northwest. That meant there was no chance the images on his screen were caused by a dead zone.

A knot was growing in Topp's stomach. The boxes on his radar screen were multiplying, fanning out, and beginning to fade. To Topp they looked like Christmas tree lights, moving around and almost twinkling.

Topp had worked steadily through a list of possibilities, contacting air traffic controllers who were watching aircraft flying at lower elevations. He asked himself if this wasn't all just a bad dream. But none of the other controllers could see Flight 103 either.

Several minutes had passed since the little green box on his radar screen had broken apart. Topp had to shout to get the attention of his supervisor, Adrian Ford, who sat at a desk about ten yards away. Ford, cradling a telephone to his ear, held out his arm to indicate he was busy. Another pilot, operating a British Airways 757 shuttle from Glasgow to London, had reported seeing an explosion on the ground in southern Scotland. Ford was trying to reach local police by telephone, but the police weren't answering.

"I've got a problem," Topp yelled across the room to Ford.

"So do I," the watch manager responded. He told Topp about the report of an explosion on the ground.

"Well, in that case it's the Clipper 103," Topp said.

Ford stopped what he was doing and placed the telephone receiver on his desk. The phone was still ringing at the police station on the other end. He walked to Topp's desk, and both men stood staring at the radar screen. The image had changed; now a cluttered path of radar returns fanned out downwind of Flight 103's last position. Neither man said a word. But both knew what they were witnessing.

THE 747 had been flying smoothly through the winter sky, crossing into Scotland, when the conversation between the cockpit crew and flight controllers ended in mid-sentence. The cockpit voice recorder that captured the dialogue recorded a loud background noise that lasted 180 milliseconds, about the time it takes to blink an eye. Then the recorder lost power.

Inside luggage container AVE 4041 PA in the forward cargo hold, a battery had sent an electrical charge through wiring to ignite a fuse. The fuse's charge was minor, just enough to detonate about 12.25 to 14 ounces of Semtex that had been packed around it. The plastic explosive turned from solid to hot gas almost instantly, creating tremendously high pressure as the material expanded to occupy the space it needed in gaseous form. A spherical shock wave raced outward from the point of the detonation, shattering part of the base and outboard face of baggage container AVE 4041 PA. Fragments and heat from the blast pitted and scorched parts of that aluminum container and the outside of AVN 7511 PA, a fiberglass luggage container directly to the rear. The nearest section of the aircraft's frame buckled. The sphere of the blast wave grew larger, intersecting the skin of the aircraft after traveling only about 25 inches. It punched a hole in the fuselage about 18 to 20 inches in diameter, barely a pinprick in the skin of a jet 225 feet long. Only milliseconds had passed since the bomb's detonation.

Blasting the hole spent only a portion of the Semtex's force. The fuselage reflected a substantial shock wave back toward the point where the explosion had originated. When these reflected waves crashed head-on with the pulses from the blast itself, a phenomenon known as a Mach stem shock wave resulted. The interaction of the blast and reflected waves created a powerful offspring that sped along the curved surfaces of the inside of the fuselage skin like a race car through a banked turn. This Mach stem wave, a hybrid of the direct and reflected shock waves, probably was 25 percent faster than, and twice as powerful as, the waves from the explosion itself. Mach stem waves normally shoot off in odd directions, depending on the configuration of the reflective surfaces. But on a Boeing 747 there are ready-made conduits to transport Mach stem waves—in effect, to channel and intensify their effects. The Mach stem waves raced away in two main directions: down into the belly underneath the baggage containers and up the left side of the plane in the gap between the baggage containers and the inside of the fuselage wall. The power of these waves would doom the aircraft.

The Mach stem waves created tremendous overpressure in various cavities of the aircraft, some far away from the point where the bomb exploded. Consequently, at about the same time that the direct effect of the blast punched the eighteen-inch hole in the fuselage, overpressures from Mach stem waves peeled off a section of the 747's roof several feet above the point of detonation. Similarly these waves gouged a hole through the thick skin in the belly of the plane. The continuing high pressure forced the jagged edges of the holes to petal out. As the cracks spread, the holes grew bigger. The 747's air-conditioning system channeled shock waves into the cabin, where they bounced off galleys, overhead luggage racks, and other hard surfaces to bombard first-class passengers with jolts from several sides.

A cloud of high-pressure gas spreading out at supersonic speed followed closely behind the shock waves. This gas sustained the high pressures in areas that had just been pummeled by explosive shock. The bomb's effects were enhanced by the difference in conditions inside the plane, where air pressure was kept at breathable levels, and those outside the fuselage, where the air pressure at thirty-one thousand feet was only about one-quarter of what it is at sea level. In an instant huge chunks of the aircraft above and below the window line between the cockpit and wings were gone, torn away by the blast and by the resistance of the wind rushing past.

The blast warped sections of the plane containing the cables that are used to control the flaps and tail. The explosion moved the cables so that the aircraft dived and rolled to the left. By now the explosion had knocked out power, thrusting the cabin into darkness. The front of the plane continued to disintegrate from the top and bottom, leaving intact the windows on the side of the fuselage and the floor. The floor, which had been reinforced to carry military cargo in wartime, gave way next. When the plane dived and rolled to the left, the reinforcing belt that held the row of windows along the left side failed. The cockpit and forward section of the fuselage broke away, deflecting up and to the right. As this breakaway section peeled back, the right window belt that held it to the rest of the fuselage snapped, and as the nose cone tore free, it struck the No. 3 engine, knocking it from the right wing. Chunks of the forward fuselage continued to break away, peppering the tail on their way past until the tail structure was a jagged silhouette. Three seconds after the explosion, the fuselage, cockpit, and No. 3 engine were falling separately.

The fuselage was an open cylinder, hopelessly nonaerodynamic. Tornado-force winds tore down the aisles, stripping clothing off the backs of passengers and flight attendants, turning drink carts into lethal projectiles and filling the air with sharp, deadly pieces of shrapnel. The wind and the rending of metal created a tremendous roar. Some passengers were thrown to the rear. Others, tossed out into the night, joined luggage and other pieces of the plane to form a ghostly caravan that swept through the moonlit troposphere at 499 mph. These passengers were battered by a 130-mile-an-hour crosswind in an air temperature that was fifty degrees below zero Fahrenheit.

In the instant that the sealed fuselage broke apart, the air pressure inside the cabin plummeted to equal that of the atmosphere outside. Suddenly subjected to the lower air pressure, gases inside passengers' bodies expanded to four times their normal volume. Most of the passengers found themselves fighting for breath. Expanding gases caused their lungs to swell and then collapse, driving the oxygen out of their system. Fierce winds slammed into their face and chest, making it difficult to breathe.

As the plane descended to nineteen thousand feet, gravity overcame forward momentum and the fall became almost vertical. The tail fin disintegrated. Tremendous pressures tore at the structure, pulling the remaining three engines from the wings. The fuselage broke into pieces, separating from the wings. Different chunks of the aircraft descended at different speeds. The wings, slowed least by the atmosphere because of their shape, sliced downward at an accelerating rate. They reached their destination first, still laden with two hundred thousand pounds of fuel.

THE DEBRIS from Flight 103 fell directly on Lockerbie, a Scottish community of thirty-five hundred known mainly for the dairy and sheep farmers in the rolling hills near the English border. For centuries most residents of the community had led slow-paced lives in obscurity. But events in the night sky were about to make the name of the town an international synonym for disaster.

Many Lockerbie residents were settling in for the evening as the passengers and pieces of Flight 103 began their descent. Robert Miller was in his living room at 5 Sherwood Crescent, getting up to switch off the television.

Miller was sixty-four and retired, but everyone in town called him Bobbie. A plasterer for most of his life, he had saved up for years to be able to buy this house on Sherwood Crescent. It was the first home he and his wife, Jane, had ever owned. It had a sitting room, a dining room, a kitchen, a bathroom, a sun porch, a garage, and two bedrooms.

At 7:00 P.M. on December 21 Miller and his wife had begun watching the television program "This Is Your Life." But the show failed to hold their interest. She got up and headed to the kitchen for a drink of water. He got up, turned off the television, then bent down to adjust the heater mounted on the living-room wall.

Across the street at 6 Sherwood Crescent, Mary Ward was wrapping two boxes of cookies. They were a Christmas present for eighty-two-year-old Jean Murray, her friend and neighbor. Murray lived four doors away at No. 14, and on this Wednesday evening four days before Christmas she was watching television. Murray was in a good mood. Her nephew had just invited her to spend the holidays with his family.

Across from Murray at No. 11, Mary Lancaster, an eighty-one-year-old widow who lived alone, moved about with the aid of a cane. Lancaster had been using the cane ever since she was fitted for an artificial hip earlier in the year. A former resident of England, she had lived on Sherwood Crescent for fifteen years.

Next door to Murray, at No. 16, Tom and Kathy Flannigan had finished supper with their two children Steven and Joanne. In several days the family would be celebrating a reunion. The Flannigans' oldest son, David, had been away from home since an argument with his father three years earlier, but this year he had promised to come home for Christmas. After supper fourteen-year-old Steven took his sister's BMX bicycle to a neighbor's garage to repair one of its tires. His parents and his sister remained inside the house, which stood at the southern end of Sherwood Crescent.

Across the street from the Flannigans, at No. 15, ten-year-old Lynsey Somerville was at home with her parents and twelve-year-old brother. Lynsey and Joanne Flannigan were best friends. The two girls went to Brownie meetings together, and both attended Holy Trinity Church. The previous day they had sung Christmas carols together at school.

Next door to the Somervilles, at No. 17, John and Janet Smith, a retired couple in their mid-seventies, were sitting in their living room, waiting for the program "Coronation Street" to come on television.

Around the corner Robert Hunter left his 29 Sherwood Park home and walked toward the center of town to meet some friends at a pub. Hunter had two daughters, two and four; as he left home, one of them was already in bed. The other was about to be tucked in for the night.

At 13 Sherwood Crescent, Dora Henry was preparing supper for Niall Scott, the Henrys' lodger. Scott, a twenty-year-old constable, was due in at any minute. At home with Dora was her husband, Maurice, who had retired from the construction business after suffering two strokes. In retirement the couple enjoyed showing friends their collection of antiques.

The first thing most people noticed was the sound. One man described it as the low rumbling of thunder; another said it was like the rush of twenty express trains coming into the station all at once.

The fuel-laden wings of the Boeing 747, joined by a section of fuselage, slammed directly into 13 Sherwood Crescent, where Dora Henry was preparing supper for her lodger. The wings were descending at between 506 and 575 mph, and the more than a hundred tons of fuel they carried exploded on impact, gouging out of the earth enough dirt to create a V-shaped crater 155 feet long and 40 feet wide—about half as long as a football field. The blast killed Maurice and Dora Henry and vaporized their house, including its foundation.

Tom and Kathy Flannigan died in their house along with their daughter, Joanne. Their son Steven survived to witness the devastation from his neighbor's garage.

Joanne's friend Lynsey died with her parents and brother at 15 Sherwood Crescent.

Eighty-two-year-old Jean Murray died alone at No. 14, sitting in front of her television set. Mary Lancaster, the eighty-one-year-old widow who walked with a cane, died, too.

Pieces of the plane fell upon the neighborhood like a deadly rain, ripping through roofs, crushing walls. A bathroom sink from the plane knifed through the Millers' roof and wedged itself inside a gable. Globs of flaming aviation fuel fell with the debris, igniting fires as far as a thousand feet downwind.

The shock wave from the explosion flattened houses closest to the impact and ripped off roofs of others up to 75 yards away. More than 125 yards away at 29 Sherwood Park, where Robert Hunter's two toddlers were going to bed, the air pressure from the blast blew in doors and lifted the first-floor ceilings.

A towering orange fireball boiled up out of the crater, displaying its brilliant colors against the black sky. It flashed through houses and scorched vehicles in the two southbound lanes of the A74. A Lockerbie policeman, Michael Stryjewski, thought it looked like the mushroom cloud from a miniature atomic bomb.

"It was extremely noticeable for miles around. It just kept going up," Stryjewski said. "It rose quite slowly—I was surprised how slowly—but I couldn't see the top. I would estimate it went up at least a thousand feet." Against the orange of the cloud he saw the black silhouettes of thousands of tiny particles raining down on the earth. He picked up the telephone to call 999, the number for emergency services, but his line was dead.

The blast lobbed more than fifteen hundred tons of debris skyward in sweeping arcs that subjected rooftops to a second pounding. The debris included chunks of roadway and houses. A four-foot block of concrete crashed through the Millers' roof and landed on the couple's bed.

John Smith, the retired man who was watching "Coronation Street" with his wife, sensed the approach of an airplane. He was turning away from the television to say to his wife, "This plane's very low," but before he could get the words out, something hit the roof of his house. A sheet of flames rolled down from the ceiling above his head. The Smith house was two buildings away from the center of the blast.

"Suddenly there was a loud bang and everything was on fire," Smith said. "Something fell on top of me—I don't know if it was part of the house or from the plane—and I fell down on my knees, trapped. I tried to move it. The first time it wouldn't budge, but the second time I got free. I went into the kitchen to try and find a way out, but it was full of smoke. So was the bedroom." Smith struggled out the front door, then called for his wife. She said she couldn't move, so he went back inside to get her. She had collapsed on the floor. "I couldn't see her, but I managed to grab hold of her and led her out of the house. There were flames everywhere. Even the lawn was on fire." Rescuers pulled the Smiths over a garden wall to a safer part of the neighborhood. Both John Smith and his wife suffered severe burns.

Up the street, in the house where Mary Ward had been wrapping boxes of cookies in Christmas paper, pieces of blazing wreckage crashed through the roof, showering her with chunks of masonry. She managed to escape through her front door. Her cat, Misty, survived, too.

At 5 Sherwood Crescent Bobbie Miller heard the rushing sound of the falling debris and turned away from the heater he had started to adjust. The explosion blew in the window behind him and knocked him headfirst into the television screen across the room. Miller suffered cuts on his scalp. He and his wife scrambled toward the back of the house. They kept the back door locked, with the key in the door so it could be opened only from the inside, but the blast had knocked the key out of the door and at the same instant put out the lights, locking them inside in the darkness. They managed to climb out through broken porch windows, and as they came around to the front of their house, the heat from the far end of the street forced them north. "When we come out, all the gravel, everything, the road, everything, was all on fire with the fuel," Jane Miller said. Their surviving neighbors spilled into the street and joined them. "When we got out, everything was burning. Everything. The whole crescent," Miller said.

For a moment the world was silent. The shower from the night sky had stopped, and no one spoke.

The fires threatened to block the Millers' escape route. Fuel from the plane had ignited the area immediately behind the Townfoot Shell station more than two hundred yards away, where old tires had been piled among a wrecker and two trailers. The fire consumed an aboveground thirty-three-hundred-gallon diesel fuel tank and lapped at the rear of the garage. If the fire had reached the underground fuel storage tanks, the resulting blast could have rivaled the explosion caused by the wings.

As they approached the Shell station, the Millers remember plenty of people shouting.

"The cry was 'Keep moving, Keep moving. Head for the Dumfries Road,' " Bobbie Miller said.

Inside the Shell station worker Ruth Jamieson was petrified. "The whole sky lit up; then everything came flying through the roof," she said. "I was terrified that the fuel tanks were going to go. We had a delivery the night before, and if they had went, there would not be much left of Lockerbie."

Eleanor Hogg had been walking with her sister in front of the drugstore at the center of town. "At first we thought it was thunder," she said. "Then the sky lit up, and there was a terrific bang." Against the orange sky she spotted a falling object she recognized as a jet engine. From where she was standing it looked as though it would land on the town's movie theater. The engine missed the cinema, slamming into the soft ground of Mains Meadow, a pasture between the buildings on the main road at the southern end of town and the rail line that linked London to Glasgow. Two other engines, falling at 300 mph, hit the field about the same time. One impaled itself on a fence post.

At the railway station the train from Edinburgh had just arrived. To people crossing the footbridge over the tracks, the explosion at Sherwood looked like fireworks. Some people ran under the bridge for cover, while others sought shelter in the station.

The impact of the falling debris caused monitoring stations operated by the British Geological Survey in southern Scotland to register a seismic event measuring 1.6 on the Richter scale.

The first fire call came in just before 7:05 P.M., when a Lockerbie resident telephoned the Dumfries and Galloway Fire Brigade to report a "huge boiler explosion" at Westacres, a neighborhood about two hundred yards on the opposite side of the four-lane highway from Sherwood Crescent. Other calls flooded the switchboard almost at the same moment. The wife of an off-duty fireman reported a plane crash, while another caller said there had been "an explosion and ball of fire" at a cheese plant west of town.

People who had been inside the houses and pubs that line Main Street ran outside and surged toward the glow at Sherwood. The flood of people immediately halted traffic, and cars quickly backed up beyond the town's limits.

The plane's No. 3 engine, knocked free moments after the aircraft had begun breaking apart, plummeted to earth on the north side of town. Robert Riddet, who had run out his back door and was looking at the fireball at Sherwood Crescent three miles away, suddenly realized that whatever was happening was not over. As fuel and pieces of luggage fell down around the row of houses set into the hill around him, he heard noises above him. "It built up into a tremendous crescendo of sounds," he said. He looked almost straight up and saw the engine tumbling wildly toward him, making a screaming sound. "It was still running full pitch," he said. Just as the noise became unbearable in Riddet's ears, it abruptly stopped. The engine had slammed into the pavement of a parking lot in front of an apartment house about two blocks away. The impact drove the engine almost entirely underground, rippling the pavement in a circle around the edge of the hole. The engine narrowly missed cars, houses, and people. It damaged a twelve-inch sewer line but just missed the water and electric lines that serve the neighborhood. Like many other Lockerbie residents, Riddet assumed that two jets had collided above Lockerbie.

Riddet's son, Alan, an off-duty fire official from a neighboring district who was visiting his parents, got in his car and drove directly to the Sherwood Crescent neighborhood.

About two miles northeast of Sherwood Crescent a large piece of the plane's fuselage slammed into 71 Park Place, where Ella Ramsden was home with her dog and bird. The fuselage section—extending from the rear of the wings about halfway back to the tail—contained the bodies of some passengers still strapped into their seats.

Ramsden had been feeling sad all day. Her son and his family, who had celebrated the holiday with her a week early, had left that morning to return to Germany. After the Scottish television soap opera "Take the High Road" had ended at 7:00 P.M., Ramsden turned off the set, got down on her knees in front of her living-room heater, and began opening the day's batch of Christmas cards. That's when her dog, a terrier named Cara, started to growl.

Ramsden heard a low, droning sound. It was coming from the sky, but it sounded too near to be an airplane. She got up from the heater, walked to the window, and opened the curtains. The whole sky was lit up with a bright orange glow. Somewhere she heard an explosion.

"First of all I thought it was the petrol station. So then my next thoughts were, *What am I going to do? Am I going to get out of here or am I going to stay in the house?* I don't know whether I was thinking or saying out loud to Cara, 'I think I would be better out amongst other people.' So I picked her up under one arm, and I came from my window to my back door, which was in the kitchen. And as I put my hand on the door to open it, it wouldn't go; it was jammed. And the lights went out."

She heard a whooshing sound and felt wind pulling at her legs. She bent down to see if the rug at the back door had become wedged into the doorframe. Then Ella Ramsden's house began to fall in on her. The noise was long and deafening. Ramsden became convinced she would never get out. Then the noise stopped as suddenly as it had started. She wasn't sure if she was alive or dead. The back door was still there, but when Ramsden looked up at where the ceiling used to be, she could see stars in the night sky. Ramsden edged over to a cupboard to her left, gripped a pan in one hand, and smashed the glass on the back door. The overwhelming silence returned, and Ramsden whispered for her neighbors.

"John, Martha, are you there?"

No one answered. There was debris all around her, and Ramsden could not move. This time she shouted, "Please help, please come get my wee dog. Someone please come and help me."

Finally she heard a shout that struck her as rude: "She's alive. She's fucking alive."

It was her neighbor's son-in-law. He had seen something fall into Ramsden's garden and had come to the house to see if she was all right. Two other men were with him. Ramsden was still holding on to her dog. She worried that if she put it down, it might run away. She handed the animal to one of the men. Then she grabbed a chair and, with the help of the three men, began climbing through the door. Given Mulligan, Stewart Kirkpatrick, and Graham Moffat pulled Ramsden through the door, over a fence, then carried her onto the roadway. Because there was debris lying everywhere, the men held her high, so that her feet did not touch the ground.

When she got out of her house and was standing on her lawn, she turned to look back. "I still couldn't think what had happened. I looked up, and the bedroom on the left-hand side—there was nothing but the wardrobe in it. My two grandchildren had slept there for nearly a week. I mean, they had been in that room at nine o'clock that morning. I still didn't know really what had happened. Thankfully for me, it was dark, and I didn't see the horrors that were in my garden." But she did catch a glimpse of the body of a man lying on the road behind her house. Although she knew all her neighbors on Park Place, she didn't recognize this man. She asked if anyone had called to get him an ambulance.

The magnitude of the disaster was not apparent to Ramsden or to her neighbors, who had begun to assemble around her. Everyone assumed a Royal Air Force jet had crashed. No one had any idea how big a plane it had been.

Jimmy Beattie, a forty-four-year-old contractor, was watching television with his wife, Mary, at their home in Tundergarth when he heard a roar that made him think his chimney was on fire. He and his wife walked into the backyard and saw that the night sky all around them had turned to red. Objects were falling everywhere; some were on fire. Beattie and his wife ran back inside to get their children, James, five, and Margaret, six, who had just been put to bed. He feared the house would be ignited by the rain of flaming debris. The children, who had heard the noises and seen the lights from the fires, began screaming. The family ran outside. For perhaps a minute everyone stood in the yard beside the house. The fire consuming Sherwood Crescent glowed in the distance. A factory must have blown up, Beattie thought. Then he looked up and saw a huge black object, larger than a truck, silhouetted against the red sky. It was falling to earth, spinning like a top. It landed less than a hundred yards from where they stood, making a weighty thud Beattie felt in his feet.

Beattie ran inside and grabbed a flashlight from the kitchen. When he came back outside, he noticed there were papers blowing through his yard. Some had Pan Am's logo on them. He walked up to the fallen object. It was an airplane cockpit, resting on its side, misshapen but remarkably intact. The windshield wipers had barely budged. Blue letters spelling *Maid of the Seas* were still legible. There were openings at either end of the cockpit. Beattie directed the beam of his flashlight inside and saw twisted metal and a tangle of wires. Then he saw the bodies. There were several of them, and they appeared to be naked except for underwear and socks. Some were covered with blood. He saw a human scalp and a leg that had been severed. Clothing and body parts were everywhere.

The crumpled body of a woman in a Pan Am uniform lay near the nose cone. Mary Young, a fifty-three-year-old local resident who had been attending to her horses in a nearby barn, came across the woman and began searching for signs of life. She found a pulse, weak but regular. She laid a coat over the injured flight attendant, then went to find some rugs, which she thought might make the injured woman more comfortable. The woman wore several beautiful rings, which glimmered in the beam of a flashlight. When Mary Young returned ten minutes later, the flight attendant was dead.

By 7:10 P.M. the first fire truck—dispatched from a station at the center of town—reached Park Place. The fire fighters smelled the odor of natural gas from a broken main and began to evacuate residents. By 7:11 P.M. Alan R. Riddet, the off-duty fire official, had made it from his parents' house to Sherwood Crescent. He radioed the first assessment of the damage to brigade headquarters in Dumfries, a city about thirteen miles west of Lockerbie.

The nightmare was only beginning for fire fighters. The explosion had destroyed the three-inch water main that served the neighborhood, including its fire hydrants. The absence of water pressure near the crash forced fire fighters to tap into hydrants distant from the affected area, but many of them were dry, too. Later they discovered that one of the plane's engines, falling in a meadow near the railroad tracks, had severed a six-inch water main that served the entire southern end of town. While public works crews rigged up a temporary bypass, fire fighters called in milk tankers to haul water.

On the A74 highway, which bypassed the center of Lockerbie, truck driver John Young left his rig to help people out of their cars escape the flames. Then he cut across a field to the burning houses.

"As I got to a house, I saw an old lady slumped on the road," Young said. He and others helped her up and moved her to a safer place. When the first firemen began to arrive, Young and other volunteers helped run out the hoses.

Robert Hunter, the Sherwood Park resident who had been walking to a pub, turned around and headed for home when the debris from Flight 103 began descending on Lockerbie. A few minutes ago his wife had been putting their two daughters to bed. Now he did not know if they were alive. Police stopped him at the gas station, where normally he would have been able to see his house. But the lack of power to streetlights and the smoke from the fires made it impossible to assess the damage. "I didn't know if the house was still standing," Hunter said.

He walked away from the horde of townspeople who had surged down Main Street to Sherwood Crescent, thinking he could get into the neighborhood from the north side, through a street called Douglas Terrace. But that road was littered with knee-deep flaming rubble. Police stopped him there as well. It was not until 9:30 P.M. that Hunter learned that his family was safe. They had escaped the carnage and made it to a relative's house.

Fire fighters continued their work, scattering to extinguish the flaming wreckage that had fallen randomly about the town. They made their way into the field between the Rosebank Crescent and Sherwood Crescent neighborhoods, where three of the plane's engines had landed. Two were in flames and had to be doused with a high-pressure hose reel and portable fire extinguishers. On the north side of town, at the corner of Alexandria Drive and Sydney Place, fire fighters sprayed the smoldering engine that had punched a hole through the pavement.

Royal Air Force search helicopters arrived at 8:40 P.M. and began sweeping the hillsides with searchlights, trying to discern some sort of pattern to the wreckage. One of the first duties of the helicopter crews was to scan the railway line that bisects the town to make sure it was not blocked by debris that would derail the next passenger train. Pieces of the plane lined the embankments, but none was on the track.

The crisscrossing helicopter flights ensured that anyone in Lockerbie who tried to sleep that night would find it pointless. Ella Ramsden had gone to her brother's house on the north side of town. Cara, her dog, refused to leave her side, even for an instant. Every time one of the Chinook helicopters rumbled overhead, the terrier growled.

Telephone circuits were overloaded throughout the evening, compounding the confusion. Ramsden, lucky for the second time that night, managed to get a line out to let her family know she had survived.

By 10:09 P.M. Lockerbie Firemaster J. Barry Stiff had twenty pumpers on the scene. A series of fires burned in Lockerbie over an area more than a mile long and half a mile wide. The worst blaze was in the southwest corner of town, in the area of Sherwood Park and Sherwood Crescent. There were dozens of smaller fires in the eastern end of town. More fires, and dozens of bodies, were being reported at Tundergarth, several miles to the east. Before the night was over, calls went out for twenty-one pumpers and eight rescue trucks or other special units. More than 350 Lockerbie residents, most from the Sherwood and Rosebank areas, were evacuated.

The passengers had fallen in clusters. About sixty of them fell near a golf course on Lockerbie's eastern end. About fifty bodies landed with the fuselage in Ella Ramsden's garden. Others landed farther east, in the countryside known as Tundergarth. The bodies of ten passengers never were recovered.

For most passengers the six-mile free fall lasted about two minutes. Some may have lost consciousness almost instantly. The thin air at thirty-one thousand feet, combined with the tremendous winds, extreme cold, and injuries resulting from flying debris, may have had a cumulative traumatic effect on passengers, causing them to black out. But others may have remained alert for thirty to forty-five seconds. And some passengers who blacked out may have regained consciousness as they fell into oxygen-rich atmosphere closer to earth. As many as half were alive when they hit the ground, then were killed by the force of the impact. One passenger was found clutching a child, a clear indication of consciousness during the terrifying descent. Two passengers remained alive briefly after impact. Medical authorities later concluded that one of these passengers might have survived if he had been found soon enough.

Christopher Jones, the Syracuse University student who had to report to work at a bookstore the next day, landed on his back in a sheep pasture overlooking the Lockerbie golf course. He came to rest on the side of a hill, near a ridge of trees. His body, like most of the others that had fallen free of the fuselage, bounced once, leaving a deep depression in the spongy, rain-moistened earth.

Melina Hudson, the Albany high school student with dark blond hair, fell to earth on Park Place, near Ella Ramsden's house. Geordie Williams, the army lieutenant, and Karen Hunt, the student loaded down with gifts for her family, landed nearby. Glenn Bouckley landed on Park Place, too. The receipt from the rental car he had returned before boarding the plane was tucked neatly into his wallet. His wife, Paula, seated across the aisle from him in the same row, landed on the Lockerbie golf course. Her wristwatch was still working.

Khalid Jaafar, the young man returning to Michigan from Lebanon, landed on the Lockerbie golf course.

Major Charles ("Tiny") McKee, the spy working in the Middle East, landed in Tundergarth.

Three-year-old Suruchi Rattan landed east of town at Halldycks farm.

ALAN TOPP, the air traffic controller at Prestwick Airport, stayed at work through the end of his shift. After it had become clear that Flight 103 had exploded in midair, Topp was relieved by a supervisor and told to take a moment to collect himself. He went to the canteen, where he drank a cup of hot coffee. Then he returned to the air traffic control room.

Topp picked up one of many ringing telephones and spoke to a local radio reporter who was pursuing a promising news tip. Someone had reported that a small aircraft had crashed near Lockerbie, the reporter said. Did Topp know anything about it? Topp looked over at Ford, who was writing down the first information anyone in the office had been given about Flight 103. In Ford's handwriting, Topp saw that there had been about 250 passengers and crew on board the plane. He told the reporter the airport lacked detailed information about the downed plane, then got off the phone.

Topp's shift ended at 10:45 P.M., and he went home. Videotapes of the crash already were being broadcast on television. For several hours Topp had followed the unfolding disaster from the air traffic control room, peering at radar screens and taking reports over the telephone. Now, as he stared at his television, he saw footage of the houses that had been incinerated by the falling jumbo jet. For the first time he saw the horrors that the tiny green boxes on his radar screen had only hinted at. A comment by a television reporter particularly haunted him. The reporter described the huge scale of the damage and speculated that the crash might have been caused by two airplanes colliding in midair. The mere mention of that possibility terrified Topp; it was an air controller's worst nightmare. Before going to bed, he took his four-year-old collie mix, Teddy, outdoors for a walk. Again and again Topp played in his mind what he had seen on the radar screen back in the control room.

Tom Fraser, the air traffic control assistant, left the airport about an hour after losing radio contact with Flight 103. He went home and had a drink. It failed to calm his nerves.

CHAPTER 6

TRAGIC NEWS

W HEN JASWANT Basuta returned to the Pan Am check-in desk at Heathrow Airport after missing Flight 103, all his relatives had gone. A Pan Am ticket agent told him there was no way he could get to New York that night. She said he had two options: He could stay overnight in the passenger lounge at Heathrow, or she could arrange for a taxicab to take him to a nearby motel. Basuta thought of a third option: He could call the relatives who had just dropped him off at Heathrow and ask them to come back and get him. At first that idea didn't appeal to him.

"They'll think, *stupid jackass,*" he thought.

The Pan Am agent noticed how agitated he was and tried to comfort him.

"Don't be nervous. You're not the first passenger to miss a flight."

"Lady, this is very important," Basuta replied. "I had to be there because of my job."

Eventually Basuta decided he would stay overnight in a motel, even though it would mean sleeping without a change of clothing. He planned to call his relatives in London to tell them he had missed the flight, but he figured they probably had not arrived home yet. So he settled back in a chair in the passenger lounge, feeling sorry for himself. In all his agitation he failed to notice that the Pan Am agent had booked him on a flight to New York City the following day.

At first the two London policemen who approached him were an annoyance.

"Are you Mr. Basuta?" one of them asked.

He said that he was.

"Did you miss Flight 103?"

He said that he had.

"Do you know what happened to that flight?" the officer said.

Basuta believed the policemen were trying to oust him from the passenger lounge, and he thought about telling them to leave him alone, but all he said was "All I know is I missed it."

"Do you know what happened to that flight?" the policeman said.

Basuta repeated his answer.

He thought the policemen were joking when they said the plane had crashed in Scotland. But they were staring directly at him, and their expressions bore no trace of humor.

"You'll have to come with us to the Heathrow police station to explain to us how you missed the flight," one of them said. Basuta followed them to their car, still trying to comprehend what he had just been told.

CHRISTOPHER JONES'S mother, Georgia, and her husband, Tony Nucci, reached John F. Kennedy International Airport about 5:30 P.M. and pulled their Ford Bronco into the parking area. Nearly three and one-half hours had passed since Pan Am Flight 103 descended on Lockerbie in a shower of bodies, jet parts, and aviation fuel, but the Nuccis were oblivious of the disaster. They had driven down the Taconic Parkway with the car radio off.

Georgia Nucci had brought some homemade chocolate chip cookies for her son to eat on the drive back home. She carried her camera and an album of photographs of her daughter into the airport terminal but left the cookies in the Bronco.

The Nuccis planned to meet someone for dinner at the Pan Am terminal. The previous year had been agonizing for the Nuccis. In the frantic days of Jennifer's sudden illness in Ecuador, they had scrambled to find a charter jet ambulance that would fly her home. Mrs. Nucci found an ally in Audrey Wilson, a medical director for the American Field Service's foreign exchange program. Wilson lived and worked in New York City, and although she had never met Mrs. Nucci or her daughter, she was the one who broke the news that Jennifer had become ill. Through telephone conversations the Nuccis felt they had gotten to know Wilson intimately. So when the day came to pick up their son, they called her and invited her to join them for dinner at the Pan Am terminal so they could meet in person. The Nuccis planned to show Wilson the photo album and introduce her to Jones.

As they walked through the terminal toward the restaurant, the Nuccis noticed a roomful of television cameras.

"What's going on?" Mrs. Nucci asked a female security guard.

The guard was gruff, telling them to move along. Mrs. Nucci remembers looking at the television screen listing information on arrivals and departures. Her son's flight was not listed yet.

Audrey Wilson knew what the commotion was, and as she looked for the Nuccis in front of the restaurant, her uneasiness grew. At work that afternoon Wilson had heard a radio report about the crash of a Pan Am flight from London. She had leaped out of her chair and cried, "Oh, my God, oh, my God! No, no, no," but then she told herself that her reaction was premature since she didn't know what flight Christopher Jones had taken. She tried calling, but the Nuccis had already left for New York.

The Nuccis did not know what Wilson looked like, so they had decided on a precise meeting point outside the restaurant. Mrs. Nucci was scanning the crowd for a woman she pictured as a short, dumpy white housewife with glasses and a bad haircut, a mental image of Wilson derived from her Brooklyn accent. When a tall black woman in an African robe walked toward them, Nucci approached her tentatively. The woman wore beads piled high around her neck like a collar.

"Audrey?" he asked.

Wilson looked, saw them smiling, and felt overwhelming, immediate relief. She concluded that Jones must not have been on the flight that crashed. They introduced themselves, hugging and kissing.

"Where's Christopher?" Wilson asked.

"He's still up there, flying around in the sky," Georgia Nucci said.

"When is his flight supposed to get in?"

"Eight-thirty."

"What flight is he on?" Wilson persisted.

"Pan Am 103," Mrs. Nucci said.

Just as quickly as she had felt relief, Wilson now was terrified. She felt as if someone had pulled a black hood over her eyes, as if the world were going dark.

"That flight crashed," Audrey Wilson said, a reflex response that she wanted back. She gasped and placed both hands over her mouth.

The moment burned itself into Georgia's memory. Time stood still as her mind struggled to cope. Wilson's surprising looks were fresh in her thoughts, and she connected that impression with the horrible news this stranger was bringing her. *This is an impostor,* she thought in a vain attempt at denial. *This is a joke.* But comprehension crashed through. She took off her glasses and handed her camera to her husband. She walked to a wall, placed one hand against it for support, closed her eyes, and prayed. At forty-six she had outlived both her children.

Tony Nucci and Audrey Wilson supported each other in an embrace. Mrs. Nucci reminded herself to stay calm, that she had already lived through this once before, but her thoughts were interrupted again as her mind flashed back to Jennifer's death. It had been one year before, and she was on her way to her daughter's bedside in Ecuador. She was in the Miami airport, and officials of another airline would not let her use a private phone to call ahead to Ecuador to find out if her daughter was still alive. She had stood in line at a public pay phone, tears streaming down her face.

The memory made her angry: angry that the security guard outside the press conference had neglected to tell her moments ago that a plane had crashed, angry that her loss of a year ago had not somehow exempted her from another loss so soon. By now the Pan Am television monitors had begun posting an ominous message for people arriving to meet Flight 103: "SEE AGT." Mrs. Nucci turned away from the wall, walked to another security guard, and grabbed him by the sweater.

"Now tell me what happened to 103," she demanded.

The guard asked if she was waiting for someone on that flight.

"My son," she said. "Did it crash?"

"Yes."

"This is unfair. My daughter died this year," Mrs. Nucci said. "It's not fair."

"What are you doing here?" the guard asked, knowing that other relatives had gathered in a lounge in the arrival area. "My God. Why are you in the departure area?"

"Get me to a private place," she said. The guard placed his arm around her, and they began the long walk to the lounge where relatives had been sequestered by Pan Am.

To Georgia Nucci, the walk down the airport corridor seemed endless. A bottleneck of journalists formed at the guarded entrance to the first-class lounge where the families were gathering. The reporters' hunger for information had increased when they found little news forthcoming from Pan Am. The media stood between Georgia and the door.

As the Nuccis and Wilson approached, the television lights came on, and the horde collapsed around them. A female still photographer circled Georgia, snapping photographs within inches of her face. A handsome male television reporter approached her. Mrs. Nucci remembered that he had a beard. But mostly she remembered what he asked: "How do you feel?"

"That's a really stupid question," she responded.

By doing so, she became one of the few relatives to have broken the silence, and the reporters' interest in her rose even higher.

"Is there anything you would like to say?" the bearded reporter asked.

"Yes," she said. The crowd moved closer. A photographer's tripod rested on her foot.

"You're all in my way."

Georgia Nucci would not remember what happened next, but friends who saw the scene on television told her she swung her arms to clear a path to the door. She hit the female photographer and crashed past equipment. The next morning she found a burn from a television light on the back of her left hand. Among those who saw Georgia Nucci on the evening news that night was her father. That was how he learned his grandson was dead.

Mrs. Nucci escaped the media frenzy inside the terminal by making her way into the comparative quiet of the lounge that Pan Am had turned into a reception center for victims' relatives. Small coffee tables were set up at intervals in the large room to create areas where families gathered. The room swarmed with more than a hundred people. In addition to relatives, there were nurses, doctors, priests, and Pan Am agents. In their midst wandered telephone technicians, heavy equipment belts sagging at their sides, plugging phones into wall outlets so that each family had its own place to make calls. As bad as it had been outside, Georgia Nucci found the noise in the lounge unbearable. With every new arrival it started again.

"Screaming, absolute screaming," she said. "It was sobbing and screaming. The screaming seemed to echo. It rained over you, this screaming."

"People were saying, 'I don't want to live,' " Nucci recalled. " 'I don't want to wake up tomorrow. We're going to have to sell the house; I'll never be able to go back there again.' "

Others huddled under blankets, moaning. Audrey Wilson heard the cries of mothers: "My baby, my baby, my baby. It should have been me." One woman was threatening to kill herself. Another lay on a table, curled in a fetal position. Pan Am workers brought out sandwiches, soft drinks, coffee, and a supply of scotch, rye, and bourbon. Georgia Nucci consumed quantities of Coca-Cola, and others drank coffee, but few people ate. And all night long Mrs. Nucci saw only one person take a drink of liquor.

The Nuccis stayed at the Pan Am terminal until about 1:00 A.M., then went to a nearby Holiday Inn where the airline had reserved rooms. Mrs.

Nucci, unable to sleep, spent much of the night pacing. In the morning Pan Am hired a chauffeur who drove them to Claverack. A young airline employee followed behind in the Nuccis' Ford Bronco. The chocolate chip cookies Georgia Nucci had made for her son were still there, unopened.

DECEMBER 21 was a busy day for Eleanor Hudson. Her daughter, Melina, was coming home from England, and she wanted to be near the telephone when the flight arrived in New York City in case she had trouble making the train to Albany. Hudson had to hurry to finish her last-minute Christmas shopping; she spent part of the day buying Melina a pair of black Calvin Klein pajamas.

Melina Hudson was coming home earlier than planned. In November her mother had booked her on Flight 103 for December 22, and Melina called her father on December 20 to relay her travel plans. Paul Hudson took down the information on a paper napkin near the phone.

"El—Melina called. She's on Pan Am Fl. # 103, arriving NYC JFK 7 p.m. Thurs. The flight is not confirmed. I told her to confirm but you better do it also from this end. Call the school at 58712 or 54188 to leave message."

Those travel plans were later changed, for reasons neither she nor her mother understood. "Something happened. They couldn't put me on," Melina Hudson told her mother the next time they talked by telephone. Instead of coming home on December 22, she would take Flight 103 on December 21. Eleanor Hudson called her travel agent to inquire about the switch and considered calling Pan Am but decided against it. What difference would it make, anyway, if she came home one day sooner?

At 3:30 P.M. on December 21 the headmaster of Albany Academy for Girls called the Hudson house and asked for Paul.

"Well, is this personal or is this business?" Mrs. Hudson asked.

"I just need to speak to him."

Eleanor Hudson called her husband's office to relay the message, but he was not there. The receptionist said there had been a family emergency. Mrs. Hudson was puzzled. The telephone rang again. It was a family friend who had heard the same news about a family emergency and was calling to ask what was going on. Hudson's mind raced: Melina was in the air; her two youngest sons were with her. The only child she could not account for was her oldest son, Stephen, a student at Skidmore College. Perhaps he had had an accident in one of the family's cars. Her husband came home a few minutes after 4:00 P.M., accompanied by a business associate. He found his wife in the kitchen.

"Eleanor, I have to tell you something. Please come upstairs." He turned and began walking ahead of her. She followed him.

"What is this family emergency?" she shrieked at his back.

"I think Melina's plane went down."

She was stunned. What did he mean, their daughter's plane had gone down? Someone turned on the television, and she saw flames and wreckage. The travel agency through which Eleanor Hudson had purchased the ticket confirmed that Melina Hudson had been on the plane, as did officials at the school in London, but the Hudsons did not need that confirmation. The moment they saw the television footage of the flaming debris in Lockerbie, they knew their daughter was dead.

BEULAH McKEE spent the afternoon of December 21 baking cookies for her son, Army Major Charles McKee, who had called the day before to say he would be home for Christmas after all. She made his favorite, brown sugar drop cookies with chocolate chips, and she doubled the recipe because he ate them by the handful.

Her son's flight into Pittsburgh was due at about midnight. At 4:30 P.M. the daughter with whom she lives, fifty-two-year-old Marjorie McKee, came home with a worried look on her face.

"Oh, Mother, I've had the radio on. Have you heard about the plane?" she asked.

"I don't think Chuck could have been on that plane," Mrs. McKee said. She had seen the news reports on television, and she knew the plane that crashed was heading for New York City. McKee had said nothing about coming home through New York, but Marjorie McKee wanted to be sure. She called Pan Am; the lines were busy. When she finally got through at 7:00 P.M., a Pan Am employee told her McKee was not scheduled to be on the flight.

The two women arrived at the Pittsburgh airport about 11:30 P.M., after visiting Mrs. McKee's other daughter, Nancy. McKee's plane was one of the last arrivals of the night, and a crowd of about fifty people was waiting to meet passengers. Mrs. McKee noticed that two Pan Am employees in blue jackets were quietly circulating among the crowd. As the passengers entered the terminal, Mrs. McKee caught a glimpse of a bald head. She thought she had spotted her son, but when the man turned around, she saw that he had a big black mustache. Her son was clean-shaven. Suddenly the McKees realized they were the only ones still waiting. A Pan Am employee told them everyone was off the plane. She gave the two Pan Am workers her son's name, and they asked her to come into the office. Perhaps he missed his flight, one of them said.

Intuition told her what was happening the moment the door to the office opened. There were four women in white uniforms inside; Mrs. McKee recognized them as nurses.

"You're telling me my son was on *that* plane," Mrs. McKee said to the man who had escorted them to the office.

"I'm sorry, ma'am. Yes, he was."

They guided Mrs. McKee to a chair, where she collapsed and began to cry. A nurse became concerned and gave her a sedative. The airline called her daughter Nancy and her husband, and they immediately drove to the airport. The airline offered to take Mrs. McKee home, but Marjorie McKee said she would do it. She drove her mother and sister home to Trafford, where they arrived at 2:00 A.M. Marjorie McKee had been composed during the hourlong drive, but as soon as they closed the door behind them, she burst into tears. The three women could not sleep. In the early hours of the morning Nancy made a pot of coffee, and they waited for dawn.

GEORDIE WILLIAMS'S high school friend Duane Tudahl had been undecided about going home to Maryland for Christmas. Tudahl shared an apartment in California with Bob DeFrank, another friend from their high school days. DeFrank told Tudahl that Williams had obtained a holiday leave from the army that allowed him to come home from Germany for Christmas. DeFrank was hoping the three of them could get together back in Maryland for a wild party on New Year's Eve. Tudahl liked the idea.

When Tudahl called friends in Maryland on December 21 to let them know he was coming home, he was told that a plane had crashed, a plane Williams might have been on. He called Williams's father.

"Whip, is it true?"

"Yeah," George Williams replied.

After he had talked to Williams's dad, Tudahl called a mall where DeFrank was Christmas-shopping and had his roommate paged. DeFrank could tell right away something was wrong. He insisted that Tudahl tell him, over the telephone, what had happened. Tudahl told him Williams was dead. A few minutes later police approached Bob in the parking lot, where they found him screaming. Later that day Duane Tudahl, Bob DeFrank, and Chris Corvese—another high school friend who lived in California—gathered to watch the news together. When pictures of grieving relatives at Kennedy Airport appeared, they turned off the television.

BERT AMMERMAN, the assistant principal of Northern Valley Regional High School in Old Tappan, New Jersey, was mingling with other school administrators at a Christmas party when a waitress came through the crowd, asking, "Is there someone named Bert here?"

Ammerman stepped toward her.

"There's a phone call for you."

That's impossible, Ammerman thought. *The only person who knows I'm here is my secretary.* The phone call was from Carolyn, his brother Tom's wife. She told him that Tom had been in a plane crash and that Bert should leave immediately to be with his mother.

Within five minutes he was at the family home in Haworth. Margaret Ammerman met her son at the front door and instead of receiving comfort from him, began soothing him.

"Don't worry about it," she said. "Everything's OK." Carolyn had called and told her Tom hadn't been on the plane that crashed.

Ammerman felt relief, but it was a feeling he did not trust. Carolyn had talked to him only five minutes ago. Cautiously he asked his mother when Carolyn had called her.

"About an hour ago," she said.

He immediately felt certain that his brother was on the plane. He ushered his mother inside. As they walked toward the kitchen, Ammerman was distracted by the television playing in the family room. It was displaying some of the first pictures from Lockerbie, and they showed a town that had been turned into an inferno. He told his mother he would call the shipping company Tom worked for, just to make sure he was OK.

"Bert, what's wrong?"

"Nothing," he told her, but he could sense her fear.

He called, and someone at the company confirmed what he already knew. He hung up and told his mother his brother had been on the plane. She became hysterical.

Ammerman reacted differently, slipping into an administrator's mode. He began organizing his thoughts, hoping to keep himself from being overcome by painful memories of his brother. He compiled a list of tasks he needed to accomplish. First he would call their priest and ask him to come stay with his mother. Then he would call the rest of the family. Then he would drive to JFK to find out more information. The rest of the family could not understand his need to go to the airport, and he had a hard time explaining. He didn't fully comprehend it himself. He just knew he had to find out what had happened—and why.

Ammerman smoked a cigar on the drive to JFK. Alone in the car, he talked aloud to his father, who had died four months before. He worked through what he wanted to find out. *Are there survivors? If there are, is Tommy among them?* What should he do next? The radio was turned on throughout the drive, and Ammerman listened intently for information, but all he seemed to hear was one word: "Crash . . . crash . . . crash . . . crash."

Ammerman headed for Pan Am Terminal A, where a radio report had said airline employees would be available to greet arriving relatives. But when he arrived, he discovered he was on his own. No one outside the terminal had any idea where he was supposed to park. No one even seemed to know there had been a crash.

Finally he left his car, a Pontiac Firebird, illegally parked at the curb. When he went inside the terminal and rounded the first corner, he knew he was where he needed to be. More than a hundred reporters and photographers swarmed over one another. He walked to the counter and quietly said, "I'm one of the relatives of the people on Pan Am Flight 103."

Immediately the video camera lights went on, punctuated by still photographers' flashes. Reporters began yelling questions. Before Ammerman knew what was happening, six or seven Pan Am security people pulled him into an elevator. In the silence of the elevator he remembered his car. "Just tell us what make it is and we'll take care of it," a guard said. Ammerman started to tell them, then paused. At that point he couldn't remember what kind of car he had been driving for the past four years.

"I know it's blue," he told them. "I know it's blue."

ROBYN HUNT, thirteen, came home from Webster Junior High School in a suburb of Rochester, New York, and turned on the television. She was the only one home. Her parents were at work, and her sister, Karen, was on her way home from a semester of study in London. Karen was due to arrive in Rochester at 11:30 P.M. Robyn had called her older sister a week earlier, full of excitement, to tell her she had made the cheerleading team at school. Now, as she stared at the television screen, Robyn's jaw dropped. A plane had crashed on its way from London to New York, the news announcer said. Robyn picked up the telephone and called her mother.

Peggy Hunt worked at a Xerox Corporation distribution center in Webster. When Robyn told her about the news reports, Mrs. Hunt said, "Take it easy. Try not to upset me at work like that. It's probably nothing. I'll check into it and don't worry about it." But after hanging up the receiver, Mrs. Hunt could think of nothing else. Someone in the office turned on a radio, and she heard the reports for herself. Her fears grew. When she could no longer stand the feeling, she put on her coat and went home.

Her husband was out of town on business and was not supposed to get home until evening. She was uncertain about what to do. The television was identifying the crashed plane as Pan Am Flight 103, and she knew her daughter was flying home on Pan Am, but she could not recall the number of Karen Hunt's flight. Mrs. Hunt tried calling Pan Am, but the line was busy. Finally Robyn got through to the airline. She gave a Pan Am representative her sister's scheduled arrival time, asked for the designation of the Pan Am flight that arrived in New York City at that time, and braced for the answer. Robyn pulled the receiver away from her ear.

"What did you find out, the flight number, Robyn?" Mrs. Hunt asked.

"Flight 103," Robyn said. The house suddenly seemed huge and empty.

Two women from Peggy Hunt's office came by and offered to sit with Robyn and her mom. Robyn, sobbing softly, slipped upstairs to her room. Mrs. Hunt remembers trying to envision what the passengers felt as the plane was falling from the sky. Her husband, Robert, got home at about 8:00 P.M.

Hunt's boyfriend at Syracuse University had spent the afternoon preparing for her return. Mark Esposito was a member of the school's gymnastics team, and he and Hunt had been dating for two and a half years. After she had gone to London, he telephoned her regularly, running up huge phone bills. His most recent bill was for about three hundred dollars. Esposito was an art major and didn't have enough money to pay for the calls, so he had been forced to take on jobs for students who were required to submit artwork with their final exam projects. On top of all that, Esposito had his own finals. By the time exam week rolled around, he had gone without sleep for three days. Esposito planned to drive to Rochester to meet his girlfriend's plane, but as he looked in the mirror on December 21, he saw that he looked pale. He wanted to look his best for her return, so he went to a tanning salon at a local shopping mall. He also stopped to buy her a dozen red roses.

Esposito was beneath the tanning lights, listening to piped-in radio music, when a radio announcer said that a flight originating in Frankfurt had crashed in Scotland, apparently leaving no survivors. He felt a lump in his stomach and momentarily lost his balance. But then he remembered that Hunt's flight started in London, not Frankfurt. Still, he was bothered by a coincidence: Her flight and the flight that had crashed were due to arrive in New York City at the same time. He finished up in the tanning booth, left the shopping mall, and went home to his apartment. His roommate pulled him aside the moment Esposito walked in the door and told him to sit down.

"What, about the plane?" Esposito asked. "Don't worry, it was out of Frankfurt, West Germany."

No, his roommate said, it was Hunt's plane, and it was flying out of London. Esposito didn't believe it, so he called his brother, who had been monitoring television accounts of the disaster all afternoon. His brother confirmed the bad news. Esposito placed Karen Hunt's red roses in the refrigerator.

Dozens of people telephoned the apartment that night, but Esposito wouldn't speak to any of them. At one point about thirty of his friends were in the house. Esposito found himself getting drunk. At 2:00 A.M. two of his best friends knocked on his door. They knew Karen Hunt had been on the plane and had driven all night from New York City after learning of the disaster. Esposito got about four hours of sleep. He woke up at 8:00 A.M. and, with his two friends, drove to his family's house outside Albany. Before leaving the apartment in Syracuse, he took the roses out of the refrigerator. They were his companions during the long ride home.

MARION ALDERMAN had a long day ahead of her when she woke up on the morning of December 21. She had an appointment with an eye doctor, and she wanted to visit her ninety-seven-year-old mother. Then she was going to the Syracuse airport to pick up her daughter and son-in-law, Paula and Glenn Bouckley. It was 4:00 P.M. by the time she had visited her mother and done her other errands. She still had plenty of time before the flight arrived, so she decided to visit her daughter Lisa, who rented an apartment in a Syracuse suburb. The moment she pulled into the parking lot of Lisa's apartment complex, Mrs. Alderman thought something must be wrong. Parked outside Lisa's apartment was the light blue Honda Civic owned by another daughter, Laura. Laura worked nearby, but it was way past lunchtime.

Lisa's boyfriend, Gary, met Mrs. Alderman at the door and told her to come upstairs with him. There had been an airplane accident, and it appeared to have involved the Bouckleys' flight, he said. Gary, a commercial airline pilot, reassured her that he was doing everything he could to find out if the Bouckleys had been on the plane. Mrs. Alderman called her travel agent, who confirmed that they had reservations for Flight 103. Slowly others began taking control of things for her. Mrs. Alderman found herself waiting for the telephone to ring and hoping that it would be Paula and Glenn, calling to say they were not on the flight after all. She waited all night.

SUDHAKAR DIXIT was wrapping presents in the living room of his home in Ohio when he heard on the evening news that a Pan Am aircraft had crashed shortly after takeoff from London. For an instant he was overcome by a feeling of panic. Five members of his family who were coming home from India that day were traveling on a Pan Am flight. But he quickly calmed himself, remembering that they were taking a direct flight from Frankfurt to New York City. He went on wrapping presents, then drove to the Cleveland airport about 8:00 P.M.

Dixit was expecting to meet his parents, his sister, and his sister's two children. When their flight arrived and they were not on it, a Pan Am representative said his family probably was on the next flight from New York, scheduled to arrive in Cleveland at 12:15 A.M. One Pan Am worker set his mind at ease even more when she said Dixit's family had a reservation for the later flight. He went to a friend's house to pass the time and called his sister's husband, Shachi Rattan, in Detroit to explain the delay. Having returned to the airport at midnight, he again failed to find his family among the disembarking passengers.

Slowly he realized something was terribly wrong. He knew his father would have called if there had been a change in plans.

His family had been scheduled to take Pan Am Flight 67 from New Delhi to New York City, with a refueling stop in Frankfurt. In New York they were supposed to board a nonstop flight to Cleveland. Dixit turned to the Pan Am counter, where someone suggested that the family had missed connections in New York. Perhaps they were spending the night at a New York City hotel.

Dixit returned home and telephoned three or four hotels in New York City, only to learn his family was not staying at any of them. He and his brother-in-law tried calling Pan Am, but both kept getting busy signals. When at last Dixit was able to get through, the airline had no information for him. Unable to sleep, he called his wife in India, who said the family had boarded Pan Am Flight 67 in New Delhi. Dixit returned to the hospital at 6:30 A.M. to start his shift. He had worked less than four hours when his name was paged. His brother-in-law was calling from Detroit. Dixit took the call at a bank of desks shared by ward physicians.

"Something is really wrong," Rattan said. Earlier Rattan had called Om and Shanti Dixit's house, and the woman who had been staying at the house while Dixit's parents were in India said Pan Am officials had been trying all morning to reach Sudhakar. She had not known what to do because Dixit's home telephone number in Cleveland was unlisted. Dixit called Pan Am, gave them his unlisted phone number, and waited by the phone. The call came in the early afternoon. A Pan Am representative read the names one by one: Om Dixit, Shanti Dixit, Garima Rattan, Suruchi Rattan, Anmol Rattan. Dixit hung up and wept.

FOURTEEN-YEAR-OLD Rony Basuta came home from school in Tarrytown, New York, at 3:30 P.M. and was watching television when the phone rang. It was a woman from the local travel agency, asking what time Rony's father was due to arrive at Kennedy Airport that night. After he answered, she quietly explained to Rony that his father's flight had crashed in Scotland. When Rony asked if she was sure, the travel agent suggested he turn on the television to see for himself. Rony called the hospital where his mother, Surinder, was employed, but she had already left for the day.

Rony was waiting outside the front door of their apartment when his mother got home. When he told her what had happened, she screamed and ran into the kitchen. She telephoned her father in London, who confirmed the news. Almost everybody in the family had been at the airport when Jaswant Basuta waved good-bye and began running for Gate 14, her father said. That was the last anyone had seen of him. In the long hours that followed, Surinder Basuta found herself staring for a moment at the clock on the kitchen wall. The clock bore the image of a Sikh prophet. Mrs. Basuta made a promise to the prophet: If her husband survived, she would hire Sikh priests to perform a special forty-eight-hour prayer ceremony in which she and the rest of her family would express their gratitude.

The Basutas had no relatives in New York, so Surinder Basuta and her children were alone for most of the night. They never bothered to turn on the bright lights adorning their Christmas tree, and they kept most of the other apartment lights off, too. A woman who lived in the same complex noticed the dark apartment and stopped in to see if everything was all right.

For a time she stayed with Mrs. Basuta and tried to comfort her and her children.

Across the Atlantic at the police station at Heathrow Airport, Jaswant Basuta heard the same questions over and over again. Why did you miss the flight? When did you come to England? What was the purpose of your visit? Why didn't your wife attend the wedding with you? Basuta responded to each of them, then happened to mention that his brother-in-law had been married in Belfast. The face of the police officer who was questioning him turned bright red. The officer—apparently associating Northern Ireland with terrorism and with the Irish Republican Army—called in other associates, who became more aggressive with Basuta. They wanted to see his tickets, his passport; they wanted to know his brother-in-law's address. *This is turning into a nightmare,* Basuta thought. He had missed supper and was hungry, so at 11:00 P.M. someone brought him a ham and cheese sandwich and a glass of milk. Later an officer told Basuta he would have to stay in the Heathrow police station overnight. There was a crowd of reporters and photographers outside, the officer said, and it was unsafe to let him leave. Basuta looked at the wooden bunk he had been assigned and decided he had had enough.

"I want a motel and a guard, if you think my life is in danger," he said. "You're trying to put me in a cell, and I'm not going to sleep in a cell. If you can't pay for a motel, I'll pay for it, but I'm not going to sleep in a cell." The officers repeated that it was unsafe for him to leave and said that if he didn't like the bunk, he was welcome to sit up with them all night. Basuta had been in the station for more than four hours, and he was getting tired, but he had enough presence of mind to ask for a supervising officer. He told the supervisor he wanted to place a telephone call to the U.S. ambassador in London. The officer got him a phone, and Basuta explained his predicament to a marine guard on duty at the embassy. The guard apologized and said the ambassador and all the other high-ranking embassy officials had left for Lockerbie. If he was still being held in thirty minutes, the guard told Basuta, call again.

When Basuta got off the phone, the police supervisor said the investigators were almost done with their questions. Not long after that he told Basuta he was free to go. The supervisor asked Basuta if he had called his family and apologized for not making the inquiry sooner. Basuta gave the officer his home telephone number in Tarrytown and asked the officer to place the call. Basuta feared that if he got on the line first, the sound of his voice would come as a shock to his wife. Rony answered the telephone and turned it over to his mother.

"I know what you're calling about," Surinder Basuta said after the police officer had identified himself. "He was on the flight. There's nothing more to talk about."

"No. I have good news for you," the officer said. "Your husband is with me; he missed the flight."

Mrs. Basuta froze. "Tell me what he looks like," she said.

The officer described a bearded man wearing a white turban, a red checked shirt, and black pants. Mrs. Basuta began to scream, so loudly that the officer held the phone away from his ear.

Basuta took the receiver and tried to calm his wife. "Listen to me. Don't cry. Listen to me. I'm OK, I'm here." He explained how he had missed the flight and said the police had prevented him from calling sooner.

Dozens of relatives in England still thought he was dead, and reaching them proved to be difficult because many of them were on the phone with each other. Every time a police officer dialed one of the numbers on Basuta's phone list, the line was busy. Finally a telephone operator agreed to break into one of the conversations. The police officer handed the receiver to Basuta.

"Who's speaking?" Basuta asked.

"Who are *you*?" the voice on the other end said. It was his sister-in-law's husband, Bant.

"I'm Jessi," Basuta said, using the name by which he was known within his family.

Bant was confused. "Which Jessi?" he asked.

Frustrated and tired, Basuta said, "How many Jessis do you have in the family?"

"We *had* only one."

"I'm the same Jessi . . . I'm here at Heathrow Airport."

Basuta recounted how he'd missed the flight and how he'd been held in police custody for several hours. In the background Basuta could hear his relatives crying and screaming.

"Please tell them not to worry," Basuta said. "God has helped me. I'm just somehow saved."

Basuta left the Heathrow police station at about 2:00 A.M. on December 22. An officer drove him to a relative's house, and eventually the family gathered at the home of Basuta's father-in-law. No one could sleep, so they made breakfast. Before Basuta knew it, the sun had come up.

CHAPTER 7

SEARCHING FOR THE KILLERS

THE FULL-FLEDGED criminal investigation into the crash began on the morning of December 22, at about the time Bill Bumpus, suspended in midair, was eased headfirst into the wreckage of the 747's cockpit section. Several other people had inspected the cockpit before him, but none of them had Bumpus's trained eyes. As a specialist at the Federal Aviation Administration, Bumpus could tell just by looking at the 747's instrument settings what had happened in the instant before the plane broke apart.

Bumpus arrived in Lockerbie with Bob Mosca, an airworthiness inspector at the FAA's regional office at JFK. Mosca had worked for Pan Am for eleven years before taking a government job in 1971, and Bumpus had been an air force pilot for twenty-one years.

While Bumpus inspected the cockpit, Mosca joined a team that was searching Park Place and Sherwood Crescent. There was almost nothing of the aircraft's structure left to examine. Mosca looked at a mass of crumpled metal and saw bodies and pieces of bodies sandwiched in its folds. He realized it was the plane's rear fuselage section. Hundreds of shoes were strewn around him; they had been ripped off the victims' feet by tremendous G forces.

The destruction was so complete that Mosca's British counterparts initially had difficulty determining where one of the 747's wings had landed—an improbable dilemma, since the plane had a wingspan of 196 feet. It was only after Mosca had counted the number of large steel flapjack screws in the crater at Sherwood Crescent that they knew that both wings, not one, as first thought, had landed there.

If Mosca and Bumpus had determined that a structural defect caused the midair breakup, Mosca would have started a process that could have led to the grounding of other 747s for inspections. But Mosca suspected his findings would not result in such a directive. FAA records indicated that *Clipper Maid of the Seas,* as part of the Civil Reserve Air Fleet, had recently received an almost three-million-dollar overhaul, making it unlikely that structural wear and tear had caused the disaster.

To do things by the book, Bumpus needed to examine the cockpit controls before the wreckage was disturbed. In this case, that meant he had to be suspended and eased into the crumpled nose section of the plane through a hole in its side, before any bodies were removed.

The nose section, floating somewhat as it spun to earth, had made a relatively soft landing. When it hit, Bumpus estimated, the nose cone was falling at a forty-degree angle to the horizon, tilted eighty degrees to the left. As Bumpus was eased into the nose section, past the bodies of first-class passengers still strapped in their seats, it became immediately clear that the crew had virtually no time to respond to the disaster. No emergency procedures had been started. The pressure control and fuel switches were set for cruise. The nose wheel, which would have been down in an emergency landing attempt, was still up. There had not even been time for Captain James B. MacQuarrie and the crew to use their oxygen masks, which would have been deployed within five seconds of the emergency. It took six days of recovery and laboratory testing of blast-scarred luggage before investigators felt confident enough to announce what was already obvious to these FAA experts: The crash had nothing to do with the age of the plane or the abilities of its crew. Only a terrorist's bomb could account for this destruction.

The regional police force that patrols Lockerbie is known as the Dumfries and Galloway Constabulary, and it had never experienced anything like 270 simultaneous murders. The year before, it had captured 626 stray dogs and investigated 456 suspected cases of the sheep disease anthrax (none was confirmed). Now it was at the center of what was becoming the largest criminal investigation in the world. Inspector George Stobbs, a white-haired man who headed the Lockerbie section of the constabulary, was at home planning a trip for the local Boy Scout troop when he heard about the disaster on television. He asked his wife to pack a bag with food and clothes and headed for the police station, about seven miles from his house.

The Lockerbie police headquarters is a modern one-story building in the

Christopher Jones with his girlfriend, Erica Elefant, during their semester in London. (family photograph)

Sixteen-year-old Melina Hudson posed for this photograph in the fall of 1988, while she was in England as a high school exchange student. (family photograph)

Army Major Charles Dennis McKee, Christmas 1987. McKee's mother and sister found out about his death when they went to the Pittsburgh airport to meet his flight. (family photograph)

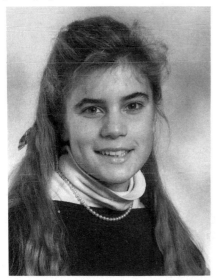

Suruchi Rattan, three, was traveling home to the United States with four members of her family. They switched flights and boarded Pan Am 103 after her brother became sick during a stopover in Frankfurt. (family photograph)

Glenn and Paula Bouckley were married in England in 1986. After visiting relatives there, the couple boarded Flight 103 to New York, to spend Christmas with Paula's family in Syracuse. (family photograph)

Army First Lieutenant George "Geordie" Williams got a late start from his girlfriend's apartment in Germany and missed his scheduled plane home for Christmas. He took Flight 103 instead. (family photograph)

Two Scottish police officers survey the downed Boeing 747's cockpit, one of the few recognizable pieces of wreckage from Flight 103, at a sheep pasture in Tundergarth, Scotland, on a hilltop east of Lockerbie. (Tom Foster)

The impact of the Boeing 747's fuel-laden wings gouged a crater in the earth at Sherwood Crescent in Lockerbie. (Martin Cleaver, courtesy of AP/Wide World Photos)

An airport security guard escorts Georgia Nucci, whose son, Christopher Jones, was on Flight 103, through a crowd of reporters and photographers at John F. Kennedy International Airport in New York the night of the crash. (Reuters/Mark Peterson, courtesy of Bettmann Archives)

Eleanor Hudson, mother of Melina, holds the balloons that she and her family released in Albany, New York, on what would have been Melina's seventeenth birthday. The family repeats the ritual every year. (family photograph)

Paul Hudson talked to his daughter on the telephone the day before her death and used this paper napkin to leave a note for his wife, Eleanor. As the message shows, Melina planned to come home on Thursday, December 22, but her plans changed and she ended up boarding Flight 103 one day earlier. (family photograph)

Victims' family members urge President Bush to implement aviation security reforms. Pictured from left are Victoria Cummock, who lost her husband, John; Paul Hudson, who lost his daughter, Melina; Bert Ammerman, who lost his brother, Tom; President Bush; Transportation Secretary Samuel Skinner; Wendy Giebler, who lost her husband, William; and Joe Horgan, who lost his brother-in-law, Michael Doyle. (The White House)

Justice Department photographs released at the time of the 1991 indictment against the two Libyans charged with carrying out the attack against Pan Am Flight 103. Left: Lamen Khalifa Fhimah. Right: Abdel Basset Ali al-Megrahi. (courtesy of U.S. Justice Department)

 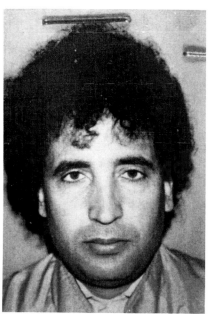

Cockpit
Captain: JAMES BRUCE MACQUARRIE
First Officer: RAYMOND RONALD WAGNER
Flight Engineer: JERRY DON AVRITT

Cabin Crew
MARY GERALDINE MURPHY
MILUTIN VELIMIROVICH
ELISABETH NICHOLE AVOYNE
NOELLE LYDIE BERTI
SIV ULLA ENGSTROM
STACIE DENISE FRANKLIN
PAUL ISAAC GARRETT
ELKE ETHA KUEHNE
MARIA NIEVES LARRACOECHEA
LILIBETH TOBILA MCALOLOOY
JOCELYN REINA
MYRA JOSEPHINE ROYAL
IRJA SYHNOVE SKABO

Passengers
First Class
01A: ROBERT GERARD FORTUNE
01B: ELIA G. STRATIS
01J: JOYCE CHRISTINE DIMAURO

02A: MARK ALAN REIN
02B: TOMAS FLORO VAN TIENHOVEN
02H: ROGER ELWOOD HURST
02J: WILLIAM CHASE LEYRER

03A: JOHN BINNING CUMMOCK
03B: GABRIEL DELLA-RIPA
03H: JAMES RALPH FULLER
03J: LOUIS ANTHONY MARENGO

04A: ROBERT ITALO PAGNUCCO
04B: HARRY MICHAEL BAINBRIDGE
04H: INGRID ANITA SMITH
04J: ROBERT VAN HOUTEN JECK

05A: JEAN MARY BELL
05B: JAY JOSEPH KINGHAM

Clipper Class, Upper Deck
06B: DANIEL EMMET MCCARTHY

07A: HERNAN CAFFARONE
07B: FABIANA CAFFARONE
07J: ROBERT EUGENE MCCOLLUM

08A: DAVID PLATT
08B: DIANE MARIE MASLOWSKI
08H: GREGORY KOSMOWSKI

09A: FRANCIS BOYER
09B: MICHAEL JOSEPH DOYLE
09H: WILLIAM ALLAN DANIELS

Clipper Class, Main Deck
10A: JEROME LEE WESTON
10B: JOSEPH KENNETH MILLER

11A: ANDRE NIKOLAI GUEVORGIAN
11B: FRANK CIULLA

12A: DAVID WILLIAM TRIMMER-SMITH
12B: MARK JAMES ZWYNENBURG

13A: NICHOLAS BRIGHT
13B: IRVING STANLEY SIGAL

14A: ALFRED HILL
14B: PETER THOMAS STANLEY DIX
14E: WILLIAM JOHN MCALLISTER
14F: THERESA E.J. SAUNDERS
14J: MATTHEW KEVIN GANNON

15A: WILLIAM GARRETSON ATKINSON
15B: JUDITH ELLEN ATKINSON
15E: JAMES RALPH STOW
15F: CHARLES DENNIS MCKEE
15H: MARTIN LEWIS APFELBAUM
15J: LAWRENCE RAY BENNETT

16A: THOMAS EDWIN WALKER
16E: THOMAS JOSEPH AMMERMAN
16H: RODNEY PETER HILBERT
16J: RICHARD ANTHONY CAWLEY

17A: CHRISTOS M. PAPADOPOULOS
17H: BERNT WILSON CARLSSON
17J: MICHAEL PESCATORE

Economy Class
18G: STUART MURRAY BARCLAY

19A: ARVA ANTHONY THOMAS
19C: ELIZABETH SOPHIE IVELL
19D: GWYNETH YVONNE MARGARET OWEN
19D: BRYONY ELISE OWEN (child)
19G: EVA INGEBORG MORSON
19H: MICHAEL GARY STINNETT
19J: CHARLOTTE ANN STINNETT
19K: STACEY LEANNE STINNETT

20A: KAREN ELIZABETH NOONAN
20B: PATRICIA MARY COYLE
20C: ASAAD EIDI VEJDANY
20D: ALEXANDER SILAS LOWENSTEIN
20G: BARRY JOSEPH VALENTINO
20H: RONALD ALBERT LARIVIERE
20K: PETER VULCU

21A: DANIEL SOLOMON BROWNER (BIER)
21C: GIANFRANCA DINARDO
21D: WILLIAM PUGH
21E: JULIANNE FRANCES KELLY
21F: FREDERICK SANDFORD PHILLIPS
21G: ALEXIA KATHRYN TSAIRIS
21H: THEODORA EUGENIA COHEN
21J: DANIEL PETER ROSENTHAL
21K: MIRIAM LUBY WOLFE

22A: RAJESH TARSIS PRISKEL RAMSES
22C: DAVID J. GOULD
22D: JOHN CHARLES STEVENSON
22E: GERALDINE ANNE STEVENSON
22F: HANNAH LOUISE STEVENSON
22G: RACHAEL STEVENSON
22H: DIANE ANNE BOATMAN-FULLER
22K: HELGA RACHAEL MOSEY

23A: SUZANNE MARIE MIAZGA
23D: GARIMA RATTAN
23E: SURUCHI RATTAN
23G: AMY BETH GALLAGHER
23H: JULIAN MACBAIN BENELLO
23K: NICOLA JANE HALL

24A: OM DIXIT
24B: SHANTI DIXIT
24C: ANMOL RATTAN

24D: SCOTT CHRISTOPHER SAUNDERS
24G: HIDEKAZU TANAKA
24H: MRIDULA SHASTRI
24K: VALERIE CANADY

25A: JOHN DAVID AKERSTROM
25C: WALTER LEONARD PORTER
25D: JOE NATHAN WOODS JR.
25E: JOE NATHAN WOODS
25F: CHELSEA MARIE WOODS
25G: DEDERA LYNN WOODS
25H: DANIEL EMMETT O'CONNOR
25K: CHARLES THOMAS FISHER IV

26A: TIMOTHY BARON JOHNSON
26D: EDINA ROLLER
26E: JANOS GABOR ROLLER
26F: IBOLYA ROBERTINE GABOR
26G: ZSUZSANA ROLLER
26H: MARC ALEX TAGER
26K: PAMELA LYNN POSEN

27A: JEWEL COURTNEY MITCHELL
27D: ANDREW ALEXANDER TERAN
27G: JAMES ALVIN SMITH
27H: JANE SUSAN MELBER
27K: MARTIN BERNARD CARRUTHERS SIMPSON

28A: PATRICIA ANN KLEIN
28B: NICOLE ELISE BOULANGER
28C: TURHAN ERGIN
28D: WENDY ANNE LINCOLN
28E: RICHARD PAUL MONETTI
28G: ROBERT THOMAS SCHLAGETER
28K: ANTHONY LACEY HAWKINS

29A: MELINA KRISTINA HUDSON
29D: LOUISE ANN ROGERS
29G: DIANE MARIE RENCEVICZ
29H: SOPHIE AILETTE MIRIAM HUDSON
29J: WILLIAM MARTIN CADMAN
29K: JAMES ANDREW CAMPBELL PITT

30A: ESTRELLA CRISOSTOMO QUIGUYAN
30B: WILLIAM DAVID GIEBLER
30C: JOHN MICHAEL GERARD AHERN

PETER ALLEN/The Syracuse Newspapers

Sources: Lockerbie police and Georgia Nucci, editor of Victims of Pan Am Flight 103 memorial book.

Pan Am Flight 103

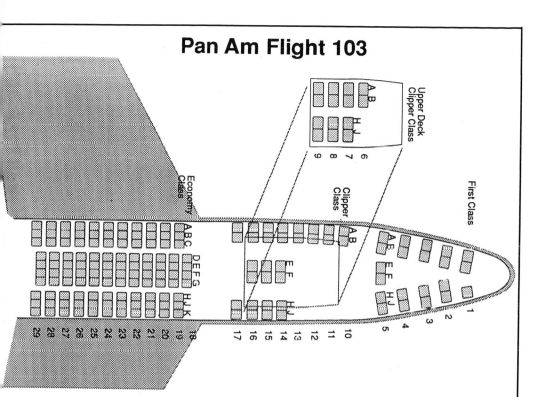

Upper Deck Clipper Class

Economy Class

Clipper Class

First Class

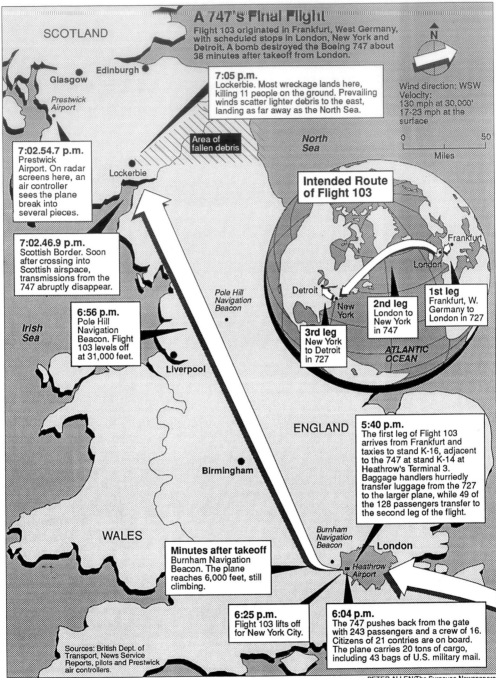

A 747's Final Flight

Flight 103 originated in Frankfurt, West Germany, with scheduled stops in London, New York and Detroit. A bomb destroyed the Boeing 747 about 38 minutes after takeoff from London.

SCOTLAND

Glasgow
Edinburgh
Prestwick Airport

7:05 p.m.
Lockerbie. Most wreckage lands here, killing 11 people on the ground. Prevailing winds scatter lighter debris to the east, landing as far away as the North Sea.

Wind direction: WSW
Velocity:
130 mph at 30,000'
17-23 mph at the surface

0 — 50
Miles

Area of fallen debris

North Sea

7:02.54.7 p.m.
Prestwick Airport. On radar screens here, an air controller sees the plane break into several pieces.

Lockerbie

Intended Route of Flight 103

7:02.46.9 p.m.
Scottish Border. Soon after crossing into Scottish airspace, transmissions from the 747 abruptly disappear.

Frankfurt
London

Detroit
New York

2nd leg
London to New York in 747

1st leg
Frankfurt, W. Germany to London in 727

3rd leg
New York to Detroit in 727

ATLANTIC OCEAN

6:56 p.m.
Pole Hill Navigation Beacon. Flight 103 levels off at 31,000 feet.

Irish Sea

Pole Hill Navigation Beacon

Liverpool

ENGLAND

5:40 p.m.
The first leg of Flight 103 arrives from Frankfurt and taxies to stand K-16, adjacent to the 747 at stand K-14 at Heathrow's Terminal 3. Baggage handlers hurriedly transfer luggage from the 727 to the larger plane, while 49 of the 128 passengers transfer to the second leg of the flight.

Birmingham

WALES

Burnham Navigation Beacon

London

Minutes after takeoff
Burnham Navigation Beacon. The plane reaches 6,000 feet, still climbing.

Heathrow Airport

6:25 p.m.
Flight 103 lifts off for New York City.

6:04 p.m.
The 747 pushes back from the gate with 243 passengers and a crew of 16. Citizens of 21 contries are on board. The plane carries 20 tons of cargo, including 43 bags of U.S. military mail.

Sources: British Dept. of Transport, News Service Reports, pilots and Prestwick air controllers.

PETER ALLEN/The Syracuse Newspapers

center of town with a handful of parking spaces. By the time Stobbs arrived, the building overflowed with people and confusion. The streets were clogged with traffic and debris, and emergency vehicles were having trouble getting through. Stobbs decided to take over Lockerbie Academy, the public school at the north end of town, which was closed because of the Christmas recess. The school's complex of buildings included classrooms, laboratories, a library, a central kitchen, a dining hall, an auditorium, and a gymnasium. The gym became the command center.

Stobbs's first task was to overcome chaos. The disaster had overwhelmed the local telephone network; in the first hours after the crash making a call into or out of Lockerbie was next to impossible. To cope with the clogged telephone lines, authorities did two things. First, they scattered trucks from the community's road, water, and sewer departments at intervals south of Lockerbie; vital messages were relayed from one truck's radio to the next until they reached Dumfries, where there were open phone lines. Second, British Telecom cut off about half the town's telephones to give priority use of the existing network to police and other officials.

Inside the academy large-scale maps of the region shared wall space with Christmas decorations. Wires for telephones and computers trailed across the command center's floors. On the auditorium stage, controllers using radios directed the Royal Air Force search helicopters. Soldiers moved filing cabinets into the corridors to store the reports that were already beginning to pile up. Grief counselors took over the school's computer room. Pan Am, the FBI, the FAA, and the National Transportation Safety Board also set up offices in the building. The American Embassy took over the science lab, where mice and chipmunks continued to scurry around inside glass tanks.

Police and British military officials, trying to impose order on the death and destruction, brought in dogs trained to sniff out bodies. Soldiers sifting through the debris meticulously separated human remains from the wreckage of the plane. Personal belongings found amid the rubble were placed in green plastic bags; the bodies and dismembered body parts went into black sacks.

Crews recovered thousands of chunks of the 747, some no larger than a paper clip, and police carefully cataloged them all. If a criminal case against the bombers was going to be built, it would be from these shards of metal and burned plastic.

Searchers found the cockpit voice recorder, but except for the loud sound in the instant before the device stopped working, the recording proved to be of little use. The crew's conversation revealed no signs of trouble, and the tape was hard to understand. In fact, it was so noisy in the 747's cockpit during the ascent that on two occasions the crew had been unable to hear the comments of the air traffic controllers. To make matters worse, the recorder had not been operating properly. The tape on which the sounds were recorded ran in a continual loop, and the new recordings were supposed to erase earlier sounds. But the earlier sounds were not completely gone, and when there should have been silence, investigators could hear eerie voices, faint echoes of previous conversations.

EARLY ON, in the passenger lounge where relatives had been herded at JFK, a Pan Am supervisor had pulled Bert Ammerman aside.

"I know you want to go to Lockerbie," the supervisor said. "You are going to be told that you can't go, that it's not advisable. But if you pursue it and you force it, they will let you go."

The day after the crash a small group of relatives who had gathered in New York City began to force the issue. They wanted to travel to Lockerbie, and at first they received cooperation from everyone. Pan Am had provided them with hotel rooms and agreed to fly them overseas. The State Department quickly processed passports for those relatives who needed them. On December 22, when it came time to go back to JFK to board the early-evening flight to London, the airline skillfully avoided reporters lingering at the airport by ushering the relatives through a series of tunnels and side doors. But all the time it assisted them, the airline gently urged this group of forty to fifty relatives to stay in New York, at least for a while. Pan Am also convinced some relatives not to make the trip at all.

Only the most persistent flew to London, where Pan Am again urged them to go no farther, warning that the scene in Scotland would be gruesome. The airline offered these relatives first-class accommodations in London. After spending a sleepless night on a plane, all but a handful of relatives accepted the offer and agreed to wait another day before flying to Scotland. The smaller group, whose members insisted on continuing to Lockerbie, was quickly pulled aside and loaded into a shuttle bus that took them to the British Airways gate and a connecting flight to Glasgow.

In the opinion of some relatives, Pan Am's warnings were probably intended to stall as many family members as possible, since the relatives who reached Lockerbie first and saw the destruction in person would likely become the most troublesome for the airline. Of the forty or fifty people who began the journey in New York, only two families were now seated on the shuttle bus. Paul Hudson, the father of sixteen-year-old Melina, sat with his father, William. Nearby was Bert Ammerman, the school administrator whose brother, Tommy, had been on the flight. He was accompanied by Tommy's wife, Carolyn, and by a brother-in-law, Brian Barry of Roswell, Georgia.

Hudson and Ammerman had no way of knowing this, but their short trip on the shuttle bus was the first leg of a pilgrimage that was to last for years. Within months the two men began leading a movement that was to reform the aviation industry in both the United States and Great Britain. They marched on the Capitol, testified at congressional hearings, met with the president, and confronted Pan Am and federal regulators. They also became embroiled in a bitter personal dispute. On their way to Lockerbie, however, Hudson and Ammerman knew only that they wanted more information.

It had been a grueling trip, and Ammerman's patience was wearing thin. A few moments before boarding the shuttle bus, Ammerman had spoken to a man from the U.S. Embassy who he hoped would provide details of the disaster. But the man knew nothing. To make matters worse, the man kept complaining about how long he had been awake. Ammerman thought about telling him, "Look, asshole, I'm not here on a vacation. I don't give a crap how long you've been up. My brother's dead up there. Just give me information." Instead he kept quiet and headed for the bus to the British Airways terminal.

Before the bus pulled away, two more people came out to catch the flight to Glasgow. They were Tom and Dorothy Coker of Mendham, New Jersey, parents of twin sons, Eric and Jason, who were returning from the Syracuse University overseas study program.

This smaller group pressed on. When they reached Glasgow late in the morning, there was more of the same from Pan Am. The airline wanted the relatives to stay in Glasgow and rest. Then they were told there was no one available to drive the bus on the two-hour trip south to Lockerbie. Ammerman told an airline employee that he would drive the bus himself, and eventually a driver appeared. About five minutes away from Lockerbie, the bus pulled off the road and stopped at a school. Once more the relatives faced another attempt to stall their arrival as they were herded toward tables of food. Their impatience gave way to anger.

"Listen to me carefully," Ammerman said. "We have been traveling for almost twenty-four hours. We are not here to rest. We are not here to eat. We are here to find out what the hell has happened. We want to go to Lockerbie, and we want to go now."

As their bus approached the headquarters of disaster operations at Lockerbie Academy, the relatives saw a group of reporters outside that rivaled the pack they had left behind at JFK. A bearded reporter walked beside Ammerman, begging him to say something into his microphone. "Jesus Christ, give me a break" was all Ammerman said before police pushed the reporter away.

Inside the academy detectives sat down with the relatives and began the first of what became thousands of interviews. They needed information to identify bodies. Hudson told his interviewer, Constable Alex Smith, about the rods that had been inserted in Melina's spine to correct scoliosis and about her luggage. He told him that on one finger she wore a ring given to her by her grandmother, who had died the previous summer. In his brief-case Hudson carried X rays of her back and her dental records. As Smith took notes in tiny script, Hudson noticed that his hands were shaking. Hudson thought the policeman was nervous because it was one of his first interviews. Later he learned that Smith and his father, Archie, a retired police inspector, had escaped their home on Sherwood Park, the street that leads to Sherwood Crescent, minutes before it was engulfed in flames.

About 10:00 A.M. on the day before Christmas Ammerman set out for Sherwood Crescent, ignoring the advice of police, who had urged relatives to avoid the site. Ammerman was accompanied by his sister-in-law and brother-in-law. Sherwood Crescent was blocked by police, so the trio climbed over backyard fences until they could approach the neighborhood from behind, walking up the slope that separated the houses from the expressway. At first they could see little of the site. Barry picked up a plane fragment lying in the grass and, thinking someone in the family might want it as a remembrance, told Ammerman to put it in his pocket. But when they crested the hill and walked down a driveway, Sherwood Crescent spread out before their eyes. Ammerman pulled the piece of the plane from his pocket and absently dropped it at his feet.

Thousands of similar shards of metal lay on the ground in front of them. Ammerman had been holding on to the faint hope that his brother had survived, but the scene at Sherwood immediately erased all doubt. He said aloud, "He's not alive."

On a separate trip to Sherwood it became equally clear to Hudson that there would be little for him to recover. Hudson had hoped to find Melina's body and cut a lock of her hair to bring home to his wife. But all he could see was a deep gash in the ground. The stench of aviation fuel was everywhere.

Though he headed an Albany realty corporation, Hudson's background was in law. He had worked as an environmental attorney for the New York Public Interest Research Group, a Ralph Nader affiliate, and as a victims' rights lawyer for the New York State Crime Victims Board. In the latter job he wrote the regulations for New York's "Son of Sam" law, which prevented criminals from profiting from their crimes by writing about them. Hudson was now the victim, and although he was still grieving, he also was taking notes. He was already trying to find out why the airline had been unable to prevent the crash and was critiquing the authorities' handling of the disaster.

Over the next several days Hudson and Ammerman spent their waking hours in Lockerbie, talking to the authorities at Lockerbie Academy and visiting the places where wreckage and bodies were being recovered. Hudson became concerned about the length of time it was taking to identify bodies. After learning that the police were operating with only one or two forensic dentists, he asked if the authorities would consider bringing in additional dentists, perhaps from the United States, a request they politely refused. Later he saw that Scottish authorities were trucking the bodies to London instead of flying them there. He believed that caused further unnecessary delays.

Hudson and Ammerman also were frustrated by the authorities' failure to share information with the relatives. When Hudson questioned police at Lockerbie Academy, they refused to provide even the most rudimentary information about the investigation. When he read in the newspapers that the crash had been caused by a terrorist's bomb, a detail that Hudson and Ammerman had been denied, Hudson asked that he and the other relatives in Lockerbie be given the same briefings as those being provided to reporters. The authorities also approved Hudson's request for a room at Lockerbie Academy, which he and the other relatives could use as a base of operations. They were given the art room, on the building's upper floor.

Christmas Eve was three days after the crash, and Hudson was determined to find some flowers to leave in memory of his daughter. Though most businesses in Lockerbie were closed, Hudson eventually found a grocery store that sold arrangements. He bought sixteen white flowers, one for each year Melina Hudson had been alive, and three pink flowers, one for each day she had been dead. Hudson took the flowers to the center of town, where a war memorial dominated a small traffic circle in front of the town hall. On the sidewalk, behind metal railings put up by police, Hudson added his bouquet to a growing pile of flowers.

The following morning, Christmas Day, Hudson learned that his daughter's body had been among the group that had landed with the main fuselage section at Park Place. He wanted to visit the area, but the street was cordoned off by police. Someone suggested he try viewing the area from a house that sits on a hill overlooking the neighborhood, so at 9:00 A.M. Hudson knocked and introduced himself to a man who appeared at the door in his bathrobe. The man had been celebrating Christmas with his family, but when he learned of Hudson's purpose, he said he would be glad to admit him to his backyard. From the stranger's hillside property Hudson got a clear view of the main fuselage section, which had come to rest on Park Place.

Two days after Christmas Hudson again bought flowers in Lockerbie, but not for his daughter. This time he bought twenty-one white flowers for a twenty-one-year-old woman he did not know: Lynne Hartunian, a student at the State University of New York College at Oswego. Hartunian had been assigned a left window seat fifteen rows behind Melina's. During a telephone conversation that morning Eleanor Hudson told her husband that she had spoken with a neighbor of Hartunian's parents, who lived about twenty minutes from the Hudsons' home in Albany. The neighbor said Hartunian's mother was overcome with grief. Someday in the future, Eleanor told Paul, the Hartunians might receive some comfort knowing that someone had left flowers in Lockerbie in Lynne's memory. Hudson placed the flowers beside the bouquet he had purchased for his daughter three days earlier.

SURUCHI RATTAN'S father, Shachi, and her uncle Sudhakar Dixit also decided to go to Lockerbie. On the afternoon of December 24 they arrived at Lockerbie Academy, where they met several other relatives. The two also spoke for about an hour with a detective, who gathered information on the five members of their family. Although they knew it was unlikely, Rattan and Dixit still hoped their family had not been on Flight 103. They kept reminding themselves that their relatives had had reservations for Pan Am Flight 67, which flew from Frankfurt to New York City without stopping in London.

On Christmas morning Lockerbie police turned down a request from Rattan and Dixit to view bodies that had been recovered. The two men spent the rest of the morning wandering the village. From the crest of a hill they watched as lines of searchers combed the countryside. The temperature was in the forties, unusually warm for Christmas Day in Scotland. A light rain was falling, and the grass beneath their feet was wet. Soldiers were everywhere, and heavy rescue vehicles returning from the fields coated the streets with mud. Dixit felt as if he were walking through a nightmare.

At Lockerbie Academy the two men were offered Christmas meals, but they were unable to eat. So they went back outside and walked across Glasgow Road to the makeshift morgue at the village ice rink, planning to ask again about viewing the bodies. Police Sergeant Robert McNeil guarded the door, and when the two men showed him pictures of their family, he told them he remembered a little girl. Authorities showed them a toe ring, nose rings, earrings, and a chain, which Dixit recognized instantly. The police changed their minds and allowed the two men inside.

It was an eerie place. Pathologists and others in surgical garb hovered over the rows of bodies covered by sheets. Here and there a naked foot stuck out, an identification tag tied to one toe. The workers were examining bodies, removing clothing and jewelry, and meticulously recording everything they saw. Rattan tried to avert his attention as he and his brother-in-law were guided to a room at the rear of the building. Workers lifted a sheet from a body on a cot in the center of the room. It took about twenty seconds for Dixit to identify his mother. He no longer doubted that all five of his relatives had died. A police detective named Millan had recovered Shanti Dixit's body at 9:00 P.M. on December 21 at Tundergarth. The two men later identified three of the other bodies—Suruchi, Anmol, and Dixit's father, Om, whose body had been found in Tundergarth, not far from his wife's. Suruchi had a large gash on her scalp, but none of the others was badly disfigured. The two men were unable to find the body of Suruchi's mother, Garima.

It was after dark on Christmas night when Dixit and Rattan boarded a chartered bus that had been hired to take relatives from Lockerbie to the airport at Prestwick. The two men were returning to London, where they planned to meet Dixit's bride, Sandhya, who was flying in from India. As the bus passed through a small town, Dixit noticed that hardly any Christmas lights were burning in the windows of the houses. He thought the countryside seemed subdued, almost dead. And he realized that he had completely forgotten about Christmas.

At their hotel in London Dixit telephoned a distant relative who told him that newspaper reporters were writing stories about a man named "Chas." who had been on the Frankfurt to London leg of the flight and who had sent flowers and a note to Lockerbie in memory of a little girl in a red dress. He immediately thought of Suruchi. He knew she had been wearing red. That fact and her friendly nature convinced Rattan the flowers were meant for Suruchi. The two men discussed returning to Lockerbie, to search for the note and to make another attempt to identify the body of Garima Rattan. Both were tired and depressed, however, and the conversation turned into an argument that dragged into the night.

Eventually the brothers-in-law returned to Scotland and on the morning of December 27, after searching through mounds of bouquets in front of the town hall, they found what they had been looking for. The ink on many of the cards was beginning to run, but the words written in black marker on one card were clearly visible. "To the little girl in the red dress who lies here who made my flight from Frankfurt such fun. You didn't deserve this. God Bless, Chas." Dixit took several photographs.

Police still had not identified Garima's body, so late in the day the two men returned to London, where they were met by Dixit's wife, Sandhya, and several of her relatives. On December 28 the group left London for the United States. The four bodies Dixit and Rattan had been able to identify already had been flown home. Funeral services for the four were held in Dayton, Ohio, on December 29. Garima's body was not identified until two days later, on New Year's Eve.

THE DAY after the bombing, the duty office of Alert Management Systems at Frankfurt's airport was in turmoil. The staff had been called in early. Oliver Koch, Alert's head of training at Frankfurt, was in the office at 6:00 A.M., using the computer terminal on top of the desk of his boss, Ulrich Weber. As he shuffled some papers, Koch uncovered a document that brought his work to a halt. It was a security bulletin that read like a chilling prophecy of the prior day's attack. On December 5, the message said, a man with an Arabic accent had called the U.S. Embassy in Helsinki, warning that within the next two weeks a bomb would be planted on a Pan Am flight from Frankfurt to the United States. What the document did not say was just as disturbing. The notice had never been stamped as received. That meant Weber had not disseminated it to the staff. Koch turned to his boss.

"What is this after Lockerbie?"

"Oh, my God, don't worry, don't worry," Weber said. "It's nothing. Forget it."

"How can I forget it?" Koch persisted. "This is a warning of a potential bomb. It is my job."

"Just forget it," Weber said. "Be quiet or you will get into trouble."

But Koch would not forget. He held on to the warning, which he showed the following day to Beate Franzki, the senior duty officer and Weber's second-in-command. She had not known about the warning notice either and was equally disturbed to see it now, unstamped. In Franzki's view, Weber should have passed it along for distribution to the workers who screened passengers before takeoff. As it was, she said, Pan Am's security firm had taken no special precautions.

After the existence of the Helsinki warning had become widely reported by the media, Pan Am was criticized for failing to take adequate precautions in response to a fairly specific threat. U.S. authorities later labeled the threat a hoax, saying the caller was the same man who had made previous bogus threats against El Al. But that reassurance did little to quell the criticism because the security alert prompted by the Helsinki threat had never been rescinded. Airport and airline security teams should have been treating it as credible.

Paul Hudson and Bert Ammerman had learned of the Helsinki threat shortly after their arrival in Lockerbie. They were stunned that such a specific threat had existed and upset that the police and Pan Am officials had said nothing about it. They had heard of its existence just as they had learned every other piece of vital information about the investigation: They read about it in newspapers.

Hudson's and Ammerman's anger increased when they discovered the government had warned its own personnel of the threat, but not the general public. U.S. officials publicly downplayed the significance of their internal travel advisories, but there were clear indications behind the scenes that government workers paid attention to such warnings. William von Raab, a high-ranking U.S. Customs official, had been booked on Flight 103 but luckily switched to an earlier flight at the last minute. Learning of the Helsinki warning the day after the crash, a furious von Raab telephoned William Green, the assistant commissioner of internal affairs. Why had he not been informed of the threat against Pan Am? Why was customs not on the list of federal offices that receive such warnings?

In all the debate over the credibility of the Helsinki threat, no one had even speculated that Pan Am and Alert might have failed to pass along the information to the frontline security employees who screened passengers. Not only would such a revelation be a terrible embarrassment, but it could have expensive ramifications for Pan Am, which would soon be facing lawsuits filed by relatives of the flight's victims. In Frankfurt Weber immediately began to cover his tracks. He took back the warning from Koch's briefcase, then stamped it as received and backdated it to December 9. But he failed in his attempted cover-up. Koch had made a copy of the unstamped warning before Weber took back the original.

Some Alert employees were not surprised by Weber's actions. They had come to view the entire Alert operation at Frankfurt as window dressing arranged solely to allow Pan Am to comply with FAA regulations. Alert had been formed in 1986 as an autonomous subsidiary responsible for security. From the start, however, Pan Am's control over the subsidiary virtually assured that security would be compromised. In theory, Pan Am was Alert's customer; in practice, it was Alert that played the subservient role, said Franzki, who supervised the Frankfurt security staff. She said Pan Am told Alert how security should be handled. If Alert's procedures threatened to delay a flight, Pan Am's desires were given priority. For example, Pan Am flight crews were supposed to wait outside the aircraft until Alert staff members had finished going over the cabin, but on some occasions crews became impatient and ordered security workers off the plane before they finished their work. "The security for Pan Am was only because of the FAA," Franzki said. "But they themselves—it was not necessary in their eyes. They did it just as a performance."

After the bombing Weber scrambled to make Alert's operation appear more effective than it had been. "Many changes took place," Franzki said. "For example, we could hire as many security people as we wanted. Before Lockerbie it was always very expensive. They had no money. But after that we could hire as many people as we needed."

Oliver Koch was so outraged at Weber's handling of the Helsinki warning that he went to Weber's boss, John Ridd, who oversaw Alert's operations throughout Europe. Koch thought Ridd might take disciplinary action against Weber. Instead, Weber found out about Koch's complaint and promptly fired him.

WITHIN DAYS of the crash the FAA experts, satisfied that neither pilot error nor structural failure had caused the crash, had joined search crews combing the hillsides and forest for wreckage. On Christmas Day the team Bob Mosca had joined was searching an area about thirteen miles east of Lockerbie when it found the metal frame of a suitcase that looked as if it had been scored by an explosion. The following day the team found a large piece of a valise that appeared to have blast marks on it. Other teams were making similar finds.

On December 26 this evidence was sent to the Royal Armament Research and Development Establishment, a military laboratory at Fort Halstead in Kent. Mick Charles, the chief aviation investigator for the British government, said the articles would be examined "to determine whether they exhibit evidence of a preimpact explosion." Until those results were back, however, no one would say publicly that a bomb had caused the crash. Charles, in fact, insisted that structural failure was still a possibility.

Scientists at the defense lab quickly confirmed investigators' suspicions. Parts of the framework of the metal luggage pallet marked AVE 4041 PA showed evidence of an explosion. From blast residue found on some of the damaged wreckage, the scientists also determined that a high-performance plastic explosive, such as Semtex, had been used.

As with many murder investigations, police were to learn a lot about the crime at first, less and less as time went on. In the beginning the Scottish police seemed to be making significant headway. In a January 17 press release Detective Chief Superintendent John Orr had announced "good progress" in the investigation. "We have now identified the baggage container within the aircraft in which the explosive device was placed and substantial forensic and re-constructive work is being undertaken in this regard," he said. "Approximately 10,000 items of baggage and other artifacts have been recovered." He heaped praise on investigators, who by now had taken three thousand statements from witnesses. As diabolical as the terrorists had been, there was a general sense that the apparent miscalculation that had allowed the bomb to detonate over land, where evidence could be more easily recovered, would be their undoing.

The forensic workers were faced with a task that was a lot like solving an enormous jigsaw puzzle. At a massive hangar at the Ministry of Defense depot in Longtown, near Carlisle in northern England, the bits of recovered plane wreckage were identified and sorted. A team of forensic experts under the direction of Alan Feraday and Thomas Hayes—skilled members of a British team that often dissects the work of the Irish Republican Army—began poring over the mess. Some of the pieces were as large as the cockpit; others, mere slivers. Wreckage from in and around the crater was so tiny that crews found it only by sifting through the piles of rubble that had once been houses, sidewalks, and streets. In all, searchers recovered more than four million pieces of crash debris, including about 80 percent of the Boeing 747. When the airplane fragments were spread out on the floor of the Longtown hangar in a two-dimensional reconstruction, the work clearly showed that the explosion had punctured the fuselage in front of the left wing.

The searchers had logged the spot where each piece of wreckage had been recovered, so investigators could determine the sequence of the explosion and breakup. They were able to determine quickly that at least one of the plane's engines was still working immediately after the bomb went off. Inside the No. 2 engine—the engine closest to the bomb—forensic experts found a piece of cable like the kind used in the curtain of baggage container AVE 4041 PA. They concluded that the force of the explosion had blown the cable through the fuselage. The cable, together with other debris, had been sucked into the engine while it was still delivering power, causing shingling, a unique damage pattern that occurs when foreign objects collide with a turbofan's moving parts.

Strong winds blowing northeast in the upper atmosphere spread out the debris, with lighter material being blown farthest. The plane left two separate trails in roughly parallel lines. One line began in Lockerbie, and the other began farther to the south. The southern trail consisted of objects that broke free from the fuselage in the first moments after the explosion. The cockpit and forward contents of the plane fell in this trail, as did sections of the tail that had been knocked free by debris from the plane's disintegrating nose section. Significantly, objects that showed signs of direct blast damage tended to be found along this path. The northern trail was formed by wreckage that broke loose when the plane lost its forward momentum and began to fall almost straight down. This trail, made up of chunks of fuselage and the remaining parts of the tail, extended from the Sherwood Crescent crater in Lockerbie northeast across the golf course and into the countryside.

Some pieces of the interior of the fuselage were pitted, distorted, and blackened by soot—as if a powerful shotgun had been fired into the aircraft's skin at close range. This indicated that the pieces had been adjacent to the explosion, further pinpointing the location of the bomb. To understand better the sequence of events that caused the plane to break up, investigators took a section of the plane from Longtown, where the two-dimensional reconstruction had been assembled on the hangar floor, to a facility in Farnborough, where scaffolding was erected to allow technicians to rebuild the forward cargo hold area of the 747 in three dimensions. To locate the center of the explosive damage, the team re-created an intact fuselage, using a transparent skin. Then they traced the tear lines that had been located from the pieces of recovered wreckage back to their point of origin on the see-through fuselage.

A similar reconstruction was duplicated, on a smaller scale, with two of the plane's baggage containers. Blast damage had been detected on only two containers: AVE 4041 PA, which showed severe damage on the inside, indicating it had contained the bomb, and the one next to it, AVN 7511 PA. Loading records showed the two containers had been stowed at adjacent spots along the left side of the plane in the fourth and fifth positions back from the front of the forward cargo hold. Using the recovered parts, workers reassembled the containers on wooden frameworks.

Once pieced together, the luggage containers were then placed within the reconstructed cargo hold. This allowed the team to observe the interaction between the luggage, baggage container, and fuselage. With the scene so precisely re-created, the team was able to determine that the bomb had detonated at a spot near the bottom of luggage container AVE 4041 PA. This became a crucial finding for criminal investigators because it meant the bag containing the bomb had been among the first loaded into the container.

While this work was under way, a worker employed by the British Air Accidents Investigations Branch found a tiny chunk of circuit board lying on the floor of the Ministry of Defense warehouse at Longtown. The fragment had fallen out of a corner of luggage container AVE 4041 PA, where it had been lodged by the force of the blast. The circuit board was traced to the Toshiba Corporation in Japan, and when a team of detectives went to the Japanese company, they learned the fragment came from a Toshiba Model 8016 radio-cassette player. Toshiba was the same company that made the BomBeat found in Dalkamouni's car in Germany. Investigators also found a piece of a radio loudspeaker, which had become entangled in an article of clothing. On container AVE 4041 PA's surfaces, the team found traces of PETN and RDX, two components of Semtex-H.

Police determined that between 12.25 and 14 ounces of Semtex-H had been used. As they worked, they found more and more wreckage that had been scorched by the blast, including a partially burned Toshiba instruction manual written in English and Arabic. There could be no doubt now. A Toshiba radio-cassette player packed with plastic explosive had destroyed Flight 103 from a position inside container AVE 4041 PA. But the key question remained: Whose bag had contained the bomb?

One hundred and eighty-six passengers could be ruled out automatically because they had started their journey at Heathrow, and AVE 4041 PA had not contained any suitcases belonging to those travelers. Only two types of luggage had been loaded into the container: bags owned by interline passengers who connected to Flight 103 in Heathrow and bags arriving on Pan Am's 727 from Frankfurt. Passengers in those two groups had checked as many as sixty-five pieces of luggage. Thirteen of the sixty-five bags belonged to interline passengers boarding at Heathrow. The other fifty-two came from the Frankfurt flight.

When police looked at the remains of the thirteen interline bags, they were able to rule out seven of the bags right away because the connecting flights that had carried them to Heathrow had arrived after John Bedford, the Pan Am baggage loader-driver, had towed container AVE 4041 PA out of the transfer shed. Those seven late-arriving bags had been loaded loosely into the rear cargo hold of the 747, nowhere near the bomb.

The remaining six bags checked in by Heathrow interline passengers belonged to four passengers: Bernt Carlsson, Charles McKee, Matthew Gannon, and Michael Bernstein. Some of the bags showed blast damage, but investigators soon concluded that none of them contained the bomb. Flight schedules and the recollections of baggage handlers indicated that these six bags had been placed on the bottom of the container—four standing up and two on their sides—in direct contact with the floor. Forensic reconstruction of the debris had shown that the bomb had been ten inches above the bottom of the luggage container, too high for a bag that was lying on the floor. So the bomb had not been inside any bags belonging to passengers who joined the flight at Heathrow. This allowed investigators to reach a major conclusion: The bomb bag had been among the fifty-two pieces of luggage from Frankfurt.

Only some of the Frankfurt suitcases had been placed in container AVE 4041 PA. Heathrow baggage handlers accepting the off-loaded luggage from the 727 had thrown the bags indiscriminately into the container. When it was full, the handlers loaded the rest of the bags loosely into the rear of the 747. There was no way for investigators to tell which of the fifty-two bags had ended up where, because no one had been keeping track.

Meanwhile, forensic specialists working the case from a different angle narrowed their own hunt for the bag's owner. According to the *Sunday Times* of London, workers searching for plane debris in southern Scotland had recovered suitcase fragments to which a magnet and screw had become fused, presumably by the heat of the explosion. Police determined that the magnet and screw were part of the Toshiba that had been packed with explosives. Later investigators sent a special team of searchers back into the fields of southern Scotland, where they combed a five-square-mile area near Newcastleton Forest, almost twenty-five miles from Lockerbie. The team came back with twenty-seven luggage fragments, all apparently from the same suitcase. Forensic experts then proved that the fragments were part of the bag that had contained the bomb. And they determined that the bag had been made by Samsonite.

There were eight Samsonite bags that could have been loaded into container AVE 4041 PA. Four could be ruled out because they belonged to passengers who had not been on the flight from Frankfurt. Of the four Samsonites that had come from Frankfurt, one bag, owned by Francis Boyer, a forty-three-year-old Frenchman, showed no explosive damage, so it was ruled out. One of the remaining three Samsonites was a brown hard-sided bag unaccompanied by its owner, a Pan Am pilot whose last name was Hubbard. It was recovered and ruled out because it showed no explosive damage.

That left two Samsonites: a gray suitcase owned by twenty-four-year-old U.S. Army First Lieutenant George ("Geordie") Williams and a beige soft-sided bag that belonged to a man named Weinacker.

Weinacker seemed to be a particularly likely candidate because he never boarded Flight 103 although his luggage did. Further checking with Samsonite headquarters in Denver, Colorado, however, revealed that the bag containing the bomb had been a bronze-colored System 4 Samsonite Silhouette 4000, a model that had been sold in the Middle East. Neither Williams's nor Weinacker's bag had been bronze; in fact, none of the eight Samsonites linked to Flight 103 passengers were that color. Nor had any of the passengers' relatives interviewed by police been able to identify a family member who owned a bronze Samsonite.

Police reached another major conclusion: The Samsonite that contained the bomb had not been checked in by any of Flight 103's passengers. Instead, the bomb had been shipped in an unaccompanied bag. This finding seemed to be confirmed when searchers found the lock from the Samsonite that carried the bomb. Police tried to match the lock to one of the more than one hundred luggage keys that had been recovered from the wreckage. None of the keys fitted.

While the police in Great Britain were pursuing those leads, their counterparts in Germany were engaged in some old-fashioned legwork. One of the early duties of the BKA after the bombing was to take control of Pan Am documents in Frankfurt related to the flight. While the forensics team worked to match the bomb to the Samsonite, investigators in Germany tried to find the bag's owner. A natural place to start was with Alert, Pan Am's security arm. Had the staff noticed anyone who seemed suspicious or uneasy as Flight 103's passengers were boarding that evening?

During the boarding procedure the Alert workers who screened Flight 103's passengers were supposed to single out a group of selectees who would receive closer scrutiny before being allowed to board. A selectee may be chosen for any one of a number of reasons, ranging from nationality to the way he or she answers a security guard's questions. When German investigators asked Alert personnel if there had been any selectees on the first leg of Flight 103, they were told yes—and no.

For Flight 103 on December 21, Alert employee Detlef Giertz was assigned the job of examining travel documents at the Frankfurt check-in area. He and Karin Winhold, who worked beside him, asked passengers questions designed to determine who should receive further scrutiny. By the time Giertz and Winhold finished screening Flight 103's passengers on December 21, five passengers had been identified as selectees. Their names were entered on the Selectee Control Sheet kept on a nearby table.

In addition to those five passengers, travelers connecting from interline flights were supposed to be automatically designated as selectees. But on December 21 the system broke down. None of the passengers who should have been identified as selectees received further security checks, as the FAA required. The German investigators who were hoping to find leads based on Pan Am's screening of passengers instead found nothing but errors on the part of the airline.

The documentation for the baggage, however, proved more helpful. The BKA looked especially closely at the original copies of the passenger coupons indicating how many bags each passenger shipped on the flight from Frankfurt to London. Some compelling details began to emerge when the information on these coupons was compared with other Pan Am records. Right away a major discrepancy emerged involving the group of JFK-bound interline passengers whose checked bags had been taken to the mobile X-ray machine for screening. Flight 103's manifest said the members of this group, between them, checked in ten bags. But Pan Am's passenger coupons showed these passengers had checked eleven bags. To further confuse matters, the X-ray operator's log and the duty report both showed still another number, thirteen.

THE MANIFEST and passenger coupons did not agree on the number of bags checked by Karen Elizabeth Noonan, the college girl from Maryland who had been warned about the Helsinki threat at the U.S. Embassy party in Vienna. The manifest showed she checked two bags, but the copy of her coupons kept by Pan Am indicated she had checked three. An FBI agent interviewed Curt M. Olsen, the marine sergeant who had dated Noonan's roommate, Patricia Coyle. The agent asked Olsen if he noticed anything unusual in the behavior of the two women the day before the crash. Before this line of investigation could be pursued further, however, Pan Am passenger service agent Simone Kohl—who had worked in Frankfurt on December 21—told investigators she had waited on Noonan. Noonan had checked three bags, she said, but Kohl remembered that she had mistakenly entered only two of them in the airline computer. Another lead fizzled.

Noonan's third bag allowed investigators to account for eleven bags. They soon found a twelfth interline bag—one that had not belonged to any of the flight's passengers. Frankfurt baggage handlers told investigators they had placed one bag marked "rush" on the 727. A rush bag is luggage that has been separated from its owner through no fault of the passenger. The idea is to reunite it with its owner by putting it on the next available flight, no matter what the carrier. According to records, this rush bag had come from an Alitalia flight and was traveling from Rome to Detroit. But when this bag was traced, it turned out to be a brown soft-sided suitcase that had no signs of blast damage.

What about the number of bags the X-ray operator said he had checked? Was he sure he had screened thirteen? Baggage handler Tuzcu, relying on his memory, thought he had sent twelve bags to X-ray. But he was not really sure. X-ray operator Kurt Maier, on the other hand, was meticulous. He had kept records for Flight 103 showing that he had X-rayed ten suitcases, two garment bags, and a cardboard carton. Both his log and his duty report said the same thing, and he told investigators he was sure about it. There had been thirteen interline bags.

Police had learned of this discrepancy within weeks of the bombing, but they were hard pressed to solve the mystery. On January 16, 1989, the FAA's Frank Burns reported on the progress of the investigation in a fifteen-page priority telex, which was sent to the FAA's Washington headquarters from the agency's Brussels office. FAA investigators "were unable to determine exactly why there was a discrepancy between the total number of interline pieces X-rayed and the total number of pieces accounted for," the telex said. Months later it would appear that this thirteenth bag was the bronze Samsonite that contained the bomb. But the person who slipped it into the luggage stream remained a mystery.

The discovery of the thirteenth bag was a closely guarded secret of the investigation. As the relatives searched for answers, all they found was silence from police and a cacophony of theories from the media and politicians. Conflicting stories sprouted like weeds. Soon after the attack a reporter for a Scottish radio station, David Johnston, broadcast a report that said Palestinian extremists had hidden the bomb inside the bag of a CIA officer who was returning home from Beirut. Two police officers interviewed Johnston at his Radio Forth office for hours about his story, demanding to know where he had gotten his information. When Johnston refused to reveal his source, they asked if he would divulge it to Prime Minister Margaret Thatcher. Johnston insisted that police already had the information he reported.

The police persistence with the Radio Forth reporter probably had more to do with plugging leaks than gathering evidence. Johnston's report had touched off a round of one-upmanship in the British tabloids, with each new report discounting the one just published by the competition. "I am concerned that the prominence being given world-wide to speculations and fanciful claims as to the identity of the perpetrators of this appalling crime may hinder the progress of the investigation," said Peter Fraser, Scotland's lord advocate, the prosecutor on the Lockerbie case.

The relatives were baffled and grew more frustrated. The conflicting reports were only a symptom of the schisms that had begun to emerge among the countries and jurisdictions that were being drawn into the investigation. To the frustration of the relatives, the investigation was inextricably tied to the domestic and foreign policies of Britain, West Germany, the United States, Israel, Iran, Syria, and dozens of other nations, each with its own agenda. Although police already had a good idea about how the bomb was made and knew of this mysterious thirteenth bag, the relatives were privy only to limited information released by people operating in a highly politicized environment. What was said, and not said, about the investigation became a delicate foreign relations issue.

In Montreal on February 16, during a meeting of the International Civil Aviation Organization, the aviation agency of the United Nations, British Transport Secretary Paul Channon held a press conference to announce that the bomb had been hidden in a radio-cassette player, a development characterized as a major break in the case. Reporters followed the text of a statement as Channon read, and no one questioned why one clause had been inserted in a larger typeface between two lines. The original sentence read, "THE RECONSTRUCTION OF THE BAGGAGE CONTAINER SUGGESTS THAT THE EXPLOSIVE DEVICE MAY HAVE BEEN AMONG THE BAGGAGE FROM THE FRANKFURT FLIGHT." The insert qualified that statement so that it read: "IT HAS NOT YET BEEN FIRMLY ESTABLISHED WHERE THE BAG WHICH CONTAINED THE DEVICE WAS ORIGINALLY LOADED, BUT THE RECONSTRUCTION OF THE BAGGAGE CONTAINER SUGGESTS THAT THE EXPLOSIVE DEVICE MAY HAVE BEEN AMONG THE BAGGAGE FROM THE FRANKFURT FLIGHT." West German representatives sat through the meeting without commenting on the statement. Privately, however, they were livid. Channon and West German Minister of Transport Jürgen Warnke had met the night before the press conference, and Warnke urged Channon not to make any mention of Frankfurt, despite the discovery of the unaccounted-for suitcase loaded at that airport. Warnke pointed out that the British were not making statements about most other aspects of the probe. And he argued that even if the suitcase that carried the bomb had passed through Frankfurt, the explosives could have been added to the bag in London. After all, the bags from the 727 had been left unattended on Heathrow's tarmac between flights. In addition, everyone agreed that the bomb bag had been placed in the belly of the 747 by baggage handlers at London's Heathrow Airport. And that placement had been of enormous significance since the bomb's explosive charge had been relatively small. It was the bomb's precise location—in the forward cargo hold, close to the aircraft's skin—that had ensured the plane's destruction. The British attributed this placement to bad luck, but the Germans thought that was too convenient an explanation.

The night before the Montreal press conference the stormy session between the British and Germans ended with what the British undoubtedly considered a concession: the watered-down reference to Frankfurt in the public statement. The Germans, however, left the meeting angry that Frankfurt was being mentioned at all. "We tried . . . to convince them to withhold it," Karl-Heinz Hemmer, the German aviation security chief, who had sat in on the meeting, said a few hours after the press conference. Hemmer argued that the British statement, which shed no new light on the probe, was designed to serve another purpose. Without revealing the existence of the thirteenth bag, it pointed the finger of blame at Frankfurt security, implying that a German failure had allowed the bomb to get on board.

Later the British complained that the Germans were not fully cooperating with the investigation and even suggested that German authorities had intentionally withheld vital evidence. As these turf battles began, the prospect of capturing the terrorists responsible for the attack seemed more remote than ever. Some of the relatives began to feel anger as well as grief, and they grew increasingly restless.

CHAPTER 8

GRIEF FORMS
A BOND

WHEN PAUL Hudson returned to the United States from Lockerbie, he still had confidence in the aviation security system that had allowed a terrorist bomb to kill his daughter and 269 others. "I thought the security was adequate and that the terrorists had just found some clever loophole," he said. "I thought it was a matter of plugging a loophole in an otherwise efficient system." Like many of those who had lost a family member in the attack, he expected his main task in the coming months would be to cope with his own grief. But he soon found himself extending his efforts to other areas.

Shortly after his daughter's funeral Hudson telephoned the Washington, D.C., offices of Ralph Nader, the consumer advocate. Hudson wanted information on aviation security, a subject about which he knew nothing. His call was referred to Christopher J. Witkowski, the executive director of the Aviation Consumer Action Project. ACAP was formed in 1971 as an advocacy group for air travelers, and part of its role had been to help the relatives of plane crash victims. Hudson was still unsettled over the December 5 bomb threat to the U.S. Embassy at Helsinki that made specific reference to a Pan Am flight leaving Frankfurt in the weeks before Christmas, and one of his first questions to Witkowski was about bomb threats. He asked how many of them American carriers typically receive. The answer stunned him. Of all the flights flown by American carriers in 1988, only 372 had been the subject of bomb threats. And during the whole year the FAA had issued fewer than thirty-five security advisories. Surely,

111

Hudson thought, those were numbers sufficiently small for carriers to be able to handle the terrorist threat, and he wondered aloud why more hadn't been done to protect his daughter's flight. Hudson had learned that Syracuse University was holding a memorial service on January 18 for the relatives of the university students who had been killed in the crash, and he asked Witkowski to attend the service and to discuss with the relatives aviation security and the role of the Federal Aviation Administration. Witkowski agreed to make the trip.

At about the same time, Christopher Jones's mother, Georgia Nucci, sent a letter to all the parents of the students affiliated with the Syracuse University study abroad program. The letter mentioned the possibility that some parents might want to contact others for support. "I really thought we were going to need one another," she said. Some bonds had already begun to form among the relatives of crash victims, particularly those who had been at John F. Kennedy Airport the night of December 21 and been exposed to the media pressures. Nucci's letter included a list of the names and addresses of the other parents who had children in the university group. In the days before the Syracuse University memorial service more than two dozen of the relatives gathered at the Mendham, New Jersey, home of Tom and Dorothy Coker, who had been among the first relatives to go to Scotland and whose twin sons had been passengers on Flight 103. The meeting was informal, and there was no agenda.

Bonds were forming as well between many of the other relatives, including those who began attending Flight 103 funerals and memorial services near their homes. Hudson estimates that at least a hundred thousand people went to Flight 103 funerals in the United States in the weeks following the attack. Relatives who met at these gatherings exchanged names and addresses, giving birth to a rudimentary directory of victims' relatives. Getting a comprehensive listing of victims' next of kin had proved to be a more difficult task. Hudson and others who had traveled to Lockerbie had asked Pan Am and the U.S. State Department for the names and addresses of next of kin. Hudson hoped to print a newsletter to send to the other relatives, which would bring them up-to-date on such details as the return of personal property. But Pan Am and the State Department rejected the request, stating the list was confidential.

The January 18 memorial service at Syracuse University provided another opportunity for relatives to gather, and many of them were hungry for information. The night before the memorial service Witkowski sat at the bar of an on-campus hotel and talked for five hours with Daniel and Susan Cohen, the parents of twenty-year-old Theodora Cohen of Port Jervis, New

York, and with Jim and Rosemary Wolfe, the father and stepmother of twenty-year-old Miriam Wolfe of Severna Park, Maryland. The four relatives wanted to know more about aviation security, the FAA, and airline safety. The next day Witkowski addressed a group of about fifty relatives at the hotel and distributed copies of *After the Crash,* a brochure designed to help survivors and the relatives of victims cope with the legal and insurance issues that arise following an aviation disaster. Hudson, whose daughter had had no connection to the university, talked to the group about his interest in forming a relatives' organization. He also touched on other subjects, including procedures for obtaining the return of personal property. The mood of this gathering was subdued, and many of the relatives were meeting one another for the first time. "People were still stunned," Georgia Nucci said. Before the session ended, however, many of the relatives signed a letter to the State Department requesting the names and addresses of the victims' next of kin.

By the end of the month the government had become more flexible on the issue of releasing the next of kin list. The State Department still refused to turn over the names and addresses, but it agreed to forward to the next of kin a letter of introduction written by Hudson. Those letters, which went out in late January, generated more than a hundred responses.

Within three weeks of the service in Syracuse a group of relatives held a press conference at the Grand Hyatt Hotel in midtown Manhattan. About thirty relatives attended the February 4 event, which had been organized by Hudson and others. They were outnumbered by about eighty reporters and photographers. The relatives—facing the bright lights of television cameras, many with pictures of loved ones pinned to their clothing—demanded to know why their government had not made public a threat that a flight would be bombed. They called for the resignation of T. Allan McArtor, administrator of the Federal Aviation Administration. They complained that Scottish authorities had been slow to return personal effects and spoke of the lack of respect with which some of the remains had been returned. One woman said her brother's body had been unloaded by forklift from a plane in the livestock cargo area at JFK. The relatives criticized the governments involved for failing to move more quickly to install devices to detect plastic explosives. But their main complaint was with U.S. officials, almost none of whom had attended memorial services or written letters of condolence. "Our numerous letters are not answered," a statement by the relatives said. "We see no sign of action, we are not being informed of any events which would lead to answers to many questions that remain." Their comments were broadcast around the world, and for the first time the relatives—now calling themselves the Victims of Pan Am Flight 103—sensed their power to command attention.

About thirty people attended the first formal meeting of the fledgling relatives' organization, held in mid-February, at the Hasbrouck Heights, New Jersey, home of Wendy Giebler, whose husband, William, had been killed in the Flight 103 attack. They formed into committees responsible for everything from issuing a newsletter to pursuing financial compensation from Pan Am. The group, which had no by-laws, agreed that decisions would be made by the membership and by a steering committee, whose members would consist of several committee chairmen. Hudson was appointed chairman of the steering committee. Bert Ammerman became chairman of the political action committee. Christopher Jones's mother, Georgia Nucci, began to edit and publish a group newsletter. Attorney Richard Hartunian—brother of Lynne Hartunian, the woman for whom Paul Hudson had purchased the twenty-one white flowers in Lockerbie—headed the legal committee. While others were discussing the organization's structure, four members closed themselves off in an adjoining room and prepared a short statement outlining their objectives. The statement, later approved by the rest of the group, listed these goals:

To provide support, assistance and information for all family members of the victims; to encourage Congressional committees to investigate the events regarding the bombing of Pan Am Flight 103 and the actions and policies of the FAA, Pan American World Airways, the State Department and other involved parties; to identify and provide specific recommendations for near term and long term improvements in airline and airport security; [and] to demand that changes and a more aggressive stance be implemented by our government regarding terrorism, to the end that there be no safe haven anywhere for terrorists.

After the meeting the relatives moved to a nearby restaurant called the Crow's Nest, where they held another press conference to announce their structure and purpose. Before adjourning, the group agreed to meet monthly and to hold its March gathering in Trumbull, Connecticut.

VIRTUALLY ALL the relatives at the early meetings of the group shared the conviction that their government had failed them by permitting Pan Am to operate with a security system that had allowed a terrorist bomb to get on board. They also felt betrayed by their government's failure to circulate the Helsinki warning. If Pan Am and the FAA knew of a threat against a Pan Am flight out of Frankfurt in the weeks before Christmas, why wasn't that information shared with others? Later, when the relatives learned that the threat *had* been shared with others—the small community of Americans in Moscow—their feelings of betrayal only increased. Had a double standard allowed some Americans to be informed of the threat, while others were left to die because they hadn't received the same information? The relatives also were bitter about their government's inability to help them obtain financial compensation. Civilians killed in terrorist acts get no government benefits. And unless lawyers are able to prove that Pan Am acted with "willful misconduct," the international treaty called the Warsaw Convention places a $75,000 cap on the amount of damages a relative can collect from the airline in a civil lawsuit.

The principal object of the relatives' anger was the State Department, which many relatives believed had failed them in the crash's aftermath. When an American dies abroad, the State Department is charged with seeing to it that the next of kin is notified and that the body and personal property are returned. Many relatives thought that the department had handled these responsibilities with a lack of sensitivity. Pan Am, not the State Department, had taken the lead in notifying people that a family member had been on the flight. When a relative called the State Department seeking confirmation of a family member's death, frequently a Pan Am representative, not someone from the department, had returned the call. (The department conceded months later that it didn't obtain Pan Am's list of family contacts until two days after the disaster.) The State Department also never sent family members letters confirming the deaths and explaining its role in the crash's aftermath—a violation of its own policies. Other relatives restated the complaint raised at the February 4 press conference at the Grand Hyatt Hotel in Manhattan: that the bodies of their loved ones had been returned as airfreight, without ceremony, and unloaded in airport sheds by workers operating forklifts. "There was a general insensitivity to victims," said Robert Monetti, whose son, Richard, was among the Syracuse University students on the plane. "They had no clue how to deal with people."

Some relatives had problems with lawyers seeking to represent them in claims against the airline. Barbara Matthews Weedon of New York City, whose daughter, Kesha, was killed, received an unsolicited call from a lawyer two or three days after the crash, offering to have Mrs. Weedon escorted to his Long Island office, door to door, in a limousine. She turned him down. When another lawyer appeared at her home uninvited, a relative told him Mrs. Weedon was unable to come to the door. Undeterred, the attorney asked if he could come inside to use the bathroom.

Other relatives suspected that Pan Am and its insurance underwriter, U.S. Aviation Underwriters, might be engaging in a cutthroat form of subterfuge known to aviation lawyers as early bonding or claimant control. Within a day of the bombing many relatives had been contacted by a Pan Am representative offering to be their full-time liaison. These Pan Am workers—sometimes called buddies—encouraged relatives to call upon them at any time of the day or night, even if they only wanted someone to talk to. Attorneys specializing in aviation litigation explained later that airlines often have more than humanitarian motives in providing such personalized attention. An airline buddy may act like a sponge, the attorneys said, soaking up personal information about a family that can come back to haunt them in court. After the 1982 crash of a Pan Am plane in New Orleans, a Pan Am buddy learned from a family member that the victim had made four recent trips to Las Vegas. When the family sued the airline and its insurance underwriter, defense lawyers tried to use the Las Vegas trips as evidence that the man gambled excessively. Similarly, after the crash of a Delta plane in Dallas, an airline buddy learned that one crash victim was homosexual. That information later was used to show that the victim had an increased chance of dying of AIDS at a young age, thereby reducing the damages to which he was entitled. Pan Am has denied having had an ulterior motive in trying to help the families of Flight 103 victims. Nonetheless, one mother of a Lockerbie victim broke off relations with her buddy after she heard the scratch of a pencil on paper during a telephone conversation and concluded that her "friend" was taking notes.

NOT EVERYONE in the newly formed relatives' organization had the same ideas about what the group's main function should be. Hudson believed it should become a lobbying group for improved aviation security. He helped form the group, he said later, "so that first of all, the people who were on the plane, my daughter and the two hundred sixty-nine others, did not die in vain, and hopefully that others won't die in vain." Other group members, including Georgia Nucci, were more inclined to see the organization as a means of support for grieving relatives. "To this day I feel it's the one thing I know we can do for sure," she said. "We were betrayed and we are still being betrayed . . . and the only people who will understand this is us." The group's tolerance for diversity of opinion on this point allowed it to attract and retain both types of people: those who sought change through the political process and those who came to meetings to give and receive emotional support. But by the end of the summer those different views of the group's purpose, together with personality conflicts, began to tear the organization apart. Meanwhile, they continued to struggle with their own private difficulties.

THE DEATH of Georgia Nucci's only surviving child brought back the same painful feelings she had experienced one year earlier, after her daughter had died in South America. And as had happened after Jennifer's death, Mrs. Nucci began to have trouble sleeping. At night she would lie awake in bed for hours, staring at the ceiling. On those rare occasions when she was able to fall asleep, she woke up with nightmares. In one of her nightmares she was at the John F. Kennedy Airport, waiting in the baggage pickup area and watching the bodies of her children come toward her on the luggage carousel. The bodies were fully clothed except for the feet, which were naked; around one toe someone had tied a baggage tag. In her dream Jennifer's body moved by so rapidly on the carousel that her mother could not reach it, and it was carried away around the corner. When Jones's body approached, she reached down to claim it and saw that her son was smirking at her.

Georgia Nucci was not surprised that Jennifer's body appeared in her dreams. Retrieving her daughter's body from Ecuador had been a traumatic experience. Sometimes the littlest thing—the sound of a familiar song, the sight of a blinking message light on a hotel telephone—could trigger a flood of memories and transport her back to that awful week at the end of 1987.

The Nuccis were in Schenectady, New York, attending a production of the play *Cats,* the night an official from the American Field Service program called their home to say Jennifer was in a coma. They had rented a hotel room so they wouldn't have to drive home after the show, and when Georgia Nucci opened the door to their room, she noticed that the little red message light on the telephone beside the bed was blinking, indicating that someone had called. She was still humming the play's hit song, "Memory." The message was from her son, Christopher, who was home when the AFS official telephoned. Georgia and Tony Nucci caught a commercial flight to Ecuador the following morning.

The Nuccis had chartered a medical evacuation flight to meet them in South America and take Jennifer back to a hospital in the United States.

But she died before the plane arrived. The Nuccis decided to use the plane to take them, and Jennifer's body, back to the United States. At the airfield in Ecuador, however, government officials refused to let the group leave: Because the doors of the Learjet were too small to admit a coffin, the body had to come home without one, but the officials refused to allow the body to be transported without a coffin. For several hours, while Jennifer's body, wrapped in sheets and plastic, lay in an ambulance next to the airplane, the Nuccis pleaded with the officials. Eventually Nucci gave all the money he had with him—ninety-two dollars—to someone who cleared the plane for takeoff. The jet was so small that during the entire ride home Georgia Nucci sat with her dead daughter's feet in her lap, breathing in the smell of formaldehyde. She said to herself as the plane became airborne, "I will make it through this, and I will never be afraid of anything, ever again."

After the bombing of Flight 103, Georgia Nucci began experiencing that same sense of panic again, only now it was triggered by different things. After Jennifer had died, the panic might be triggered by the song "Memory," by the sight of a blinking message light on a hotel telephone, or by the smell of formaldehyde. Now the feelings welled up whenever she found herself unexpectedly facing bright television lights, like those she had encountered on December 21 at Kennedy Airport, or when she was exposed to the sight of a Boeing 747's distinctive humpbacked outline. In the weeks following Christopher Jones's funeral several people suggested his mother seek out psychiatric help, and when she did, she was diagnosed with posttraumatic stress disorder, the same illness that affects many war veterans. Her doctor suggested she begin taking the antianxiety medication Ativan before going to bed. She had been prescribed the same drug after Jennifer's death. She found it was the only way she could sleep.

PAUL HUDSON'S wife, Eleanor, also had difficulty functioning in the days following her daughter's death. She found herself not caring if she lived or died, and to the dismay of her family and friends, she began to pay less and less attention to her two youngest children, Paul Joseph and David, who were in grade school. The sight of her sons was physically painful to her; their existence seemed like a reminder that Melina was dead. What was the point of giving love to her two surviving sons, she thought, when there was no guarantee that someone would not take their lives, too? On a television news show she had once seen, a Jewish man who had survived the Holocaust had explained his reluctance to have children by saying that he didn't want to give the world another Jew to kill. Mrs. Hudson now understood that feeling. "It was such a betrayal of our existence," she said of the attack on her daughter's plane. "It was such a betrayal of everything we lived for, everything I tried to teach my children. To have her killed and then to feel that no one cared—they killed all of us when they killed Melina."

Melina Hudson's funeral service was held at the Catholic cathedral in downtown Albany, and one of those who attended the mass was Father Patrick Conlon, a priest from Blessed Sacrament Church in Exeter who had become friendly with the girl during her semester of study in England. The day after the funeral Father Conlon planned to travel to New York and then to California, but Mrs. Hudson found herself reluctant to let him leave. Against her husband's wishes, she decided to take the train to New York with Father Conlon, so she could spend that much more time with him. "I felt very close to him," she said. "I felt he knew Melina." On New Year's Day they rode to New York City together. Eleanor Hudson said good-bye, then boarded another train for the return trip. On her way back to Albany a fellow passenger, a young girl who was seven months pregnant, began having contractions. Mrs. Hudson noticed that the girl was about Melina's age and had the same hair color, and she sat with her. When the girl's contractions became more frequent, the conductor called for an ambulance to meet the train in Poughkeepsie. Mrs. Hudson agreed to disembark with the girl and accompany her to the hospital. "I remember I was a little worried about what Paul was going to say, but I didn't care," Eleanor Hudson said. "She was seventeen and she was blond and she didn't have anyone else. I was thinking of Melina."

She saw the girl to the emergency room, then decided to board the next train to Albany. Before leaving the hospital, she removed an ornament from a Christmas tree in the hospital lobby. The whole trip to New York seemed like a dream; she wanted the ornament as proof that she hadn't just imagined it.

In the weeks after her daughter's funeral, Eleanor Hudson found it difficult to accompany her husband and other members of the family on Sunday trips to the cemetery. She sobbed at the sight of her daughter's name on the stone marker, and when she got home, she lay in bed for hours. So she stopped going to the cemetery.

The Hudsons rarely spoke about it, but in the weeks before she had left home, Melina Hudson had told her parents she had changed her mind and did not want to go to Exeter. She had also expressed misgivings about leaving home to her brother Stephen in a late-night conversation about a week before she left for England. She said she was unhappy about leaving behind her friends. "She really didn't want to start all over again at a new school—make new friends, live in a whole new culture," Stephen Hudson recalled. But her parents told her she should participate in the program anyway. Mrs. Hudson figured that Melina would get over her misgivings and that England would be a good experience for her. But Melina had been very homesick at Exeter. When her mother visited her in England in the fall of 1988, Melina had begged to be allowed to leave school and accompany her mother to Italy, where Mrs. Hudson planned to visit relatives. But Mrs. Hudson encouraged Melina to stay in England and finish her studies. These events came back to haunt Eleanor Hudson in the months after her daughter's death. She asked herself, "Why didn't I take her to Italy with me? Why didn't I take her home with me?"

Friends and family members began to voice concern for the welfare of the Hudsons' two youngest boys. "I really didn't care for them in the sense of a mother," Eleanor Hudson said later. "Initially it was hard for me to be a mother to them. I didn't cook for them. I didn't check their homework. I didn't wash their clothes. I didn't want them." The family's part-time housekeeper soon took over all the household tasks. Other duties Mrs. Hudson used to perform simply fell by the wayside. She stopped taking her sons to Little League games. David had to stop playing altogether, and Paul Joseph continued only because his Little League coach agreed to give him rides to and from his games and practices.

Although Paul Joseph had always been an excellent student, after his sister's death he received a failing grade in mathematics. Eleanor Hudson lashed out at her ten-year-old son when she saw his report card. "After all we've been through, how could you possibly do this to us?" she said. A school nurse who noticed changes in the boy's demeanor contacted the family, and Mrs. Hudson agreed to seek counseling with Paul Joseph and her husband. The three family members attended about ten counseling sessions, which Mrs. Hudson believed improved life in her household. "The psychologist said, 'Who is going to love this boy? Who is going to play with this boy?' " she said. " 'Don't judge him, don't care about his schoolwork, just nurture him, play with him, have a good time with him.' " Friends and family members also spoke to her about her children, but her response—at least at first—was fatalistic. "I knew that people meant well, and I knew that they were right, but there was nothing I could do. I didn't want to take care of them."

Most of her energies were poured into the work of the relatives' organization—Pan Am work, as she began to call it. At Hudson's downtown real estate office an entire room had been turned over to the work of the group. Two four-drawer file cabinets were set up to hold correspondence and records, and photographs of the flight's victims hung from the walls. Eleanor Hudson embraced the group's mission with a passion. Some weekends she and her husband would ask Stephen to come home from college and watch his brothers so that they could devote all their energies to the organization. If Stephen couldn't help out, she left her young sons with the parents of some of their classmates. From her vantage point, the most important thing in the world was Hudson's work. "I had nothing to give anybody," she said. "All I wanted was for Paul to do this work and for no one to hurt him or attack him."

BEULAH McKEE, the mother of Army Major Chuck McKee, attended a meeting of the relatives' group in Cleveland, Ohio, a couple of months after her son's death. She was seventy-two at the time, and even as she went to the meeting, she told herself that others could carry the group's burdens better than she could. Though Beulah McKee felt drawn to the organization, she was one of the less active members, attending meetings occasionally and rarely speaking. She viewed herself as a spectator. "There are so many young people there, who are so much more able," she said. Prior to one meeting she learned that a twenty-one-year-old victim of the bombing, Beth Ann Johnson, had grown up nearby in Greensburg, Pennsylvania. Soon she struck up a relationship with Beth Ann's parents.

Mrs. McKee had turned down the opportunity to review her son's remains, and as time passed, she began to second-guess that decision. "I still have moments when I think, *Well, was that really Chuck?* I know he's dead, but yet not having seen a corpse . . . It was very difficult for me."

Mrs. McKee also became lonely. Her husband was dead, and another of her four children had died nearly twenty years earlier as a result of a heart ailment. With McKee's death, her family had dwindled to half its original size.

Chuck McKee had been in the military for a long time, and it had been many years since he had been a daily part of her life. Still, Mrs. McKee occasionally found herself looking up quickly, thinking she had seen him out of the corner of her eye. She felt his absence most strongly at night when the telephone rang. "I would wonder, *Was it Chuck?*" It was months before she accepted the reality of her son's death.

* * *

OTHERS FOUND a more open expression of their grief in gathering outside the Pan Am Building in New York City on the twenty-first of each month. They demonstrated with placards, handed out flyers explaining the purpose of their organization, and periodically read aloud the name of each of the flight's victims. Their presence, they said to anyone who stopped to ask, was a reminder to the world of the lives that were lost in the Flight 103 bombing.

Soon Victims of Pan Am Flight 103 began to emerge as a special-interest group that was difficult to ignore. On March 14 Hudson, Ammerman, and several other members of the organization testified before a special hearing of a subcommittee of the Senate Committee on Appropriations. At the hearing, which was chaired by New Jersey Senator Frank R. Lautenberg, Hudson proposed that American carriers begin conducting hand searches of all airline luggage—both checked and carry-on—until more effective bomb detection equipment was available. "We believe that the 270 lives lost on Flight 103 could have been saved; that this bombing could have been prevented," he told the panel. "We believe that those who conclude that little or nothing can be done about terrorist attacks on airlines are grievously wrong, motivated in some instances by commercial considerations and in others by an effort to conceal and tolerate inadequate efforts and actual dereliction of duty." One week later he and others testified at a hearing before the House Subcommittee on Aviation. At the March 21 session, Hudson pointed out that three months after the bombing airlines still were allowing passengers to transport radios and other electronic devices that could be easily modified to conceal plastic explosives. "The plastic is invisible to the present X-rays used, and the wiring cannot be distinguished," he said. The failure of the industry to ban such devices, Hudson continued, "goes on beyond negligence, beyond incompetence, and we are now in an area of incredibly reckless behavior."

Other members of the group began making themselves available for television interviews. In late March Wendy Giebler, Dorothy Coker, and Bonnie O'Connor, sister of victim John Ahern, appeared on NBC's "Today" show. At about the same time Daniel and Susan Cohen were interviewed on ABC's "Good Morning America."

Melina Hudson's older brother, Stephen, returned to Skidmore College in January to complete his freshman year and soon realized he was having difficulty adjusting. For one thing, he couldn't concentrate on his studies. After classes he would return to his dormitory, borrow a friend's telephone, and begin calling television news organizations, trying to interest them in the Flight 103 story. If he went to the school library to study, he found himself photocopying the addresses of U.S. senators and representatives, then writing them letters complaining about the state of aviation security. He also had trouble readjusting to dormitory life. When a distraught friend described how he had been rejected by his girlfriend, Hudson found it hard to generate any sympathy. Not long after that, he decided to withdraw from school and devote all his energy to the work his parents were doing.

Although he hadn't been particularly interested in political science in school, Stephen Hudson decided to become an unpaid full-time Flight 103 lobbyist in Washington, D.C. He moved to the capital area, living first with Christopher Witkowski, the executive director of the Aviation Consumer Action Project, and later with an aunt in a Washington suburb. He also bought an olive green suit and a briefcase, which he thought would make him look like a lobbyist.

At first Stephen Hudson had no office and carried all his materials in his briefcase. Eventually, however, he was allowed to use a conference room at the offices of the national headquarters of Ralph Nader's public interest research organization. The arrangement was awkward—when staff members needed the conference room, Hudson had to pick up his belongings and leave—but the room had a telephone, and it gave him a base of operations.

Stephen Hudson coordinated his work with his father in Albany. His first task was to poll senators on their support for an independent investigation of the Flight 103 bombing. Through this work he began to develop a relationship with legislative staff people. Another of his early tasks was to look through campaign contribution records, to see which senators had received money from aviation industry political action committees. As he learned more about Washington, he began to feel his confidence grow.

Stephen Hudson attended many of the congressional hearings on aviation security. He also worked as an advance man, setting up meetings for his father. If he learned that a senator was undecided about supporting a Flight 103 investigation, he would speak with a Flight 103 relative from that senator's state and request that he or she contact the senator. He had learned from experience—more specifically, from the dozens of unacknowledged letters he had written to lawmakers from other states—that a senator or representative who won't acknowledge correspondence from out of state is almost certain to respond to a constituent. Stephen's parents gave him money for food and for the metro and supplied him with train or airplane tickets when he needed to return to Albany.

As spring approached, the relatives grew concerned that interest in the Flight 103 story was flagging. So they planned a major demonstration in Washington, D.C., on April 3—the 103d day after the attack on the flight. Hundreds of family members and friends traveled to the capital for the demonstration and for a vigil in Lafayette Park, across the street from the White House. Near the end of the vigil, the relatives came forward with white carnations labeled with the name of each victim. They wove the flowers through the boughs of an evergreen wreath, then turned and walked toward the White House gate. A guard cautiously pulled open the gate, accepted the wreath, and began to swing it shut on the relatives, but Eleanor Hudson, standing near the front of the group, thrust out her arm and told the guard there were more flowers to deliver. The crowd surged forward, and the guard, now alarmed, hurried to close the gate.

"Wait!" Mrs. Hudson shouted. "There are more flowers. Take the flowers."

She turned from the guard and yelled back to the crowd. "Pass up your flowers! Hurry! Pass up your flowers! They're closing the gate!"

Bouquets came forward in waves, passed hand to hand over the heads of the relatives and friends of the victims. By now Eleanor Hudson was hysterical. "Take the flowers!" she cried. "Take the flowers! Take . . . the . . . flowers!"

On the same trip Paul Hudson and four others of the victims' relatives, including Bert Ammerman, met inside the White House with President Bush and several of his key advisers, including National Security Adviser Brent Scowcroft, Chief of Staff John Sununu, and Secretary of Transportation Sam Skinner. The meeting had been arranged through the efforts of group member Victoria Cummock of Coral Gables, Florida, who was friends with a Bush family member and who sat in on the meeting. Mrs. Cummock's husband, John, was a victim of the bombing. Bert Ammerman had hit upon the idea of establishing an independent civil investigation of the disaster, and in their meeting the relatives asked Bush to support that concept. The session, scheduled to last fifteen minutes, went on for more than an hour but ended without any commitments from the president. While that meeting was taking place, other relatives fanned out through the Capitol to lobby members of Congress. Karen Hunt's parents and sister, Robyn, traveled from Rochester to meet with New York Senator Daniel Patrick Moynihan. In the course of the afternoon members of the organization visited the offices of all one hundred U.S. senators.

Later in the month the relatives learned that Bush had rejected the idea of a special investigation. It was disappointing news, but they refused to give up on the idea. Following up on the group's meeting with the president, Transportation Secretary Skinner announced that the United States would speed up deployment of sophisticated bomb detection equipment at foreign airports. This news, too, came as a disappointment to the relatives, who saw it as an attempt at appeasement. The new equipment used a technology called thermal neutron analysis (TNA) to detect plastic explosives but had not been widely put into service. And there had been concerns that the machines' price tag of nearly a million dollars each and their high false-alarm rate would make them too costly and troublesome to be practical. Skinner said the new program would be paid for by airlines and probably would boost ticket prices by between twenty cents and one dollar per ticket. The transportation secretary also announced that airport X-ray machines and metal detectors would be upgraded and that the FAA would add 120 employees to bolster security at domestic and foreign airports.

Convinced that the government reaction was inadequate to meet the threat posed by terrorism, the relatives resumed their efforts to urge Congress to support an independent probe of the bombing. By the summer of 1989 they had persuaded about seventy senators to support a civil investigation. They still had a long way to go, but they were beginning to feel that the government just might be getting serious about improving airline security.

WHILE SOME relatives chose to work through the family group, others struck out on their own to find answers to their questions about the bomb attack. Bruce Smith, a Pan Am pilot whose wife, Ingrid, died in the bombing, wrote to the relatives of 160 other victims to urge them to settle their litigation against Pan Am for the hundred thousand dollars the airline was offering, then pool their money and match a government reward for the capture and prosecution of the terrorists who planted the bomb. Although he communicated with the relatives who had organized themselves, Smith eventually became a lone activist, spending much of his free time in Washington lobbying for legislation to increase the reward fund. "Our enemies are the people who put the bomb on the plane, not the people who failed to prevent it," Smith said. "Talking to some relatives, you'd think Pan Am actually did it."

Another man whose wife died on Flight 103 took a different approach. German businessman Frank Rosenkranz not only wanted to know who killed his wife, Pan Am flight attendant María Nieves Larracoechea, but also wanted to know why his wife's employer had failed to stop the bombing. Rosenkranz, who operated an insurance and real estate business in Madrid, devoted all his energy to investigating his wife's murder. He and his sister-in-law, Marina de Larracoechea, began working with the relatives' organization. Eventually Rosenkranz became a member of the group's board of directors, holding the title of international vice-president and serving as the board's eyes and ears in Europe. "I stopped my business," he said. "My secretary had to work only on this."

In Germany Rosenkranz tried to duplicate the success of those relatives in the United States who had used media coverage to put pressure on the government to conduct an independent investigation. He telephoned reporters throughout Germany but was unable to generate any stories. His lone success was a letter to the editor published in *Der Spiegel* in March. Unlike the case in the United States and Great Britain, where there had been public outcries over the security failures that led to the attack, there had been no comparable reaction in Germany. "I wanted to provoke some," Rosenkranz said, but his letter failed to do that. "I thought this cannot be. We had the airport. We had the terrorists in Germany." Failing with the media, Rosenkranz tried to convince politicians in Bonn to push for answers. Some were not interested, while others, including a well-known human rights activist in parliament, Petra Kelly, said they lacked the time to pursue the issue. In April, while attending the vigil at the White House, Rosenkranz tried to persuade staff members of several U.S. congressmen involved in foreign affairs to put pressure on their German counterparts. Again, no results.

At the end of April a German magazine reporter called Rosenkranz. Rosenkranz had called dozens of reporters; this was the first time a journalist had contacted him. Thomas Osterkorn, who worked for the publication *Stern,* wanted Rosenkranz's help in securing photographs of victims for a story that would personalize the bombing by describing the routine activities of some of the passengers in the days before the flight. Rosenkranz said *Stern* made it clear the magazine was not interested in joining the relatives' political fight to launch an investigation. Rosenkranz agreed to help. He took a New York-based *Stern* photographer to a relatives' meeting in the United States and explained the project to the other family members. Largely thanks to his efforts, the magazine obtained more than a hundred photos. A nervous Rosenkranz went to *Stern*'s headquarters in Hamburg to check on the story before publication. "I don't want to have any sensationalism and no naked woman," Rosenkranz said he told the editors.

"Occasionally *Stern*, they put a naked woman in. I said this cannot go, not with this issue. Maybe with the next one, but not together with Lockerbie."

Although the *Stern* story was not the kind of investigative report Rosenkranz had sought, it had tremendous impact. In the narrative of the events leading up to the takeoff of Flight 103 from Frankfurt, the story mentioned that Pan Am's Frankfurt employees had held their Christmas party the night of the bombing. The story prompted Pan Am to write a critical letter to *Stern*'s editor, insisting its security was working efficiently that day. Actually Pan Am's security subsidiary, Alert, had held its Christmas party on a different day, so the party on December 21 was for nonsecurity personnel. But the question of who attended the party soon became moot. Challenged by Pan Am, *Stern* dug deeper and uncovered the story about the backdating of the Helsinki memo and the widespread criticisms by former Alert employees about poor training and management at Frankfurt. "Because of the reaction of Pan Am in Germany, *Stern* really started to fight back to Pan Am," Rosenkranz said. "So they really made a mistake, Pan Am."

As THE criminal investigation continued, many of the relatives became frustrated by what they were reading in the newspapers and watching on television news shows. Their organization kept voluminous files of newspaper clippings, in addition to videotapes of television shows devoted to the bombing, and as a result, group members were extraordinarily well informed about the investigation. In the early part of 1989 the news that frustrated them the most concerned events in West Germany.

Marwan Khreesat, the PFLP—GC bomb maker, had turned out to be a much more complicated man than he appeared to be when the West German police placed him under arrest in the fall of 1988. Investigators had long suspected that Khreesat had had a hand in crafting the bomb that blew up Flight 103. Months after the attack it became clear that he also had been a spy for Jordan, feeding information on the PFLP—GC to the government of King Hussein, which in turn forwarded the data to the West German intelligence agency, the Bundesnachrichtendienst (BND). Khreesat's information had been valuable, and his arrest during the Autumn Leaves sweep had been a mistake—a result of the same lack of interagency communication that earlier had allowed Ramzi Diab to slip through the Germans' grasp.

Sometime in the first week of November, while he was still in police custody, Khreesat placed a call from prison that was later traced to an intelligence contact in Jordan. The call may have indicated that Khreesat considered his cover completely blown because under normal circumstances a spy would never use a nonsecure telephone to make such a contact. Then a judge concluded that there was not enough evidence to continue holding Khreesat. After fifteen days in custody the bomb maker went free, in spite of his obvious link to the sophisticated bomb found inside the Toshiba radio-cassette recorder in Neuss. Khreesat returned to Jordan, where he informed authorities that in addition to the Toshiba bomb found in the green Ford in Neuss, he had made three other bombs for the PFLP—GC and had worked on a fourth. Khreesat said the four missing bombs probably were still in the apartment where he and Dalkamouni had been staying. The German authorities had searched that apartment and five other places where they thought Khreesat might have left the devices but had found nothing. The West Germans had long ago ceased their surveillance of the organization Dalkamouni had headed; they were apparently confident the immediate danger from the terrorist group had passed since most of the captured terrorists left Europe within days of their release. "They sort of disappeared from our screen," said one U.S. government official familiar with the German operations.

Scottish and U.S. police realized Khreesat's importance to the Lockerbie probe, so two investigators—one from the FBI and one from the Scottish police—traveled to Amman to meet with Jordanian officials, who they hoped would arrange a meeting with Khreesat. They learned after arriving that the session had been called off without explanation. Later a Scottish detective tried to meet in Washington, D.C., with a source in Jordanian intelligence believed to have been Khreesat's handler, but that meeting, too, was canceled at the last minute. Their reason for wanting to speak to Khreesat was obvious. "There can be little doubt that Marwan Abdel Razzaq Mufti Khreesat is the bomb-maker for the PFLP—GC, that he was brought to West Germany for that express purpose and that there is a possibility that he prepared the [bomb] which destroyed PA103," Scottish police notes obtained by the *Sunday Times* of London said. "As such he should not be at liberty but should be closely questioned regarding his activities with a view to tracing his associates in the attack."

U.S. authorities eventually spoke with Khreesat in Jordan, and after they had learned of the additional bombs he had made in West Germany, they and the Scottish police pressed German authorities to make further searches. On April 13 special investigators from the BKA returned to the Neuss flat of Dalkamouni's brother-in-law, Hashem Abassi, at 16 Isarstrasse, and to Abassi's business, a grocery at 14 Neumarkt. In the basement of the market, where Dalkamouni's and Khreesat's belongings had been stored, police found what they were looking for. They seized two stereo tuners and, on a subsequent trip, a Sanyo computer monitor. Although they looked normal, the devices had been rigged with explosives. Dalkamouni's brother-in-law had denied any knowledge of the PFLP—GC activity under his roof. "I had no idea about the bomb," the grocer said. "I don't get involved in politics. I just run the shop." Investigators appear to have accepted Abassi's claims perhaps because he had had so much time to get rid of the bombs and had failed to do so.

German police had allowed three terrorist bombs to lie undetected for nearly six months. It is hard to believe they could make any bigger mistakes, but they did. The tuners and Sanyo monitor were taken to the BKA offices in Meckenheim on Thursday, April 13. No special precautions were taken in transporting the devices, which were loaded into a BKA investigator's car and driven over bumpy roads. In Meckenheim the bombs sat on a desk until Monday, when a senior official placed one of the tuners on the desk of a technician and walked away without comment. A slip of paper attached to the device bore the phone number of another high-ranking BKA official. The technician assumed that the device was broken and that he was supposed to repair it. As soon as he opened up the housing on the tuner, however, the technician spotted extra wiring. He carefully took the device over to an X ray machine normally used to examine mail addressed to government ministries. The X ray confirmed his suspicion that the tuner was a bomb. The technician called the office's criminal director to ask about the device and was told to take it, by car, to experts in the demolition of explosive devices in Wiesbaden. Although the standing orders for handling an explosive device called for the area to be evacuated, that never happened. The technician requested that a bomb team come to Meckenheim to pick up the device, but his wishes were overruled. He put the tuner in his trunk and drove to Wiesbaden. The device was turned over to Hans Jürgen Sonntag, thirty-five, a veteran at disarming bombs, and Thomas Ettinger, twenty-nine. As the two men worked to dismantle it, the device exploded. Sonntag and Ettinger were rushed to Mainz University Clinic. In two hours Sonntag died. Ettinger was left crippled and blind.

The Meckenheim chapter of a group representing German police detectives—Bund Deutscher Kriminalbeamter or the Association of German Criminal Investigators—complained about the casual handling of the three devices in an April 24, 1989, letter to the director of the BKA's Meckenheim office. "It is more than cause for alarm when life-

endangering objects are handed around with no indication of how poten-
tially explosive they are," the association wrote. The German police
further bungled the probe by intentionally blowing up the second tuner,
destroying valuable evidence. The Sanyo monitor was deactivated by a
private explosives expert from Cologne, Helmut Bauer. Inside the monitor
Bauer found 13.75 ounces of TNT and a detonator. He was later critical of
the BKA's handling of the bomb. "No one should ever transport a finished
explosive device," Bauer said.

NEWS THAT West German police were killing themselves with terrorist
bombs did little to restore the relatives' confidence in the criminal investigation. Some of them began to consider hiring guides to lead them on their
own exploration of the intelligence underworld. In April three relatives—
Paul Hudson; Rosemary Wolfe, the stepmother of Syracuse University
student Miriam Wolfe; and Kathleen Flynn, mother of Colgate University
student John Patrick Flynn—attended a Washington meeting set up by the
national officers of B'nai B'rith. There they met Juval Aviv, a shadowy forty-
two-year-old figure from the legendary world of Israeli counterterrorism.

Aviv's past was cloaked in intrigue. According to the 1984 book *Vengeance: The True Story of an Israeli Counter-Terrorist Team,* after Black
September terrorists had killed eleven Israeli athletes at the Munich Olympics in 1972, Israel's Golda Meir had handpicked a man to lead a specially
trained squad of assassins to track down and kill the Munich terrorists.
From 1972 to 1974, the book says, the squad killed or injured fifteen
people in shootings and bombings in Rome, Paris, Cyprus, Beirut, Athens,
Switzerland, the Netherlands, and Spain. Juval Aviv claimed to be the man
who headed up the squad. In the book, however, he was given the pseudonym Avner, the idea being that he needed to be disguised for his own
protection. (Aviv surfaced as the protagonist through an obscure lawsuit in
New York stemming from a dispute over the rights to his story. The lawsuit
involved both the book's publishers and Home Box Office.)

Seventeen years after the Munich Olympics, Aviv was making a living as
president of a security consulting company in New York known as Interfor
Inc. His firm, Aviv told Hudson and the other relatives with whom he met,
could obtain information on the bombing because of his connections to the
international intelligence community. As part of his pitch to be hired, Aviv
claimed that two U.S. government agencies had prior knowledge of the
attack on Flight 103 and had done nothing to prevent it.

The relatives learned later that Aviv's credibility had been seriously challenged. In some circles, in fact, he had long since been dismissed as a fraud. Before *Vengeance* appeared on the shelves, it generated more than five hundred thousand dollars in advance sales, but once it was published, it created an uproar in the intelligence community, and its authenticity was widely questioned. The publishers offered serial rights to the *New York Times'* Sunday magazine, the German magazine *Der Spiegel*, and the Canadian magazine *Maclean's*. All three said no. *Maclean's* went a step further, assigning a reporter to assess the credibility of the book. The magazine reported that before convincing Canadian journalist George Jonas to write the book, Aviv—whose name at his birth in Israel had been Yuval Abayov—had tried to peddle the story to a series of other writers, each of whom had turned him down. The magazine also said that during the time Aviv supposedly was hunting down terrorists, he actually was working as a cabin steward and security guard for El Al. Israeli officials had denounced Aviv as a "crook and impostor," and after the Flight 103 bombing, Yigal Carmon, a counterterrorism adviser to the Israeli prime minister, said Aviv had never had any connection to Mossad.

Although the relatives were unaware of these challenges to Aviv's credibility, they chose not to hire him. Aviv kept shopping around, and soon he found another client for his services.

MOST OF the relatives had decided to pursue legal action against Pan Am, and as the months wore on, the attorneys they had hired began to make progress in their efforts to collect damaging testimony against the airline. After Oliver Koch had told reporters how his boss, Ulrich Weber, had backdated the Helsinki memo, the attorneys for the families, headed by New York lawyer Lee S. Kreindler, obtained a deposition from Koch to use in their lawsuits against the airline. One day after New York attorney James Shaughnessy, the airline's point man in the defense against Flight 103 lawsuits, traveled to Frankfurt on a mission related to the litigation, Pan Am fired Weber. The airline insisted Weber's firing had nothing to do with the quality of the security operation he supervised; rather, it said, Weber was let go because of an internal audit that showed that he had used the company's Eurocard account at a Munich bordello and to buy Christmas presents for his children.

Weber's firing in June 1989 signaled a realization by Pan Am that the relatives were winning the public relations war. Six months had passed since the bombing, but for the airline Lockerbie continued to be a daily nightmare.

Flight 103 relatives, some of whom still picketed Pan Am's corporate headquarters, were succeeding in keeping Lockerbie from becoming a forgotten aviation statistic. "Surveys show that the perception of a crash lasts in the public memory about two months," a Pan Am official said. "Lockerbie was different." Although the relatives' efforts hurt the airline's image, Pan Am knew that any effort it made to challenge the group's claims was likely to backfire. If there was one thing the airline did not want to do, it was to position itself opposite a group of grieving relatives.

As the summer of 1989 approached, the civil case against Pan Am appeared to be strong. What the airline needed was a defense that would shift blame away from itself, both in the courtroom and in the minds of the flying public. In June Juval Aviv's security firm, Interfor Inc., quietly went to work for Windels, Marx, Davies & Ives, the law firm that had been hired by Pan Am's insurer, U.S. Aviation Underwriters.

Within three months Aviv produced a twenty-seven-page report on his version of what happened to Flight 103. In a foreword Aviv wrote that his preliminary findings on the bombing had revealed a "complex and murky background to the disaster." That characterization would be the only subtlety in the report. Indeed, many knowledgeable parties dismissed the report as fiction, and two years later the U.S. Justice Department asked a federal judge to impose a million-dollar fine on Pan Am's lawyers for wasting the government's time on "patently unreasonable and false allegations," including those contained in the Interfor document.

Nonetheless, Aviv's Interfor report received a fair amount of attention. It recounted a colorful tale of drug runners, spies, and a renegade CIA team—all woven into the fabric of the Flight 103 bombing. His story began a few years before the Lockerbie attack with the governments of Iran, Syria, and Libya trying to develop ways of striking at U.S. targets in a way that would keep the attacks from being traced back to them. The solution they came up with, he wrote, was to form a coalition that would offer covert support to several terrorist groups. The PFLP, PFLP—GC, and Abu Nidal Organization—normally rivals within the terrorist world— began coordinating their efforts, meeting with Ali Issa Duba of Syrian intelligence and with unidentified Iranian radicals.

According to the report, the three terrorist organizations began raising money and seeking out secure routes for smuggling weapons and agents. Although these were activities they had engaged in individually before, they were now working in unison. Eventually the three terrorist groups set up a web of drug- and arms-smuggling operations throughout Europe. In time members of what Aviv called the Interterror Group began to specialize, with Abu Nidal controlling the arms and drug smuggling and Ahmad Jibril of the PFLP—GC focusing on terrorist attack planning. A key player in all facets of the Interterror Group's operations, Aviv claimed, was Monzer al-Kassar, a Syrian whose brother-in-law was the head of Syrian intelligence.

As part of their smuggling network, the terrorists had established a route through Frankfurt that relied upon the cooperation of a passenger and a baggage handler. According to Aviv's report, one frequently used drug "mule" was Khalid Jaafar, the young man from the Detroit area who was visiting relatives in Beirut. The baggage handler, the report said, was a Turk whose name was not known. When the terrorists wanted to make a drug run, the Turkish baggage handler would remove a suitcase checked in by the passenger and replace it with an identical case containing the contraband. The passenger then claimed the bag at the end of the trip. "It is not known how this method passed through arrival customs where such existed, but this route and method worked steadily and smoothly for a long time," the report said. Jaafar's family angrily denied he had ever played such a role.

The Aviv report stated that the CIA, the U.S. Drug Enforcement Administration, and the BKA knew about the drug route and kept it under surveillance. "As they realized the extent of the operation they decided to try to channel the operation into less numerous areas so that they could concentrate their surveillance focus," it said. The BKA made arrests and increased police visibility at other smuggling points in West Germany, hoping to channel the illicit activity toward Frankfurt.

The Interfor report suggested that the Frankfurt CIA team, referred to in the report as CIA-1, was a renegade unit that failed to communicate some of its activities to CIA headquarters: "It appears that it eventually operated to some or a large extent as an internal covert operations without consistent oversight, a la Oliver North." In March 1988 CIA-1 received reports through the BKA of a secret meeting in Vienna between French and Iranian delegations. After the covert session Iran received a shipment of weapons, and French hostages held in Lebanon were released.

Despite the revelations of the Iran-contra arms for hostages scandal, CIA-1 decided to strike a similar deal to free U.S. hostages, the report said. The renegade CIA team had identified al-Kassar as both an intermediary in the French exchange and a major figure in the drug routes under surveillance. Now it offered to protect his smuggling operation in return for his cooperation. According to the report, al-Kassar helped send weapons to Iran to further the release of U.S. hostages. In return CIA-1 gave him a free hand. "It is believed that U.S. Customs at JFK were ordered by CIA to allow certain baggage to pass uninspected due to national security interests," Interfor stated.

By the fall of 1988 the terrorist leaders were under pressure to attack an American target largely because Iran wanted revenge for the downing of Iran Flight 655 by the USS *Vincennes*, the report found. It also noted that Ahmad Jibril of the PFLP—GC—aware of the success of the drug route operated by al-Kassar but unaware that it had CIA protection—met twice with al-Kassar, once in the presence of Abu Nidal at a hotel in Warsaw and once at a restaurant in Paris. Jibril's goal was to use al-Kassar's smuggling route to plant a bomb on a commercial airliner. The PFLP—GC leader recognized the Frankfurt smuggling route as a perfect channel, especially because drug mules had not been previously associated with terrorism. Al-Kassar and Abu Nidal knew the outline of Jibril's plan, but neither was given the specific details. They suspected he would attack a plane flying out of Madrid or London.

According to Aviv's report, al-Kassar brought the bomb into Germany in a car he rented in Paris. He had picked up the explosives in France from his sister-in-law, who in turn had received them from a Syrian living in Bulgaria. The report named all the alleged bomb couriers, even listing a telephone number for the Syrian contact in Sofia, Bulgaria. Jibril initially targeted American Airlines, said Interfor, but a fast-paced series of events beginning in early December changed the plan and resulted in the bomb's being placed on Pan Am Flight 103. First, an agent for Mossad tipped off his superiors that a major attack was being planned at Frankfurt against a U.S. carrier. Then Mossad warned the CIA and BKA. The CIA team in Frankfurt wanted to steer the threat to where it could be best observed, so the presence of police and security officers was visibly increased around all U.S. carriers except Pan Am, the report said. By now al-Kassar and Nidal realized Jibril was going to use the Frankfurt airport to carry out his attack, and they deduced that the target might be Lufthansa, American Airlines, or Pan Am. They wanted to protect their drug route, so on or about December 18 al-Kassar and Nidal informed the BKA that a bomb would be placed on one of Pan Am's regular Frankfurt to London to New York flights. "Unwittingly, these terrorists tipped off the authorities to what proved to be the very act," said the report. The BKA informed CIA-1, and the threat eventually was relayed to CIA headquarters. At about the same time a BKA undercover agent made a separate report to his superiors outlining the plan to bomb a Pan Am jumbo jet. Warnings were sent to various embassies, but not to Pan Am.

One or two days before the bombing al-Kassar's Turkish baggage handler in Frankfurt went to the airport parking lot and picked up a suitcase that had been left inside a black Mercedes. The baggage handler carried the bag inside the airport and placed it in an employee locker area. "This was his usual practice with drugs," the report said. The day of the bombing a BKA agent on surveillance duty noticed that the drug courier's suitcase, a brown Samsonite, was different from luggage used in past runs. The report stated: "He, like the other BKA agents on the scene, had been extra alert due to all the bomb tips. Within an hour or so before takeoff he phoned in a report as to what he had seen, saying something was very wrong." The BKA alerted the CIA-1 team but was told to let the suitcase pass through.

The Interfor report went on to say that in Lebanon a separate CIA team led by Army Major Charles McKee was gathering information on the location of Western hostages. In the course of its investigation the team uncovered the work of the CIA-1 unit and the protected drug route in Frankfurt. Angered by the dealings of the CIA-1 team in West Germany, and believing that the team's work would jeopardize both their mission and their lives, the members of the unit in Lebanon broke off their work. The eight-person team decided to return home and bought tickets for Flight 103. Interfor identified five of the intelligence officers on board Flight 103 as Beirut CIA deputy station chief Matthew Gannon, agents Ronald Lariviere, Daniel O'Connor, William Leyrer, and McKee. The other three were unnamed.

The bottom line of Aviv's report was that the U.S. government had not only failed to stop the bombing but had actively, if unwittingly, participated in it by protecting the drug courier who slipped the bomb on board. Pan Am was just an innocent bystander. To disprove the allegations, U.S. intelligence services might have to reveal details of sensitive spy operations, a move they were unlikely to make. The report may have read like a cheap spy novel, but it provided Pan Am with its strongest defense to date against the relatives' civil lawsuits.

THROUGHOUT THE summer of 1989 the relatives continued their efforts to convince Congress and the president to establish an independent investigation into the bombing. After Bush had rejected the idea, the relatives began considering other options. First, they tried to convince Congress to establish a joint House-Senate investigations panel, similar to that which had probed the Iran-contra affair, but it died as the result of insufficient support. Next, they lobbied for creation of a special Senate committee, an idea rejected by the Senate. Then they tried to convince an existing Senate or House panel to conduct its own probe; that idea did not find support either.

Finally, Senators Frank Lautenberg of New Jersey and Wendell Ford of Kentucky proposed a bill that would establish an independent commission to examine aviation security and the circumstances surrounding the bombing. The relatives, although generally pleased with the bill, worked with the sponsors over the summer to change portions they found objectionable. The original proposal, for example, would have named Transportation Secretary Samuel Skinner the panel's chairman and would have provided seats on the panel to the Department of Transportation, the Central Intelligence Agency, and a representative of the airline industry. The relatives believed a panel that included those members would not be independent at all. "It was like a grand jury where a majority of the members were relatives of the suspects," Paul Hudson said. The group also wanted the panel to have subpoena power. But the proposal soon became moot. At 4:30 P.M. on August 4, as Congress was leaving Washington for a summer recess, President Bush signed an executive order creating the President's Commission on Aviation Security and Terrorism. The commission's mission was to evaluate aviation security, using the Flight 103 bombing as a starting point. It also was charged with examining the treatment afforded to the relatives of victims of terrorism and with scrutinizing the government's policy of not publicizing threats against aviation carriers. The commission lacked subpoena power, and it was under a strict directive to steer clear of intelligence operations and the criminal probe; still, the relatives greeted its creation as a victory. Hudson said the executive order was a realization of the organization's first major goal. Bert Ammerman said, "We commend the president for finally taking the leadership role. We now can really look at it, we can find out where the warnings fell through the cracks, we can find out where Pan Am's security was lacking. All of these findings can only help us prevent this preventable massacre from occurring again."

IN LOCKERBIE, meanwhile, Scottish police, who had scoured 845 square miles of countryside for clues and conducted thousands of interviews, still needed some luck to piece together leads in their investigation of 270 murders. As the summer of 1989 wore on, they got it.

On August 16 a parcel from BKA headquarters arrived unannounced at the Lockerbie incident control center. Inside was a computerized baggage loading list for the Frankfurt to London leg of Flight 103. It had been eight months since investigators had discovered the existence of the mysterious thirteenth bag X-rayed by Alert Management employee Kurt Maier; now they had the document that might reveal its secret.

The loading list contained what looked like a smoking gun: documentation that a previously undetected bag, headed for a destination in the United States, had been transferred onto Flight 103 unaccompanied by a passenger.

The baggage sorting computer system used at Frankfurt's airport is one of the most sophisticated in the world. Four separate computer networks make up the system. One tracks outgoing bags, one tracks incoming bags, one serves as a backup, and the fourth, known as the KIK system, allows airport employees to locate a bag anywhere in the system.

The computer operator on duty the night of Flight 103 heard about the crash on the radio on her way home. The following day she used the KIK system to make a printout of every bag that had been loaded on the Frankfurt to London leg of Pan Am 103. The computer commands took only a few seconds, and in four minutes, from 5:32 to 5:36 P.M., the operator had unknowingly produced a vital piece of evidence for Lockerbie investigators. Had she not made the printout the information could have been lost forever, because the computer system purges such data after eight days.

The coding for one bag, which included the numbers B8849 and S0009, indicated that the suitcase had been transferred to Flight 103 from a location within the airport known as station 206. The bag was coded at 1:07 P.M., and airport records showed that Air Malta Flight KM180 was being unloaded at that station from 1:04 to 1:10 P.M.

It was an interline bag, which meant it should have been among the luggage sent to Maier's X-ray machine. It also was an unaccompanied bag—none of the thirty-nine passengers on Air Malta Flight KM180 had boarded Flight 103—and so under FAA rules it should have been opened and searched by hand or else kept off the flight altogether. But Pan Am was not matching bags to passengers at Frankfurt, and the bag was loaded on the flight anyway. The sudden appearance of the loading list appeared to answer the mystery of the thirteenth bag. It was an unaccompanied suitcase transferred from Air Malta Flight KM180.

Although it advanced the investigation, the unexpected arrival of this critical piece of evidence frustrated Lockerbie investigators. German authorities had said months ago that this record had been destroyed. Its emergence in August 1989 raised additional questions about the Germans' handling of the probe. Later, Lockerbie investigators would learn that no German investigator had even interviewed the woman who had produced the computer printout.

In early September Detective Chief Inspector Harry Bell flew to Malta to track down whether this mysterious bag might be the bronze-colored

Samsonite whose shattered remnants had been found in the wreckage of the 747. It was not the first time Lockerbie investigators had been to the island nation.

British forensic experts poring through debris from the disaster had identified some of the clothing that had been packed inside the bomb bag. One article was an infant's Babygro blue cotton jumpsuit that carried the label of the Malta Trading Company. On their first trip to Malta, officers interviewed the manufacturer only to find that the jumpsuit was sold at outlets throughout Europe. That was no help. Other contents of the Samsonite included a pair of patterned pants with a label that read "Yorkie Trading Company 0005." Investigators had no idea where Yorkie was located. Other clothing linked to the bag—both by the scorch marks they bore and by the fibers found fused to the suitcase lining—included men's pajamas, a white undershirt, a gray herringbone jacket, two shirts, a herringbone skirt, another jacket, and a second pair of pants.

The discovery of the unaccompanied bag from Air Malta renewed investigators' interest in the Babygro jumpsuit that had been manufactured on the island. On the return trip to Malta, Bell brought pictures of all the clothing the forensic team had matched to the suitcase. He visited the Malta Trading Company, located in an industrial park called San Gwaan, and asked for a list of all the outlets on Malta that might have sold the Babygro jumpsuit. After obtaining that information, Bell noticed a sign in front of another factory. It said, YORKIE INDUSTRIAL CLOTHING, the name that had been sewn into the patterned pants. The detective chief inspector showed a photograph of the trousers to Alex Calleja, the company's director, who recognized them and explained that the code 0005 identified them as the fifth of a recently manufactured lot. Yorkie's records showed that the trousers had been sold to retailer Tony Gauci, who operated a store called Mary's House at 63 Tower Road in Sliema, Malta's fourth largest city.

Bell was accomplishing more in a day than other investigators had in months. He drove to Mary's House, found Gauci, and asked if the shopkeeper might possibly remember who had bought the trousers. Gauci remembered—in exceptional detail. The customer had been a man in his late forties, clean-shaven, well dressed, and about two inches shy of six feet tall. Gauci thought he looked like a Libyan—a recollection that took on tremendous significance later in the probe. The shopkeeper remembered the man because he shopped randomly, selecting an odd assortment of items. In addition to the pants, the customer had purchased a blue Babygro jumpsuit with a sheep's face on the front, a pair of brown herringbone pants, a wool cardigan sweater, and an old tweed jacket. The merchant remembered the tweed jacket in particular because he had been trying to get rid of it for years. It was raining that day, so the man also bought an umbrella. Five umbrellas had been recovered from the plane wreckage, and sure enough, when forensic experts looked closely, they discovered that one showed blast damage. Later investigators learned that fibers from the Babygro jumpsuit had been fused to the umbrella, a result of the tremendous force of the explosion.

Nearly nine months after the bombing, investigators finally had found a witness who might be able to identify one of the bombers. Gauci was placed under police protection.

Before Bell's trip to Malta investigators had been paying close attention to another pile of clothing damaged by the explosion. Although these clothes appeared to have been near the bomb, they bore no traces of plastic explosive. It was hard to tell if they had been inside the Samsonite or in a nearby suitcase. Included in this batch were a purple sweatshirt, a gray jacket with a tartan pattern, a white bra, and, most important, a pair of sweatpants with the name Noonan on them. The discovery of Karen Noonan's sweatpants especially intrigued investigators because they had learned that Noonan had befriended an Arab man named Bilbassi while studying in Europe. She also had traveled to Dublin, one of the places in Europe where Babygro jumpsuits were sold. Perhaps Noonan was a mule who had been duped by her friend into checking the suitcase containing the bomb on board. The Noonan theory was dismissed, however, when Bell came back from Malta. The interview with Tony Gauci, the owner of Mary's House, together with the forensic evidence placing the umbrella and the Babygro jumpsuit inside the bomb suitcase, pointed convincingly to the Libyan-looking man in Malta. Investigators learned later that Bell had narrowly missed catching up with the mystery customer. According to the *Sunday Times* of London, Gauci told police he had seen the man who bought the Babygro jumpsuit three times: once in the summer of 1988, once to buy the clothes, and the last time less than a week after Bell's visit.

Lockerbie investigators had their strongest evidence to date. It appeared that the suitcase bomb that destroyed Flight 103 had originated its travels in Malta, perhaps after someone had placed a New York City destination tag on its handle. Once past security in Malta, the bag had been loaded onto Flight 103, first at Frankfurt and then in London. Since no one at Pan Am was trying to identify unaccompanied bags, the bag with the bomb was allowed on board unaccompanied.

While Bell was unraveling the mystery of the bomb-damaged clothing, investigators working another angle of the case found their attention directed toward Malta, too. Sifting through the files of several suspected terrorists arrested in May by the Swedish police agency SÄPO, police came across information indicating that a man arrested in Sweden might be the indiscriminate Libyan-looking customer in Mary's House. If this were true, it could mean the investigation had established a link between the bomb and the bomber.

The new clues emanated from a bungled attempt to smuggle three men into Scandinavia in the fall of 1988. On September 5 of that year a man living in Sweden calling himself Martin Imandi had met his brothers, Ziad and Jehad, and his cousin, Samar Ourfali, at the Munich airport. They had arrived from Damascus via Syrian Arab Airlines, passing through customs without problems because of the visiting visas they had obtained from the West German Embassy in Damascus. Their visit to Germany was short; the four men left almost immediately on a northbound train for Denmark, where they apparently intended to cross to Sweden by ferry and return to Imandi's home in Uppsala, a university town north of Stockholm. They traveled with false passports furnished by Imandi, which they had altered with their own photos, but the forgeries were poorly done. A guard at the Danish border village of Rodby Havn easily spotted the alterations, and Imandi's relatives were turned back to West Germany. Danish police questioned and fingerprinted Imandi and held him for questioning. As part of their routine investigation, Danish police entered the prints in a comput-erized system to check for a match against fingerprints linked to unsolved crimes. The computer spit back a major hit, linking Imandi—whose real name is Imad Shaaban—to an attempted terrorist bombing in Denmark that had stymied investigators for more than three years.

In June 1985 a man strolling by an El Al ticket office in Copenhagen had stopped at the doorway, set down a plastic tote bag, and walked away. His manner had been so casual that a Danish woman watching him thought he had forgotten his parcel. She picked up the plastic bag and hurried after him. After she had overtaken him, the woman was surprised to see the man grab the package, run down the street, and hurl it into a canal. Police divers were called in to recover the bag, which was found to contain explosives, some Swedish-manufactured nails that would make lethal projectiles, a shopping bag from the Swedish store Ica, and an Arabic magazine. The would-be bomber, meanwhile, had been seen heading back to Sweden on the hydrofoil ferry that links Copenhagen with Malmö. Danish police provided Swedish border guards in Malmö with the man's description before the ferry arrived from its thirty-five minute crossing. He slipped past the guards, however, because of a quirk in translating Danish to

Swedish. (The man wore blue jeans. In Swedish the word *jeans* is almost the same as the English "jeans," but in Danish the translation comes out like "cowboy clothes." As a result, border authorities in Malmö had been looking for a man they envisioned wearing anything from spurs to a ten-gallon hat.)

Police were left actually holding the bag. From the Arab magazine they found in it, they were able to lift a single fingerprint. Three years later— after Martin Imandi had bumbled his way into their hands with his amateurish passport forgeries—they discovered the fingerprint was his.

Following his 1988 arrest on charges related to the false passports, Imandi was released for a court appearance and turned over to the Swedish police, who took him home and staked out his house in Uppsala. Investigators hoped the surveillance might help them solve a number of other Scandinavian bomb attacks. At about the time of the botched attack against the El Al office, bombs had exploded at a Northwest Airlines office and a synagogue in Copenhagen, killing one person and injuring twenty-two more. In April 1986 another bomb exploded outside the Northwest Airlines office in Copenhagen; no one was injured. Swedish police believed the attacks had been the work of a Palestinian terrorist group known as the Popular Struggle Front (PSF). Terrorism experts had always considered the PSF and the PFLP—GC rivals. But information gathered after the release of Imandi began to change that perception.

Imandi's three traveling companions, like him, were unaware that police had drawn a connection between him and the Copenhagen bomb. After they were turned back at the Danish border, two of Imandi's relatives, Jehad Shaaban and Samar Ourfali, looked for a new way to sneak into Sweden. The third, Ziad Shaaban, flew back to Syria. Stranded in Germany, Imandi's brother and cousin called Imandi's home in Uppsala and asked where they could go for help. They were given directions to 14 Neumarkt in Neuss, the address of a grocery store operated by Hashem Abassi, the brother-in-law of PFLP—GC operative Hafez Dalkamouni.

German police conducting the Autumn Leaves investigation later saw Shaaban and Ourfali in Neuss, although they did not recognize them at the time. On October 14 a German surveillance team outside Abassi's apartment at 16 Isarstrasse, where Dalkamouni was staying, watched a white Volvo with Swedish license plates pull up to the building. The men inside the car got out and began to load and unload packages. From the license plate, police identified the car as Martin Imandi's, and although he was not among the car's occupants, Shaaban and Ourfali were. Also, the driver was

Imandi's friend Mohammed Mougrabi. German police thought the men in the white Volvo were handling their parcels with extraordinary care. Later bomb maker Marwan Khreesat arrived at the Isarstrasse apartment. Could the passengers in the car have been delivering the explosives Khreesat would later use to build bombs? That seemed plausible, particularly after the white Volvo had left and the Germans followed Khreesat and Dalkamouni to the stores where they purchased clocks, batteries, and other bomb components.

The Swedish surveillance of Imandi that had begun six weeks earlier was continuing, and police in Uppsala apparently were not ready to make arrests. But the Autumn Leaves raid on the PFLP—GC cell in West Germany forced their hand. On November 1, less than a week after the German raids, Swedish police conducted their own sweep, arresting several people, including the Volvo's owner, Martin Imandi, and its driver, Mohammed Mougrabi. The prosecutor for the Uppsala region filed charges alleging that Imandi and Mougrabi had been preparing to smuggle explosives for use against airplanes. The Swedes were relying on the Germans to produce the evidence to support the charge, but when Mougrabi insisted that he had unloaded nothing more than clothing and gifts at the Neuss apartment, police had no way of contesting his claim. There was no proof that the group in Sweden had any connection to the arsenal of bombs and weapons the Germans had found with the PFLP—GC cell in Germany. One day after taking them into custody, the Swedes released everyone. Unlike the Germans, however, who quickly lost track of the suspects they released, the Swedes kept close watch on Imandi and his associates, and the investigation of Imandi's connection to the 1985 attempted bombing in Copenhagen quietly continued. It took more than six months, but on May 18, 1989, SÄPO arrested fifteen people in Stockholm, Göteborg, and Uppsala. Four eventually were held for trial on charges that stemmed from bomb attacks in 1985 and 1986. They were Imandi and three members of the Mougrabi family: Mohmoud, Mustafa, and their brother-in-law, Mohammed Abu Talb.

After checking with Swedish police and learning the identity of the passengers in the white Volvo, German police determined that Imandi's relatives, Jehan Shaaban and Samar Ourfali, had not been delivering explosives in Neuss at all. Apparently the two men had come to Germany with the same goal they had had in mind when they were stopped with false passports at the Danish village of Rodby Havn: they wanted to be smuggled into Sweden. Just the same, Lockerbie investigators pored over Swedish police files, banking on slim hopes that the connection to the terrorist cell in Sweden would not be a dead end. Eventually their attention was drawn to Mohammed Abu Talb.

Abu Talb had all the credentials of a terrorist. At thirty-five he was a scarred veteran of the Palestinian cause. After receiving military training in Egypt and the Soviet Union, Talb was shot in the left shoulder in Lebanon in 1976; when the pain flared up, he walked unevenly, with his head tilted slightly to the left. Talb also was a writer. In the mid-1980s, using the pen name Samer Abdul Magid, he wrote a novel about an orphaned Palestinian boy. He also had written parts of two other novels, both dealing with injustices directed at Arabs in the Middle East. Like Imandi, Talb lived in Uppsala.

Lockerbie investigators became very interested in Talb after learning about the unaccompanied Air Malta bag that had been loaded onto Flight 103. Swedish court files showed that on October 26, 1988, the same day West German police swept down on the PFLP—GC cell, Abu Talb had returned to Stockholm from Malta, where so much of the investigators' attention had recently been focused. He had traveled to Malta on a charter flight during the first week of October. His trip also took him through Cyprus, where police believe he may have met with Hafez Dalkamouni, perhaps to lay the groundwork for the Flight 103 attack. When Talb left for Malta, he told his wife he was going to visit two people: a friend who ran a bakery and the baker's brother, a man who sold clothes. The PFLP—GC operated a bakery in Malta through a front company called Miska Trading. And Talb's appearance was generally consistent with shopkeeper Tony Gauci's description of the customer who had bought clothing at Mary's House. A Swedish police report even said Talb used a brown Samsonite bag on a trip he took in 1985. Had Talb shuttled the bomb to Germany or somehow arranged for it to be planted on a connecting flight from Malta?

The answer to that question proved elusive. Still, if police could link Talb to the clothing in the Flight 103 bomber's suitcase, they would have their first hard evidence against a suspect. Police raided locations in Uppsala, including the apartment of Abu Talb's ex-wife, Jamilla Mougrabi, and seized enough of his clothing and belongings to fill eighteen black plastic bags. These clothes were taken to Malta and shown to the shopkeeper at Mary's House, in the hope that he could identify an article he had sold from his store. He could not. A second shipment of clothing taken from Abu Talb in prison also failed to produce a match. And then Gauci, the owner of the Malta clothing store, failed to identify Talb as the man to whom he had sold the clothes. The connection between a terrorist and the bomb-scarred clothing was still a long way from being established.

Talb was convicted in connection with terrorist bombings in Scandinavia and sentenced to life in prison, but the connections between him and the Lockerbie bombing grew weaker. "If it's a crime for a Palestinian to love his country, then I am the biggest terrorist of all," Abu Talb said on the last day of his trial. "For the love of my country, I have been trained to use weapons and I have participated in battles with our enemies. But I have never done these things we have been accused of here." Abu Talb's role, if any, in the Flight 103 attack remained a mystery, and an intriguing one. Among the belongings police found during a raid of his apartment was a 1988 calendar. On the page for December a circle had been drawn around the twenty-first.

CHAPTER 9

CRACKS IN THE BOND

Wᴵᴛʜɪɴ ᴀ few months of the bombing the relatives who had joined the lobbying group began to realize the power they possessed. When they showed up in Washington with pictures of dead loved ones pinned to their chests, victims of terrorism suddenly had faces and names. They were mothers and fathers, wives and husbands, sons and daughters—and they refused to be ignored. Doors opened not only in the White House but to the offices of key lawmakers on Capitol Hill who could draft legislation to implement some of the changes the relatives sought. Bert Ammerman, the group's political action chairman, thought the organization was developing some powerful momentum and should push as hard as it could, but Paul Hudson took a more cautious view. A rift between the two men began to emerge when Hudson, speaking as the group's leader, urged Ammerman to move carefully in his meetings with legislators and to get Hudson's approval before taking any action on his own. Ammerman turned him down. "I don't have time to sit down and get a go-ahead," he told Hudson. "They made me political action chairman, I'm doing my thing."

The rift widened after Ammerman had violated what Hudson saw as an important rule of the organization: that members get approval from the steering committee before meeting with any high-ranking government official and that at least two members of the group be present at such a meeting.

Following a special hearing before a subcommittee of the Senate Committee on Appropriations chaired by Senator Lautenberg, the State

Department's ambassador-at-large for counterterrorism, Clayton Mc-
Manaway, Jr., approached Ammerman and offered to arrange a meeting
with Lawrence S. Eagleburger, the deputy secretary of state. Ammerman
took him up on the offer and called Hudson to tell him about the meeting.
During the session Secretary of State James Baker unexpectedly walked in.
Ammerman seized on the opportunity to convey his frustrations to the
secretary of state. First, he told Baker that the government's handling of the
Flight 103 bombing had so alienated him that he planned to vote for
Democrat Jesse Jackson in the next presidential election, even though he
was a longtime Republican. "I hear exactly what you are saying," Baker
replied. Then Ammerman launched into a litany of complaints about the
State Department: that families had been treated shabbily, often having to
wait days to get confirmation of their loved ones' death; that bodies had
been returned like cargo, without any kind of escort from the department;
and that relatives had been generally frustrated in their attempts to get
information and help from the department. Baker promised Ammerman
his staff would correct those deficiencies. And then the meeting with Baker
was over. It had lasted about fifteen minutes.

Ammerman considered the session a major coup, and he called Hudson
to tell him about it the following day. Ammerman thought Hudson sounded
pleased. The two men laughed on the telephone, and Ammerman promised
to give Hudson all the details at the group's next meeting in Fishkill, New
York. But Hudson was angry. "We had only one rule, and that was that
before meeting with any high officials, we would bring it to the steering
committee for an OK," Hudson said later about the meeting with Baker.
"He didn't tell anybody about it until it was over. We got no publicity out of
it, no minutes; it was a total waste of our one shot." That night Ammerman's phone rang repeatedly as other leaders of the group called to talk
about the session with Baker. Ammerman had thought they might be
congratulatory calls; instead, the group's officers, some of them angry,
wanted to know what the hell Ammerman thought he was doing, talking
with the secretary of state without first checking with everyone else.
Ammerman explained how the meeting came about and defended his
actions, saying he had acted appropriately by seizing an unexpected opportunity to meet with the secretary of state. Although some of the other
officers were satisfied with Ammerman's explanation, Hudson was not; he
wanted Ammerman stripped of his committee chairmanship and thrown
out of the organization. As the group's April meeting in Fishkill approached, Hudson made preparations to force Ammerman's resignation.

From those beginnings the dispute grew into a bloody battle, with supporters of each man acting like so many spouses in a bitter matrimonial dispute. The session at Fishkill went on for seven uninterrupted hours—at one point one group member began screaming hysterically; at another a steering committee member threw some papers on the floor and walked out—and the debate continued informally for weeks. Some relatives disagreed over whether the group should cooperate with producers of a made-for-television movie about the bombing. And Hudson objected to a letter Ammerman had sent to President Bush, which Hudson described as fawning and inappropriately obsequious.

The meeting in Fishkill ended with a decision to hold an election for a newly formed board of directors, at which time the steering committee would be dissolved. But the deep-seated personality clash between Hudson and Ammerman had divided the group, and most of its leaders found themselves choosing sides.

Although many rank-and-file members stayed out of the debate, others got fed up and quit, including some people who were attending their first meeting of the relatives' group. Edward Smith, whose daughter, Cynthia, had died in the bombing, watched in frustration and decided he would attend no more meetings. "They spent the whole day on arguing and nonsense—who was going to be in charge," he said. "It was a pretty nasty meeting. . . . They made a great mistake when they split. They alienated a lot of people." The organization's May newsletter tried to describe the Fishkill gathering in a positive light, but the truth could not be concealed. "The meeting in Fishkill April 29 was difficult, intense, and above all, fruitful," the newsletter reported. "Our apologies to newcomers. . . . We had serious and difficult organizational and philosophical differences to resolve before we could continue our work. With great humility, perseverance and the collective spirit and commitment of the group, those issues were resolved by the evening and we were back on track and stronger than ever."

THE ELECTION of members to the newly formed board of directors took place in May and June 1989, through mail balloting. Fifteen directors, including Ammerman and Hudson, were chosen. The new board met for the first time on Friday, June 23, in Haddonfield, New Jersey, on the eve of a general membership meeting, hoping to elect a president and to appoint other officers. But the division that had characterized the April meeting in Fishkill was present in Haddonfield, too, and the Friday night session ended with no decision. Saturday morning the board reconvened, and four names were placed into nomination for the group's presidency: Ammerman; Victoria Cummock of Coral Gables, Florida; Hudson; and Aphrodite Tsairis of Franklin Lakes, New Jersey, whose daughter Alexia was killed in the Flight 103 bombing. Hudson and Tsairis withdrew their names from consideration, forcing a two-way contest between Ammerman, who had opposed Hudson's leadership, and Cummock, who received Hudson's support. Balloting was secret, and the two directors who could not attend the meeting voted by long-distance telephone. When the ballots were tallied, Ammerman had been elected leader of the group by a single vote, 8–7. Eleanor Bright of Massachusetts, the wife of victim Nicholas Bright, won the election for vice-president. Cummock decided to resign from the organization, despite the pleas of board members who urged her to stay on.

The issue of leadership resolved, many group members hoped to get on with their work. But the infighting was only beginning. The following month, as the group prepared for its July meeting in Williamsport, Pennsylvania, Hudson told board members he could not attend the session. He asked to be allowed to participate through a speakerphone connection. A majority of the board believed it was important for everyone to talk face-to-face, however, and when the issue was put to a vote, Hudson lost. The final blow came in September, when the organization's newsletter carried a small item on an inside page announcing Paul Hudson's sudden "resignation." The announcement ran just two sentences long: "Citing philosophical differences with the goals and methods of the organization Paul Hudson has resigned from The Victims of Pan Am 103, effective immediately, and has decided to work alone on his personal agenda in regard to the bombing of Pan Am 103. We thank Paul for his tireless initiative and energy and wish him well in his solo endeavor."

Hudson called the article a fabrication and said he had no intention of resigning. He demanded an apology and a retraction, but Georgia Nucci, the newsletter's editor, stuck by the published account. She claimed Hudson told her in an August 27 telephone conversation he was leaving the organization with some of his followers to create a second Flight 103 group. She had notes of the conversation, she said. The flap over the newsletter announcement completed the group's fissure. In a September 6 letter to the general membership, Hudson announced he was leaving the organization, taking with him five other members of the board of directors: Rosemary Wolfe and Kathleen Flynn, both of Washington, D.C.; Ted Reina, of California, whose daughter Jocelyn Reina was a flight attendant on Flight 103; Victoria Cummock, of Florida; and Johanna Hesami, of

Ohio, a friend of victim Peter Vulcu. Hudson's letter urged members to "disassociate" themselves from Ammerman's leadership and join him in forming a new group. Ammerman's faction—now left with nine of the fifteen newly elected board members—kept the original name, Victims of Pan Am Flight 103. Hudson's organization adopted a new name, Families of Pan Am 103/Lockerbie. After the division Ammerman threatened to sue Hudson, claiming he had not relinquished the original group's financial records, but Hudson denied the accusation, and no lawsuit was filed.

Even some of those who had taken sides in the split were disappointed with the way things turned out. Georgia Nucci said later that Ammerman and Hudson, with their different styles, could have made an extremely effective leadership team had they been able to put aside their differences. And she worried that the dispute had hurt the group's less active members, who relied on the organization to fight for them and to represent their interests. "Because I did the newsletter, I got calls every day from people all over the world, people we never saw or heard from. They just needed to know that there was this group there, people out to help them, maybe people stronger than they were. For this group to split—it [was] very harmful to these people."

IN THE months following the breakup each group set off in its own direction, with its own agenda. Hudson's group tended to be more suspicious of the government officials handling Flight 103 issues, less willing to compromise. Ammerman's style, at least initially, was smoother. One illustration of the difference between the two organizations was their choice of outside consultants. Hudson's group hired a well-connected Washington, D.C., lawyer to serve as its lobbyist on Capitol Hill. Ammerman's group hired a public relations firm, which it hoped would help it build bridges to the media. There were other differences, too. At the meetings of Ammerman's group many members gathered at a bar to talk, laugh, have a few drinks, and enjoy the shared company of others who had lived through the same ordeal they had survived. "People like Paul Hudson felt that was weakness. Actually that is our strength," one member of Ammerman's group said. Typically the meetings of Hudson's group had a less jovial air about them. "You're not at these meetings to drink. You're not there to socialize. You're there to remember and make sure it never happens again," one Hudson group member said. The residual distrust between the two groups was so strong that months later it threatened to derail efforts to win tougher aviation security and antiterrorism legislation.

During the split the leadership had attempted to hide the fighting from the general membership, and from the public. Now, with the split made formal through the creation of the second organization, there was no hiding the truth. Each group found itself in the uncomfortable position of having to explain the existence of a competing organization. Meanwhile, yet another group, made up of relatives of British victims and led by Dr. Jim Swire, the father of Flight 103 passenger Flora Swire, had surfaced in England. Instead of one voice for the victims, there were now three.

THE SPLIT between the relatives had a devastating effect on Eleanor Hudson, who took much of it personally. In July, the same month that her husband's request to participate by speakerphone in the organization's meeting in Williamsport, Pennsylvania, was turned down, she went to Cleveland, Ohio, where her children had been staying with her sister, Patricia. From Mrs. Hudson's vantage point, the division of the organization into two groups had involved vicious personal attacks on her husband. After the candidate Hudson supported for president lost the election to Ammerman, Mrs. Hudson's mind turned to dark thoughts. She saw the vote as an indication that all goodness had gone out of the world. Seven months earlier her daughter had been attacked and killed while coming home for Christmas; now her husband was being attacked by members of the organization he had formed to address the security failures that had permitted the bombing. In a telephone conversation with him, she told him she wasn't sure she wanted to go on living. She also hinted that she didn't want her children to continue living either. "I said I didn't want us to go on anymore—me, the kids, all of us. That's how I felt. . . . I saw no reason to live. What for, so this could happen again?" Hudson became alarmed and, with his sister-in-law Patricia's help, arranged for his wife to make an emergency visit to a psychiatrist.

The following morning Eleanor Hudson saw the doctor. When Hudson talked with her later, he told her that he had spoken with the psychiatrist and that the doctor had suggested she be placed in a hospital. Mrs. Hudson rejected the advice. She told herself she would never harm her own children. But she did agree to take a three- or four-week vacation from Pan Am work. She returned to Albany and tried to relax at home. "Your body craves peace, craves rest after something like this," she said. "The idea of resting was very nice, but not in a hospital."

*   *   *

At about the same time Eleanor Hudson decided she needed a rest, Georgia Nucci was taking a vacation of her own at a campground in Foxboro, Massachusetts. She was hoping the trip would help her lose her dependence on Ativan, the antianxiety drug she had been taking at night to help her get to sleep. Without the pills, she said, "I couldn't shut my eyes, I couldn't stop my brain from running." Her husband, Tony, had to work during her vacation, so she was alone in the family's twenty-three-foot tow-along camper. Family friends from Massachusetts stayed in an adjacent camper with their children.

Mrs. Nucci's plan was to do as little as possible while she stopped taking the medication. Most mornings after waking up, she put on her bathing suit, took a swim in the pool, then put on a knee-length T-shirt her son used to wear, one that advertised the musical group Duran Duran. Then she sat back in a lounge chair, reading spy novels and drinking coffee. The only cooking she did was on a charcoal grill, which she had positioned next to her lounge chair so she could cook and eat without having to get up. Most days she ate hot dogs. In the afternoon she switched from coffee to wine, and at night, after watching the evening news on a small portable television set, she sat around the campfire and talked to her friends at the adjacent campsite. "It was one of the best vacations I ever had," she said. And it worked. By its end she was able to sleep without Ativan.

Internal turmoil was not the only trouble eroding the relatives' cause. Earlier in the summer fissures had developed in the bond that had formed between relatives and the people of Lockerbie. The catalyst came in an unlikely form: Mickey Mouse.

The idea started innocently enough. Ed Blaus, a thirteen-year-old boy from New Jersey, had read about Flight 103 and felt bad that children in Lockerbie had missed Christmas celebrations. He decided he would like to send gifts to Scotland. His father contacted Pan Am for help. The airline liked the idea and went a step further, proposing to hold "Ed's Party," a belated holiday celebration for the people of Lockerbie. Pan Am offered to fly Ed and his family to Scotland and cover some of the expenses. But what started as a young boy's goodwill gesture quickly mushroomed into an extravaganza. Disney decided to send Mickey and Minnie Mouse, the National Aeronautics and Space Administration was considering sending an astronaut, and companies were lining up to donate food for a barbecue.

Lockerbie, a town that had come to be internationally identified with disaster, suddenly was the center of an international festival. Pan Am downplayed its role in the planning, saying it was merely giving Ed a hand. It seemed likely that the event would attract tremendous media coverage and perhaps change the image of Lockerbie as a place of death and disaster.

That was an image some relatives of the victims did not want erased, and many of them were aghast when they heard details of the party. "We do not begrudge the people of Lockerbie a chance to end their mourning period. But this is not the way to do it," said Susan Cohen, of Port Jervis, New York. "How can the happy images of Mickey and Minnie wipe out the memory of dead babies falling from the sky? And the thought of a barbecue in the town where our children died in the flames of Flight 103 is too much for us to take." Many Lockerbie residents did not like being told how to run their affairs and reacted angrily to the criticism, saying the victims' families were giving them no credit for having any common sense or decency. "The Americans who are protesting don't live here," said Lockerbie gasoline station attendant Agnes Jamieson. "They were not here on the night. We've had all the trauma and we need something to lift our spirits."

The party went ahead on June 3, attended by about five thousand people from Lockerbie and the surrounding region. As the festivities were being held, relatives and friends of the victims held protests in New York, Cleveland, Detroit, Pittsburgh, and Syracuse. "How can they do something like that—picnic where bodies were found?" asked Florence Bissett, mother of Cornell University student Kenneth Bissett, as she picketed Pan Am's New York headquarters. Because of the relatives' protest, Disney removed Mickey and Minnie Mouse from the guest list, and some companies that had planned to donate food also pulled out. For children such as young Lucy Gibson, who had worn a pink Mickey Mouse sweatshirt to the party, the dispute meant disappointment. The Disney characters she had looked forward to meeting did not show up. "A lot of children from Lockerbie will never get to go to Disneyland," said a local policeman. "This was their only chance to see Mickey and Minnie. Some of the sympathy for the Americans is going to go down the drain."

MORE THAN three months after the party, on September 27, Pan Am put its defense plan into action. Using Juval Aviv's Interfor report as a blueprint, attorneys defending the airline filed subpoenas requesting documents from the U.S. government. One of Pan Am's requests sought information on Monzer al-Kassar, a man already known to Washington journalists because of his links to the Iran-contra investigations. His name had surfaced at the time of those investigations as one of the businessmen reportedly used by Lieutenant Colonel Oliver North and others to launder profits from the covert sale of weapons to Iran; the inclusion of his name in Pan Am's subpoenas virtually assured that the court filings would make big news. If the strategy worked, the pressure to provide answers to Flight 103's troubling questions would shift from the airline to the government.

The *Independent*, a British newspaper, published a front-page story on the subpoenas on November 1, and with that story Pan Am effectively went from being the accused to the accuser. For the time being, the accuracy of Aviv's work was largely irrelevant. The CIA was unlikely to engage in a point-by-point debate on his theory; even if the agency disputed his findings, Aviv could say a government denial had been what he had expected all along. As he pointed out in his report, many of the allegations would be viewed in court as "inadmissible speculation or hearsay." But to journalists they were "publishable speculation."

Filing the subpoenas was only the first step in the strategy Aviv outlined in his report to Pan Am. He also suggested that the airline use the relatives in its campaign. "The passengers' relatives group can mount pressure on Congress if they are tipped," he said. Their recruitment "widens the field to include multiple players with different agendas." Interfor made a number of other suggestions, including one that Pan Am focus its attention on the Turkish baggage handlers at Frankfurt, who, according to the report, had been involved in the CIA-protected drug route that had been instrumental in allowing the bomb bag on board. Aviv also proposed infiltrating the Turkish community in Frankfurt, to learn more about the handlers' contacts there. "There is a chance, albeit speculative, of amassing enough circumstantial evidence to confront the culprit and induce a confession," said the report.

Lee S. Kreindler, the lead attorney for the relatives, quickly denounced the subpoenas as a "public relations gambit" by Pan Am. He said the airline was trying to deflect attention away from itself and create diversions that would delay trial on the civil suits.

But some of the relatives were unwilling to dismiss the report completely. They were very interested when, on Friday, November 3, Ohio Representative James A. Traficant, Jr., called a press conference to tell reporters he had read the report on which Pan Am based its subpoenas. Traficant described some of the details of the alleged CIA involvement, but he declined to say who had written the report. (At the time Aviv had not surfaced as its author.) The congressman also refused to provide copies of the document. Traficant had a checkered past—in 1987 a U.S. Tax Court judge had found that he had evaded taxes in connection with $108,000 in payments from organized crime figures in Ohio and Pennsylvania—and his reputation in Washington was that of a maverick with a tendency to attach himself to conspiracy theories involving the intelligence community. So his "revelations" were greeted with skepticism and received limited media attention.

The day after Traficant's press conference the Families of Pan Am 103/Lockerbie, headed by Paul Hudson, met in Alexandria, Virginia. One of the relatives' attorneys quickly dismissed the Aviv report's allegations, but some relatives began to smell a conspiracy of colossal proportions. "What we are witnessing is a lot of finger-pointing going on," Hudson said at the meeting. "Everyone has an ax to grind, but that doesn't mean that everything they are saying is a fabrication." Another member of the group, Marina de Larracoechea, summed up a suspicion widely held among the relatives that the subpoenas signaled the end of an agreement between the airline and government to cover up what really happened. "Their unity is cracking," she said. Traficant, meanwhile, decided to hold another press briefing at which he would release five pages of Pan Am's report.

Traficant's second press conference was jammed partly because Lockerbie was back in the news. British newspapers had begun reporting that Lockerbie investigators, tracking clues back to Malta, were making progress. The congressman entered the room accompanied by Victor Marchetti, the man who had given him the report. Marchetti was a former CIA agent who had cowritten a 1974 book called *The CIA and the Cult of Intelligence*; rightly or wrongly, he, too, was perceived by the Washington media as a maverick likely to see a CIA plot under every stone. Nonetheless, Traficant's second news briefing received widespread attention, causing the CIA to break its silence. "We have not seen the report," spokesman Mark Mansfield said, "but the allegations it makes are nonsense." Marchetti would not say where he obtained the report and freely admitted he had no role in its preparation. "I think this report is basically accurate," he said. "The fact that the CIA denies it convinces me I am right." The CIA denial and the counterclaim by Marchetti, a well-known critic of the agency, were at the time the only ways of assessing the accuracy of the report because no one knew who had prepared it for Pan Am.

Two weeks later the *Post-Standard* of Syracuse, New York, identified Juval Aviv's Interfor Inc. as the source of the report and summarized the findings that had not been revealed by Traficant. Later that week the *London Observer* carried an extensive article disputing the accuracy of the Interfor work, saying its reporters had disproved or had been unable to verify a variety of its details.

It had been nearly a year since terrorists had bombed Flight 103, but for the relatives the picture of who was responsible was becoming more clouded, not clearer. Police had made remarkable progress in identifying the bomb and in tracing the clothes packed with it to their origin in Malta; they had visited thirteen countries, taken 14,181 statements and more than 35,000 photographs. But they did not have enough to make their case in a Scottish court. As the first anniversary of the bombing approached, the relatives were still without the answers they were seeking.

THE FIRST anniversary of the bombing prompted memorial services in Scotland, England, and the United States. At 7:02 P.M. on December 21, 1989—one year to the minute of the bombing of Pan American World Airways Flight 103—270 candles flickered in the darkness in Lockerbie. At the same instant the Crouse College bells tolled taps across the Syracuse University campus in upstate New York. In Detroit thirteen-year-old Jim Bennett, who had lost his father in the bombing, played "Amazing Grace" on the violin. In New York City people sang "Let There Be Peace on Earth." A group of New Jersey schoolchildren released white balloons in a plea for world peace. And in the mausoleum at St. Agnes Cemetery near Albany, New York, a family friend placed seventeen roses at the foot of the crypt where Melina Hudson's body had been interred. Sixteen of the roses were white, one for each year Melina Hudson lived. The seventeenth was pink. With the flowers was a message from Melina's brother Stephen: "In a way my sister was a martyr, because her death . . . shredded our hearts, but the heart is a muscle and it rebuilds itself stronger. I love you, Melina."

PAUL AND Eleanor Hudson went to Lockerbie for the first anniversary of the bombing. Their children stayed behind, visiting relatives in Ohio. Melina's former classmates at Albany Academy for Girls had made luminaries—paper bags with candles in them, which gave off a subtle glow when the candles were lit—which the Hudsons took with them to a memorial service in Scotland.

Georgia and Tony Nucci wanted to have something else on their mind on the anniversary of the terrorist attack, so they towed their twenty-three-foot trailer to Walt Disney World in Florida, where they were joined by Tony's daughter Lisa, her husband, the couple's two young children, and an Ecuadorian exchange student who lived with the Nuccis. The weather was cold and wet when they visited Epcot Center on December 21; freezing rain coated the poinsettias at the theme park with a thin sheet of ice. Georgia Nucci spent much of the day shivering and stamping her feet to stay warm, but she had no regrets. She had wanted to get away from everyone who would have known about her son's death, and she had succeeded. "We met all kinds of people who were perfectly cheerful. People didn't look at us like 'Oh, you're the woman who lost your son.' "

Beulah McKee stayed home in Trafford, Pennsylvania. She doesn't remember precisely what she did on the anniversary of her son's death, except that she spent part of the day sitting in her son's room, looking through his belongings.

Pan Am observed the anniversary of the crash by taking out full-page advertisements in several newspapers, including the *New York Times*, the *Times* of London, and, in West Germany, *Frankfurter Allegemeine Zeitung*. The stark ads—three sentences of text surrounded by white space—described the attack as "senseless" and "barbaric" and asked for a moment of prayer for the Flight 103 victims and for other victims of terrorism.

BEHIND THE scenes, meanwhile, the airline was forging ahead with the Interfor recommendations. As Aviv had suggested, Pan Am gave polygraph examinations to three Frankfurt baggage handlers who worked on Flight 103. The polygraph operator who performed the tests asked the handlers if any suitcases that hadn't belonged on the flight had been switched with one that did. The response of two of the handlers—Roland O'Neill and Kilins Aslan Tuzcu—indicated they were lying, the operator reported. Pan Am apparently decided Scotland Yard would be interested in this information and set in motion a bizarre plot to get O'Neill and Tuzcu to travel to London, presumably so they could be questioned by those investigating the bombing. Neither man was told the real reason for his trip to England.

O'Neill was asked to travel to Heathrow Airport, where a man in a gray suit would give him a package he was to bring back to Frankfurt. O'Neill agreed. Although the package was not ready when he arrived at Heathrow, the man in the gray suit was there. He gave O'Neill thirty British pounds and told him to enjoy himself in London and to return in a few hours. When

O'Neill came back to the London airport, he was surprised to find that his co-worker, Tuzcu, also was there. Tuzcu told O'Neill he had been brought to England as part of Pan Am's investigation into the Lockerbie bombing. O'Neill eventually took possession of the elusive package, and the two men boarded the plane back to Germany. If Pan Am had hoped that Scotland Yard would question the two men, the airline's hopes were not realized.

When O'Neill and Tuzcu returned to Frankfurt, they learned they had been suspended from their jobs. And although he had previously been questioned and cleared by West German police, O'Neill faced two days of intense examination by police officers presumably because of the results of Pan Am's polygraph test. O'Neill hired a lawyer, who immediately challenged the methods used in the polygraph examinations, and O'Neill was cleared again. On January 25, 1990, an agitated officer of the West German police agency BKA was on the phone with the legal attaché at the U.S. Embassy in Bonn, complaining about the treatment O'Neill and Tuzcu had received. The officer said German police were considering filing kidnapping charges against the people who had arranged for the two baggage handlers to be flown to London. The embassy in Bonn relayed the message to the U.S. secretary of state. Pan Am quickly reinstated the handlers to their jobs.

The U.S. government also was disturbed. When James W. Keefe, the polygraph specialist who had conducted the lie detector tests, arrived at JFK International Airport in New York City, he was served with a subpoena to appear before a grand jury in Washington. The questions he was asked at the closed-door session made it clear the U.S. attorney was exploring whether Interfor had interfered with the criminal probe.

The U.S. and German governments may have reacted as strongly as they did to this strange episode because they feared Interfor's initiative would disrupt the sensitive work of the criminal investigation. But some relatives of those killed in the attack began to wonder whether the governments had clamped down because Interfor had come close to uncovering something the two countries wanted to keep buried. Paul Hudson, among others, considered unwarranted the notion of taking criminal action against attorneys in a civil case. "Kidnapping?" Hudson said. "Who are we kidding? It's absurd. The investigation is obviously stalled."

As spring 1990 approached, the Lockerbie bombing no longer held the nation's attention, and the relatives were looking for ways of jump-starting their campaign to keep the bombing in the public eye. They got some help from George Williams, the father of Flight 103 victim Geordie Williams and an active member of the group headed by Ammerman.

From the beginning George Williams had been among the most vocal of the voices in the relatives' organization calling for a full investigation of the bombing. With his salt-and-pepper hair and glasses perched low on his nose, Williams looked like a bashful schoolmaster, but that impression dissolved the moment he opened his mouth. Williams was a former marine sniper, and he could be brutally direct. The other members of Victims of Pan Am Flight 103 saw Williams as a natural candidate for what they had begun to call commando squads—groups of two or three people sent to public appearances of government officials to draw attention to the group's demands for better aviation security. The relatives hoped that by obtaining media attention, they could put pressure on government officials to denounce state-sponsored terrorism and explain what they were doing to capture the bombers. This had been an ongoing effort, but by the spring of 1990 it was considered especially important because so little seemed to be happening with the investigation.

The group's previous work in this respect had been disappointing. When members of the organization went to Great Britain, their presence in that country was overshadowed by a tragic ferry accident. Then the relatives planned a high-profile visit to Germany to focus attention on the questionable level of cooperation German police were extending to Scottish investigators. For its trip the group picked November 9, 1989—the same day the Berlin wall fell. Even on December 21, the first anniversary of the bombing, the relatives were upstaged by world events. The previous day the United States had invaded Panama. The bad luck continued when President Bush and USSR President Mikhail Gorbachev met for their summit at sea in Malta, an island that had played a role in the Flight 103 story. The leader of the relatives' group based in the United Kingdom, Dr. Jim Swire, decided to hire a boat and stage a protest beside the ships the two world leaders were using. But the island's worst storm in a hundred years scuttled Swire's plan.

The relatives persisted, setting their sights on Bermuda, where Bush was to meet British Prime Minister Margaret Thatcher to discuss the upcoming Bush-Gorbachev summit in May 1990. Although many of the family members had become skeptical about the effectiveness of drawing attention to themselves at public events, the Bush-Thatcher meeting was an especially attractive target. Not only did those leaders represent the nations that accounted for the majority of Flight 103's victims, but syndicated columnist Jack Anderson had recently fanned the relatives' smoldering suspicions about a cover-up. Anderson claimed that both U.S. and British intelligence had evidence that the PFLP—GC, backed by Iran, was responsible for the Flight 103 bombing and that Thatcher and Bush had agreed in a telephone conversation not to make the findings public. The reason, Anderson said, was that neither government could effectively punish the culprits.

Williams and Bill Marek were dispatched to Bermuda to raise a ruckus. Marek's sister, Elizabeth, had died in the bombing, and his loss was compounded when his father died a few months later.

On April 12, when Williams and Marek met at the airport terminal in Bermuda, they were woefully unprepared for their mission. They did not know where summit events would be held or where reporters were staying. Other than wiring ahead an order for a wreath of red and white carnations they planned to drop in the harbor, the two men did not know what they would do in Bermuda. They knew only that they wanted to publicize their call for a tougher stance by the United States and Britain against states that sponsor terrorism.

At the airport in Bermuda a taxicab driver approached the two travelers and offered them a ride. The three men struck up a conversation, and the driver asked about the Flight 103 buttons Williams and Marek were wearing. When they explained, the driver identified himself as Trevor E. Woolridge, said he'd followed the Flight 103 story from the start, and offered his help.

When he wasn't driving a cab, Woolridge served in the Bermuda legislature, as a Progressive Labour party senator. He knew all about the summit. He recited the schedule of events and explained where the press and visiting government officials would be staying. If the visitors hurried, Woolridge said, they might be able to catch the end of Thatcher's meeting with the premier of Bermuda. He even told the men where he thought Thatcher would stand if she held an impromptu press conference after the meeting: at a memorial outside the building. Sure enough, that is where Williams and Marek found Thatcher and a crowd of reporters. The two men remained silent as she spoke. But as soon as Thatcher got into her limousine, Williams began reading the names of the 270 victims of Flight 103. The television cameras spun around, and Williams and Marek gave several interviews, mostly to local reporters.

They continued to look for ways of getting their message to the president and to the media. At a local radio station they gave an interview that was played every half hour for four hours that evening. At the Hamilton Princess, a hotel where Bush's staff and British journalists had their headquarters, the two men slipped onto the sixth floor, where the U.S. delegation had set up its operations center. They found a message area in which rows of manila envelopes had been tacked to corkboard easels. There were envelopes for White House Chief of Staff John Sununu, White House spokesman Marlin Fitzwater, and National Security Adviser Brent Scowcroft. Williams and Marek quickly stuffed into each envelope a copy of a letter Bert Ammerman and Dr. Jim Swire had written to Thatcher and Bush. At another hotel, the Southampton Princess, they stuffed messages into envelopes reserved for messages for American reporters. They also urged the few media people they found at the hotel to question Bush and Thatcher on terrorism at the next day's press conference.

The following day the two men returned to the hotel where the U.S. journalists were working. Walking past security guards and into a bustling media room, Williams convinced several reporters, including some from Korea and Japan, to interview him.

Williams and Marek had been told repeatedly not to bother even trying to get near the Bush-Thatcher meeting at Government House. But they did try, and to their surprise a security officer peered inside their taxi and waved them through. About 150 feet up the road, Williams got out of the cab. Secret Service agents with wires protruding from their ears were everywhere, and as Williams began walking to the press table, he heard a voice behind him.

"Pardon me, sir, may I have a word with you?"

Williams turned and faced the man, who said, "Do you have an official function here, sir?"

Williams explained who he was and that he wanted to put information on the press table.

"I'm sorry sir, that won't be allowed."

Williams retorted, "Well, how 'bout you doing it for me, OK?"

With a serious tone in his voice, the security agent responded, "That's not my function."

Williams pressed a little more, saying all he wanted was to place his material on the table.

"I must insist, sir, that you evacuate the area immediately." So Williams left, although the thought of risking arrest had occurred to him. He might have done it if there had been some cameras around to record the event.

The two men went back to their hotel and stretched out on their beds to watch the press conference that followed the Bush and Thatcher meeting. The reporters shouted question after question, but no one asked the two leaders the question Williams and Marek had been urging them to pose for the past two days. When the final query came and it had nothing to do with state-sponsored terrorism, Williams and Marek looked at each other in silent disappointment. Bush finished his answer, but then he kept talking. He pulled a letter from his jacket pocket as he spoke: "May I add one word? And I wouldn't dare to speak for the Prime Minister but it—a flyer was called to my attention here about the victims of—put out by—relating to the victims of Pan American Flight 103."

Williams heard little else. He began jumping up and down on his bed, while Marek shook his head and mumbled, "I don't believe it. I don't believe it."

Bush went on to say that he and Thatcher would be happy to renounce terrorists and reaffirm their commitment to find and punish those responsible for the Flight 103 bombing.

"But we can't simply pull solutions out of the hat," Thatcher added. "It's a question of patient, continuous work on that investigation, and patient, continuous determination to try to defeat terrorism."

There was little substance to the comments by Bush and Thatcher, but Williams's and Marek's efforts had produced the payoff they were after: renewed attention to their organization's cause. The two men also had reiterated to Bush and Thatcher that the relatives were not going to let their governments stall forever on the Lockerbie investigation.

On the flight home to Maryland Williams composed a letter to his son. Later he added a postscript to tell his son about the follow-up note he received from President Bush, personally written on light blue stationery aboard Air Force One. "I know some of the families feel that I don't care— but I really do and I will keep pushing for a proper disclosure," Bush wrote. The letter to Geordie became a kind of private celebration, but it was a party Williams wanted desperately to share. "I am happier than I have been since your murder," Williams wrote. "And also nearly as despondent."

IN MID-MAY the President's Commission on Aviation Security and Terrorism released its 182-page report, filled with stinging criticisms of the FAA, the State Department, and the aviation industry. The report said that the U.S. civil aviation system was "seriously flawed" and that Pan Am was guilty of "apparent security lapses" that remained uncorrected nine months after the bombing. The report even went so far as to suggest the United States consider conducting preemptive strikes against terrorist camps to prevent attacks. "The United States must not be held hostage by a handful of outlaw nations," the commission chair, Ann McLaughlin, said at a press conference announcing the findings.

For the relatives the news was better than they had dared hope. They had anticipated the commission recommendations would not go far enough to satisfy them, and they still wanted answers they had not gotten, particularly when it came to the charges of CIA involvement and whether some air travelers had been warned away from the flight. But they were generally pleased with, and surprised by, the report's harsh tone. The relatives in Ammerman's group hastily watered down a press release—prepared before they saw the report—that criticized the commission. Hudson saw the report as establishing a national standard that hadn't existed before. "It became the Bible," he said. "It's the authoritative reference point and will be, for aviation security and terrorism, for the next ten years at least."

In the United Kingdom things were not going as well. Dr. Jim Swire, the father of Flight 103 victim Flora and the leader of the British relatives' group, envied the success the U.S. relatives were having in forcing their government to act. While the U.S. relatives had been fighting in Washington for an investigation into lax aviation security, Swire and his group, U.K. Families—Flight 103, had been pushing the British government for a similar probe in London. British officials had consistently assured him that British airlines and airports met rigorous security standards. Yet when the president's commission issued its harsh criticisms three days before he was to leave for the United States, Swire felt as if his government had failed him. While the American relatives had had a meaningful inquiry into their security problems, in Great Britain the government had not even launched an investigation into the quality of aviation security. Swire thought it was time to get things moving.

Swire devised a plan to slip a harmless replica of the Flight 103 bomb through Heathrow security and onto a British Airways jet. Even if he got caught, he reasoned, his action would draw attention to aviation security in Britain.

Swire already had studied as much as he could about the Flight 103 bomb. For a physician, he was unusually suited to understand the workings of such a device. In 1956 Swire had learned how to use plastic explosives as a member of the army's Royal Engineers in Cyprus, where part of his job was blowing up houses that had harbored terrorists. Later, when he held a job with the BBC, he received extensive training in electronics. In researching the bomb, Swire obtained access to the color brochure the Germans had distributed after their raid on the PFLP—GC hideouts in West Germany. The brochure described the Toshiba bomb that authorities had seized from the trunk of the green Ford sedan in Neuss, and it included photographs and a detailed description of the device. The brochure had been distributed to airlines and airports. Swire used it to construct a device that displayed as many of the telltale signs as possible. Because there no longer was a Toshiba radio-cassette player on the market that looked like the BomBeat, Swire used a Hitachi Model TRK 510ER, which he thought resembled the BomBeat. It was about twelve inches long, nine inches high, and three inches deep. It had a single four-inch speaker adjacent to the cassette player. The radio dial was at the top, and the row of control buttons was beneath the handle.

The warning from the Germans said the PFLP—GC bomb could be armed by placing a plug in the aerial jack. Although the plug in the Neuss bomb had been black, Swire put a bright scarlet plug in the jack on his device. "I did that deliberately so no one could miss it," he said. As a Semtex substitute, Swire used marzipan, an almond confectionery paste that has a texture similar to Semtex's. He molded a glob of the yellowish marzipan inside the cassette player's case so it would be visible through the grille on the back. Then he placed a length of brass tubing inside as a substitute for the detonator. He also tucked inside the device an electronic timer, an air pressure switch, and a set of small batteries like the ones used in 35 mm cameras. The small batteries would be impossible to confuse with the flashlight battery-size D cells that normally powered the radio-cassette player. When he finished his work, Swire's device weighed substantially more than it should have, and merely picking it up should have aroused suspicions about what was inside. Swire figured he could not have constructed a more obvious device, especially because it was patterned on a bomb with which air security personnel should have been intimately familiar.

Once his mock bomb had been built, Swire ran it through the X-ray machine in his office to see how it would appear to screeners at the airport gate. Even though he knew an X-ray examination would not detect plastic explosives, Swire found that careful screening could detect some of the components. At the very least, he decided, an X-ray operator would be able to tell that his luggage contained an electronic device, which could then be subjected to more detailed examination by hand.

Swire was on his way with Barry Flick, the brother of flight victim Clayton Lee Flick, to meet with their American counterparts to discuss strategy. When they checked in for their British Airways flight from London to New York on May 18, security workers told them that their flight had been selected for "special security" and that they would have to open their luggage for inspection. Swire and Flick hoisted their bags onto a table and opened them for viewing. Flick glanced over as a woman security officer searching their belongings uncovered a radio-cassette player in

Swire's bag. Flick's jaw dropped open. Swire looked intently at the woman searching his case. She showed no concern about the cassette recorder and in fact casually picked it up.

"Have you taken the batteries out?" she asked.

"Yes," he said, truthfully.

She did not ask any questions about whether he had been given the radio-cassette player as a gift, nor did she pose other questions that might have determined if Swire had been duped into carrying a bomb on the plane. She put the device back in his suitcase and cleared the bag for loading.

Swire had shown his mock bomb to other members of his group, but he did not tell them he planned to smuggle it onto an airplane. Possessing a mock bomb at an airport is illegal, and he did not want to involve anyone else in case the stunt backfired and he found himself in jail. "Obviously I hoped they were going to find the damned thing," Swire said. "It's very depressing, you know, eighteen months after your daughter has been blown to pieces, if you take a bomb as similar as you can make it to the one that caused her death along to an airport where you have been told repeatedly that the people in charge of security have done their own internal inquiry and beefed up security and made it foolproof. You take a bomb along and sail through with it, it's very depressing."

Swire not only flew across the Atlantic with his bomb but also transferred it with him to a domestic U.S. flight from New York to Boston, where he and Flick planned to attend a meeting of the relatives' group led by Ammerman. When Swire told the directors of that group what he had done, a lively ninety-minute discussion ensued. Initially the U.S. relatives debated the merits of the stunt, but eventually they saw that it could have publicity value. Still, the leaders of the U.S. group convinced Swire to delay publicizing his action. They were concerned the disclosure might somehow derail implementation of the security reforms recommended by the president's commission.

News of Swire's bomb stayed a secret for six weeks. Then, as several American relatives returned to Lockerbie in late June for the dedication of a chapel at Tundergarth Church, a British politician who had been told about Swire's stunt leaked the news about the false bomb, causing an immediate uproar and forcing Swire to call a press conference to tell the full story. The American relatives, who thought it inappropriate to reveal the news in conjunction with the dedication service, were caught off guard by the timing and were unprepared to capitalize on the announcement by Swire.

Swire became something of a celebrity crusader in Britain. British Department of Transport officials were not impressed, however; they launched an investigation into how he had been able to slip the false bomb onto the flight. British law bans false explosive devices from being inside airports *without due reason*. If he had been arrested, Swire was prepared to argue that he had due reason: He was trying to point out flaws in the country's aviation security system. After asking him some questions and confiscating a second false bomb he had constructed—the device he had carried across the Atlantic on British Airways was still in Boston, where he had left it—police informed Swire they would not press charges.

A television crew conducting an interview with Swire as he got off a train at Euston Station in London had to interrupt the filming when he was mobbed by well-wishers who slapped him on the back and shook his hand. British authorities apparently had decided that bringing charges against Swire would only increase his visibility.

A year and a half had passed since the bombing, and Flight 103 was still in the news, on both sides of the Atlantic.

CHAPTER 10

CONFRONTING EVIL

THE RECOMMENDATIONS of the President's Commission on Aviation Security and Terrorism were just the beginning. The relatives knew the findings could be ignored unless there was a law based on the commission's work. Then the congressional members of the commission, New Jersey Democrat Frank Lautenberg and New York Republican Alfonse D'Amato from the Senate and Minnesota Democrat James Oberstar and Arkansas Republican John Paul Hammerschmidt from the House, introduced an aviation security improvement bill to give the recommendations teeth. The legislation called for stationing federal security managers at high-risk airports in the United States and overseas, accelerating research on equipment to detect explosives, and notifying the public of credible bomb threats. But the relatives quickly learned there were no guarantees that the reforms would be enacted.

The legislation grew from the work of the commission appointed by President Bush, but agencies within his administration openly opposed major portions of the bill. Officials of the FAA and State Department said they considered the legislation unnecessary because they had already adopted most of the commission's findings on their own. FAA Administrator James Busey said his department was upgrading metal detectors and beefing up security personnel in Europe and the Middle East. Morris Busby, coordinator for counterterrorism in the State Department, said his department already had begun providing the general public with access to information regarding threats through electronic bulletin boards. The relatives, however, were not satisfied with these initiatives. They continued to see the FAA and the State Department as a major part of the problem, and they did not trust the two agencies to police themselves.

The opposition of the FAA and the State Department was not the greatest threat to the relatives' effort to enact reform. That came from within. Now, when a unified front was needed, the two groups again came down on opposite sides. Hudson and his followers opposed the legislation unless it was bolstered by a series of amendments to make it tougher. "Our position was, either strengthen it or defeat it," Hudson said. Ammerman and his group wanted some of the same stipulations but feared that pushing for them too hard would doom the legislation and leave them with no reform, so they supported the draft legislation. As the summer of 1990 drew to a close, relatives in both groups mustered the expertise and contacts they had developed over the months on Capitol Hill and braced for battle.

Ammerman and Hudson both testified at several congressional committee hearings. Ammerman's group, Victims of Pan Am Flight 103, began a sophisticated lobbying campaign that involved formulating position papers and organizing a focused letter-writing campaign with Chairwoman Aphrodite Tsairis as one of the chief organizers. The first step occurred in mid-August, when Joe and Sheila Horgan, using a computerized mailing list prepared by another group member, John Root, sent a letter to each member of Congress requesting his or her stand on the bill and the name of the legislative aide responsible for monitoring it.* After using those responses to plan their strategy, more than sixty members of the Ammerman group went to Washington in late September. Working from the Quality Hotel and Best Western motel near the Capitol, they visited the office of each U.S. senator and representative. The organization's leaders, meanwhile, met with officials from the departments of Transportation and State and with aides to key senators and congressmen. A letter bearing Ammerman's signature and delivered to each lawmaker warned of the growing threat of terrorism following Iraq's invasion of Kuwait and urged swift passage of the aviation security improvement bill. "The wheels of government must be ahead of the terrorist threat to civilian aviation," the letter said. "Since the horror of Lockerbie, 21 months ago, no significant changes in security have been addressed. We look to you to enact this legislation to begin that long-neglected process. In the words of Edmund Burke—All that is necessary for the triumph of evil is that good men do nothing." In a separate letter to President Bush, members of Ammerman's group were critical of the FAA and other administration agencies for opposing the legislation and called on the president to live up to a promise

---

* Sheila Horgan was the sister-in-law of victim Michael Doyle; John Root, a New York City attorney, was the husband of victim Hanne Maria Root.

he had given them earlier: to see to it that the commission's recommendations were not allowed to wither and die.

At the same time that Ammerman's group was pushing for fast adoption of the bill in the House, Hudson's organization, Families of Pan Am 103/Lockerbie, was working to convince members of Congress that the bill was unacceptable. Hudson's view was that it was better to defeat the bill than to adopt it as it was drafted since passage of a weak bill would create the illusion that airport security was being improved while the public continued to travel with inadequate protection. In July, testifying before the House Foreign Affairs Committee, Hudson submitted a list of twenty-nine amendments his organization believed should be added. Two of his main objections were to sections that would have delayed or even canceled the proposed deployment of bomb-detecting TNA devices and that required the FAA to obtain the "cooperation and approval" of foreign governments before imposing U.S. security regulations on U.S. carriers operating overseas. Hudson told the committee the bill was "weak, flawed and inadequate" and urged the panel to strengthen or defeat it.

During their lobbying effort members of Hudson's group had organized into smaller groups representing different regions of the country. Each group was headed by a captain. When the leadership identified a member of Congress who needed to be lobbied, the captain of the region represented by the member directed the relatives in his or her area to send the member letters and telegrams and to make telephone calls. Relatives also traveled to Washington to meet with elected officials in person. Throughout the summer Hudson's group drew on the expertise of Michael Lemov, an experienced Washington lawyer it had hired to serve as its eyes and ears on Capitol Hill.

If any members of Congress were unaware that the two groups of relatives took different positions on the legislation, their ignorance was soon erased. On August 15 members of Ammerman's organization sent a letter to each member of Congress seeking support of the bill. Within a week Hudson's organization sent a letter of its own, asking congressional leaders to withhold their support unless the bill was amended. After extensive lobbying, Hudson's group obtained several of the amendments it had sought. Most notably the House agreed to lift the section requiring the FAA to obtain the "cooperation and approval" of foreign governments before imposing U.S. security regulations on American carriers operating overseas. The House approved the bill on October 1. With those improvements, Hudson began to speak in support of the legislation although his group continued its efforts to strengthen it.

Members of the Ammerman group had devised a fax network allowing them to communicate quickly with a large section of its membership, and on October 2 Tsairis used this network to issue an update on the lobbying effort. The good news was that the House had passed the bill, she wrote. The bad news was that the version that was to be considered at a Senate hearing in two days did not include the stipulation that high-risk airports be assigned "federal security managers." The assignment of those managers was a priority for the Ammerman organization, and the group launched a drive to convince the Senate to restore the language.

On October 4 Ammerman and Hudson testified before the Senate Committee on Commerce, Science and Transportation. Ammerman, who backed the bill that had passed the House, opposed the watered-down Senate working draft. Hudson also objected to the weakened Senate draft, but more important, he went on the record with his support for the House legislation, which he said was "a much better bill now than when it was originally introduced." Hudson continued to argue for the insertion of a provision requiring the immediate deployment of bomb-detecting TNA devices at some high-risk airports.

After the October 4 hearing it was clear that both relatives' groups would be able to unite behind the same version of the aviation security bill. To the members of Ammerman's group, the agreement marked a turning point. Both organizations conceded that their feud had provided fodder for early attempts to cripple the bill. With that friction reduced, Tsairis's next fax to members of the Ammerman group was upbeat. "Bert was at his best. . . . We stood firm on the federal security manager and I believe we will prevail." By the middle of the month the Senate had largely reconciled its bill with the version passed by the House, restoring language requiring the hiring of security managers at high-risk airports. That gave the Ammerman group what it had been seeking. And eventually the Senate agreed to one of Hudson's priorities, adopting an amendment permitting the immediate deployment of bomb detection devices at the FAA's discretion.

By late October the Bush administration and Senate Democrats had signed off on the bill. But a handful of Senate Republicans were balking. Working separately, the two relatives' organizations began a round of eleventh-hour arm-twisting, focusing their attention on Robert Dole, the Senate minority leader. Days before the Senate vote, members of both groups, setting aside their personal differences, showed up simultaneously in Dole's office, seeking an explanation for the holdup.

One delay was caused by Senator Conrad Burns of Montana, who wanted to add an amendment that would allow the death penalty for terrorists. Members of the Ammerman group urged Burns to withdraw the amendment, saying they agreed with his idea but feared it would jeopardize the bill.

Another threat came when Wyoming senator Malcolm Wallop moved to attach an unrelated amendment to the bill that would make permanent a temporary program allowing heavyweight trucks to travel on Wyoming interstate highways. Although the amendment had nothing to do with aviation security, Wallop's office had placed a "hold" on the bill while he tried to get the amendment added. As long as that hold was in place, the bill could not reach the Senate floor. Leaders of the Ammerman group called upon their members to make calls opposing the amendment. A fax transmission from Tsairis listed the telephone number for the Wyoming senator and explained, "This amendment must be withdrawn today or our bill will die as ignominiously as did our loved ones." Hudson's group also worked to loosen the logjam. Hudson's wife, Eleanor, got the telephone numbers of newspapers and other media outlets in Wyoming and brought the truck weight proposal to their attention.

Wallop's office lifted its hold on the bill on October 23, after learning that the Bush administration objected to the amendment. "Rather than cause the death of the aviation bill, we pulled our amendment," Janis Budge, a spokeswoman for Wallop, said later. "We never had any objection to the aviation bill."

The two groups worked as allies to fight the amendment, but as soon as they achieved victory, they were again at odds. Each group considered its own members' actions primarily responsible for the withdrawal of the amendment.

Ammerman credited the action of Jane Schultz, a member of his organization whose son Thomas was killed on Flight 103. Schultz had developed a personal rapport with President Bush through correspondence. She had lost her only other child, Andrew, in an explosion ten years before, and the president had been moved by her experiences. Luckily for the relatives' lobbying effort, Schultz had made arrangements to greet the president at the Westchester County Airport in White Plains on the day the relatives were trying to get the Wyoming senator to release the aviation bill. According to Schultz, Bush appeared angered by her explanation of what was happening and promised to take care of the problem as he headed to his car phone. Within half an hour the bill's sponsors contacted Ammerman to apologize and to say Wallop was withdrawing his amendment.

Hudson, however, said Schultz's meeting with the president could not have played a role in Wallop's decision to release his hold on the bill. He said his group learned of Wallop's change of heart at noon, a full two hours before Schultz met with the president.

Regardless of how it happened, the truck weight proposal was withdrawn, and at 4:00 P.M. on October 23 the Senate approved the aviation security bill by unanimous consent. The final version of the bill established training standards for airport security employees, required the hiring of federal security managers at major foreign and domestic airports, required the secretary of transportation to submit to Congress an annual report on airline security, mandated that foreign airlines flying to and from the United States impose security measures similar to the ones followed by U.S. carriers, established procedures for notifying passengers of credible bomb threats, improved State Department procedures for helping relatives of victims of terrorist attacks, and delayed the installation of bomb-detecting TNA devices until tests proved their effectiveness, although the FAA administrator was empowered to deploy them if he believed they were needed.

Both relatives' groups took credit for passage of the legislation, the most comprehensive aviation bill to get through Congress in years. "We were told the bill was spared by our efforts," Hudson said later. Tsairis, in an October 23 legislative memorandum, wrote: "The success of this legislation is OUR success—The Victims of Pan Am Flight 103, under the leadership of Bert Ammerman." President Bush signed the legislation into law on November 16. In his bill-signing message the president mentioned the work of the two relatives' groups and called the law "a living memorial to those whose lives were so cruelly cut short by the terrorists responsible for bombing Pan Am 103."

BY NOW relatives feared they might never see those terrorists punished. Police knew the bomb had been concealed in the bronze Samsonite that was the unaccompanied "thirteenth bag" loaded at Frankfurt and that had been transferred from Air Malta Flight KM180. But as the second anniversary of the attack approached, there was no indication the bombers would be brought to justice any time soon.

Late in 1990 reports began to surface implicating Libya in the Flight 103 attack. Many of the relatives viewed this turn of events with deep skepticism. They feared the investigation was being forced in a direction that better suited the Bush administration. Details implicating Libya emerged at a time when the president was building a coalition against Iraq prior to the war in the Persian Gulf. A cornerstone of the alliance was Syria, home of Ahmad Jibril and headquarters of his PFLP—GC. Several relatives in both groups felt it too convenient that the progress in the investigation took the heat off the PFLP—GC and Iran. John Root said, "It's absolutely disgusting that the president of the United States and secretary of state are playing politics with the bodies of our dead ones, of our families."

This became a common view among the relatives as the investigation continued into 1991. Their concerns grew as they began getting signals that the investigation was moving further away from Syria and the PFLP—GC. Shortly before the bombing's third anniversary, the relatives learned that indictments were imminent. Fearing that U.S. and Scottish prosecutors might continue their pattern of secrecy by seeking sealed indictments, five relatives from the group led by Bert Ammerman traveled to Great Britain to urge authorities to make the police findings public. It was early November of 1991, only weeks after representatives of Israel and several Arab nations began peace talks in Madrid.

"The public has the absolute right to know the names of those responsible for this heinous crime," Ammerman said. "We will not allow government officials to quietly dispose of the results of their three-year investigation all for the political expediency of the Middle East peace conference."

On Thursday, November 14, 1991, less than a week after Ammerman's delegation returned to the United States, U.S. and Scottish prosecutors released a twenty-nine page indictment charging two Libyan men with carrying out the attack. Named were Lamen Khalifa Fhimah, thirty-five, who prosecutors said had used his job as an airline employee to store Semtex at the Malta airport, and Abdel Basset Ali al-Megrahi, thirty-nine, who had been identified by the shopkeeper in Malta as the man who bought the assortment of clothing at Mary's House. The indictment stated that both were agents of the Libyan intelligence service, Jamahirya Security Organization (JSO). Prosecutors charged that the Libyan government had provided them with Semtex and detonators, and that other conspirators, not named in the indictment, also were involved.

Investigators concluded that both men used Libyan Arab Airlines as a front and then under this cover at Malta's Luqa Airport made sure the suitcase containing the bomb was placed with luggage bound for the United States. Lamen Fhimah was a station manager and representative for Libyan Arab Airlines at Malta, a position which gave him access to Air Malta luggage tags. About two weeks before the Flight 103 bombing Abdel Basset, the former chief of the JSO's airline security section, traveled from Libya to Malta and checked into a Holiday Inn about 300 yards away from Mary's House. On December 7, 1988, he bought the clothes, including the blue Babygro jumpsuit, that were eventually packed with the bomb. He left Malta two days later.

The indictment alleged that the week before the Flight 103 bombing, on December 15, Lamen Fhimah made three entries in his diary to remind himself to obtain airline baggage tags from Air Malta. "Abdel Basset is coming . . . take taggs [sic] from Air Malta," one note said. "Bring tags from the airport," said another. In a third entry Lamen Fhimah had written "OK" adjacent to one of his earlier notes.

On December 18, the indictment said, Lamen Fhimah traveled to Tripoli, Libya, for a meeting with Abdel Basset. Two days later, on December 20, the two men went back to Malta, where Abdel Basset registered at the same Holiday Inn near Mary's House, this time using a pseudonym. The following morning, sometime between 8:15 and 9:15 A.M. local time, the two men made certain a hard-sided Samsonite suitcase with a stolen Air Malta luggage tag was placed among luggage being loaded on Air Malta Flight KM180 to Frankfurt. The suitcase contained the bomb concealed inside a Toshiba radio-cassette player. About twelve hours later, after the Samsonite had been transferred to Flight 103, the bomb exploded over Lockerbie.

Abdel Basset left the island the same day, boarding Libyan Arab Airlines Flight LN147 to Tripoli. Lamen Fhimah remained in Malta, although he, too, eventually returned to Libya, investigators concluded.

Libya, which denied any connection to the bombing, has no extradition treaty with the United States.

THE CLUES that led authorities to the Libyans emerged from scraps of fabric, fragments of plastic, and a bit of luck. The bomb-scorched clothing traced to Malta, coupled with the baggage handling list that revealed the presence of the unaccompanied suitcase from Air Malta Flight KM180, indicated that the bomb started its travels at Luqa Airport.

But another small clue, the piece of circuit board that had fallen out of a corner of luggage container AVE 4041 PA, kept leading investigators back to the PFLP—GC cell in Germany. The circuit board proved the bomb had been hidden inside a Toshiba radio-cassette recorder, just like the device seized by the Germans two months before the bombing. Investigators struggled for months to link the suitcase in Malta to the PFLP—GC cell in Germany.

Despite this compelling connection, Lockerbie investigators had been unable to find any evidence that an altitude sensor had been incorporated into the Flight 103 bomb. If there was no barometer involved, the Lockerbie and Autumn Leaves bombs had been fundamentally different: the Flight 103 bomb used a timer only, while the Autumn Leaves bomb incorporated both a timer and barometer.

A second scrap of plastic, a piece of a different circuit board, finally allowed investigators to solve the riddle. This green fragment had been discovered in the shreds of a shirt that had been packed inside the Samsonite suitcase that carried the bomb. Investigators determined that the fragment, smaller than a fingernail, was part of a timer.

Although someone had tried to scratch out the manufacturer's initials, forensic workers were able to make out the letters MEBO. That led police to a Zurich-based firm, Meister et Bollier Ltd. Telecommunications. The fragment was part of the firm's Model MST-13 electronic digital timer. The company had made only twenty of the devices in a special order for the Libyan government in 1985 and 1986.

Investigators working on the intelligence side of the investigation, meanwhile, found their own link to Libya. A CIA analyst who searched the agency's massive data base on terrorism found that the timer recovered from the Flight 103 wreckage was identical to ten timers seized from two Libyan intelligence agents in Senegal on February 20, 1988. These devices were part of the shipment of twenty Model MST-13 timers the Swiss firm had built specially for Libya.

All of the timers had gone to agents of the JSO. They had been manufactured at the request of Said Rashid Kisha, an intelligence operative who later became head of the JSO division that handled aviation security for the Libyan national airline. Another Libyan, former Minister of Justice and current Minister of Transportation Izzel Din al-Hinshiri, also was involved in acquiring the devices. The Swiss firm's records listed a man named Mohammed Naydi as the recipient.

Mohammed Naydi was an alias of Mohammed al-Marzouk. In 1988 he had been arrested along with Mansour Omran Saber at the airport in Dakar after stepping off an Air Africa flight. In their luggage police found nearly twenty pounds of Semtex, several blocks of TNT, and the ten timers. Over the objections of U.S. officials, the Senegalese government released the two Libyans on June 16, 1988. Afterward authorities traced the pair to Sliema, Malta.

Pan Am 103 and the ten timers found in Senegal accounted for eleven of the total shipment. A twelfth turned up in the wreckage of another bombing: the attack on French UTA Flight 772 on September 19, 1989, over Niger. And French authorities investigating the UTA bombing had discovered more similarities between the Pan Am and UTA attacks. High-ranking Libyan officials, including Qaddafi's brother-in-law, were present at a meeting in September 1988 in Tripoli at which attacks against U.S. and French targets had been plotted, the French believed.

U.S. and Scottish investigators now felt they had a case against Libya, and only Libya. The indictment said the attack had been an operation funded and supported by the Qaddafi regime. By coincidence or by guile, the Libyans had planted the bomb inside a Toshiba so that investigators would be drawn to the PFLP—GC cell operating in the country where Flight 103 originated. This would not have been difficult because details of the PFLP—GC bomb had been widely publicized after the October 1988 raids.

In announcing the indictment, U.S. prosecutors said that despite the activities of the PFLP—GC cell in West Germany and the intelligence intercepts discovered in the attack's aftermath, there was no evidence of Syrian or Iranian involvement. "A lot of people thought it was Syrians," President Bush told reporters the day the indictments were announced. "The Syrians took a bum rap on this."

RELATIVES WERE angered by the administration's push to clear Syria. Rosemary Wolfe said she found it hard to believe that Libyan agents had carried out the bombing alone.

"There are certainly enough indications that Iran commissioned it, and that Jibril, with the go-ahead of the Syrian leaders, tried to carry it out, and that after Autumn Leaves Jibril then worked directly with the Libyans to carry it out," she said. "There are some of us who are concerned that because of our new dealings with Syria and also with Iran the indictments may not go far enough. We've been told that politics will play no part in this. But we want to see results."

Bonnie O'Connor, the sister of victim John Ahern, also was suspicious. "This was a preventable tragedy and now they are not going to bother to punish those responsible," she said. "It is infuriating. Life will never be the same."

Bert Ammerman urged President Bush to consider a military attack on Libya, just like the one former President Reagan ordered upon learning of Libyan involvement in the April 1986 bombing of the West Berlin nightclub.

Paul Hudson was more circumspect. He wanted the United States to urge other nations to cut all air links to Libya. He also called for a trade embargo on Libyan oil. But he stopped short of endorsing a military strike. "One of the alleged motives here is the 1986 U.S. bombing raid on Libya, which in addition to trying to take out Qaddafi killed a number of Libyan civilians," Hudson said. "Another cycle of bloodshed on both sides is probably all that a military strike by the United States would engender."

Escaping notice at the time of the indictment was a lingering mystery that supported the relatives' suspicions. The movements of Mohammed Abu Talb, the man who police thought might link the PFLP—GC to the clothes in Malta, suggested the Libyans may have had help.

Talb, who lived in Sweden but who had ties to the German PFLP—GC cell, visited Malta two months before the Flight 103 attack. Police noted that during a stopover in Rome he changed his plans and decided to buy a ticket for Benghazi, Libya. He had been short of cash, however, and had been able to purchase the ticket only after a helpful Libyan named Fawzi had given him about twenty dollars. Then, for reasons that remain unclear, Talb did not take the flight, although his luggage traveled to Libya. Talb put in a claim for his bags at the Malta airport, and they were returned to him within two days. Could someone have used Talb's luggage to smuggle bomb components to him from Libya?

Investigators had other questions about Talb. When interviewed by Lockerbie investigators in April 1990, Talb said his encounter with Fawzi in Rome marked the first time he had ever seen the man. But when Swedish police probing terrorist bombings in Scandinavia had questioned Talb in August 1989, he had provided a different answer. The Swedish investigators went through every page of Talb's address book and demanded that he identify each entry. When they reached the "F" section, they asked about Fawzi. At that time, a report by the Swedish police agency SÄPO shows, Talb had explained matter-of-factly that Fawzi was a friend he had met in Libya in 1977—not someone he happened to meet eleven years later in Rome, as he told Lockerbie investigators.

Mohammed Abu Talb would remain a puzzling figure because of his connections to Libya, Malta, and the PFLP—GC as he served a life sentence in a Swedish prison for his role in terrorist bombings in Scandinavia.

Meanwhile, for Pan Am the bombing of Flight 103 was a disaster in more ways than one. Within months of the attack the FAA announced it was fining the airline $630,000 for violating security rules at Frankfurt and

Heathrow airports. The fines included a $380,000 penalty for the mixup that allowed thirty-eight passengers to board Flight 103 at Heathrow without any security markings on their ticket coupons and a $40,000 penalty for the airline's failure to follow FAA rules after Jaswant Basuta's bags went on the flight even though he showed up too late to board.

Behind the scenes there were major reforms at the airline. Pan Am moved toward an El Al-style system of security and hired a firm operated by Arik Arad, El Al's former security director at Ben Gurion Airport in Tel Aviv, to train security personnel. The airline also hired a new corporate security director, Ray Mathias, a former FBI supervisor assigned to provide security at the North Atlantic Treaty Organization headquarters in Brussels.

The words *Flight 103* had become synonymous with disaster, so Pan Am did away with that flight designation. But the damage was already done. The Pan Am Corporation, already in financial trouble, posted a $63.5 million operating loss in 1988. The year after the bombing the corporation's losses rose to $306 million. In his 1989 message to shareholders, Pan Am Chairman Thomas Plaskett called the bombing "the principal cause" of the operating losses and said it had made the public reluctant to fly U.S. carriers.

Strapped for cash, Pan Am began to carve itself up and sell the pieces. It agreed to sell United Airlines its routes to Heathrow in 1990.

By early 1991 high fuel prices brought on by the Gulf War had compounded the airline's problems, and Pan Am entered Chapter Eleven bankruptcy, a status that allowed it to continue operating while it worked out a plan to pay creditors. But the airline's problems only continued to mount.

In August 1991 a bankruptcy judge approved a $1.39 billion deal to sell most of Pan Am's assets to Delta Airlines. Under the agreement Pan Am, once the flagship U.S. carrier around the globe, shriveled to a Miami-based operation with Latin American routes. But four months later that deal fell apart when Delta stopped providing Pan Am with cash to offset its losses. The end came on December 4, 1991, when Pan Am grounded its planes, ceased operations, and prepared to liquidate its assets.* Sixty-four years after it was founded, Pan American World Airways was dead.

THE BODY of Christopher Jones was returned to the United States on January 3, 1989, a year to the day after his sister's body had come home from Ecuador. On January 6, a year to the day after Jennifer's funeral,

---

* Meanwhile, civil lawsuits brought against the airline by about 200 relatives of the flight's victims continued to move toward a trial that is scheduled to begin in 1992 in Brooklyn before U.S. District Court judge Thomas C. Platt.

Christopher was buried. The brother and sister lie side by side in a cemetery in Rowley, Massachusetts, where they grew up.

Georgia Nucci realized within days of her son's death that the bombing of Flight 103 was going to be bad for her real estate business. People began to pull their listings from her and give them to other agents, figuring that she would not be able to give them the attention they expected from a real estate agent. She closed her office in the summer of 1989 and worked out of her house, then got out of the business altogether in the spring of 1990. Mrs. Nucci closed the firm partly because of the loss of business but also because she found she lacked the patience to put up with the minor headaches that were part of the trade. "I feel entitled not to be given a hard time. 'How dare you give me grief. I've suffered enough already.' It's how I feel. I know it's not rational. So I wasn't really suited to working. . . . I just didn't have the tolerance to deal with people's problems." Her husband continued to work, however, and they also had income from real estate investments Georgia Nucci had made.

Between the lost income from her real estate business and the cost of her participation in the relatives' organization, Mrs. Nucci estimates she lost or spent about thirty-five thousand dollars in the year following the crash. Her monthly telephone bill tripled, averaging about three hundred dollars, and every time she attended the organization's monthly meeting she incurred bills for transportation, motel rooms, and meals. Like every other member of the Ammerman group, she paid these expenses out of pocket.

Her home is in a rural section of New York State, and despite all the time and energy she put into the work of the relatives' organization, she soon found herself looking for something else to do. She wanted more children, but she was past the age when she could have her own. So she and her husband decided to adopt.

In the summer of 1990, while other relatives were attending the dedication of a Tundergarth memorial, Georgia and Tony Nucci were in Bogotá, Colombia, arranging to adopt four Colombian children. In August 1990 they made a second trip to South America, and when they came home, they were accompanied by a new family—two boys and two girls. Nataly, the youngest, was four years old. The two boys, Andrew and Marcus, were six and seven years old. The oldest child, Sandra, was ten. Mrs. Nucci had to guess at the ages because the children's mother had abandoned them and no one knew their exact birth dates. When she registered the children for school that fall, a school nurse told her the children needed birth dates to enroll in classes, so she made them up. She decided Nataly's birthday would be the same as her mother's, September 25. Sandra's would be the same as her grandmother's, November 25. Andrew, she decided, would celebrate his birthday on Bastille Day, July 14, and Marcus would celebrate his on August 15, the day of the Feast of the Assumption.

Georgia Nucci continued attending emotional support meetings sponsored by the relatives' group. The sessions she attended, typically held in a Holiday Inn in Kingston, New York, were led by a grief counselor who helped group members cope with the strong emotions that continued to trouble them two years after the bombing. Like Mrs. Nucci, many group members had been on medication to combat anxiety or depression. And most described the same feelings of alienation she had experienced. More than one person said they had taken offense when a friend described it as a crash, not a bombing. Many also said they had become angry with friends who avoided mentioning the names of their dead loved ones. The grief counselor taught participants ways of avoiding these kinds of confrontations, including reassuring friends that it was OK to talk about the victims of the attack. "Grieving people often cut off their friends, take offers of help the wrong way, get upset because friends don't bring up the names of their loved ones," Georgia Nucci said. "They don't realize that people aren't being malicious. They've just never been there before."

Early in 1991 she attended a meeting of the Ammerman group in Pittsburgh at which Scottish police offered to give relatives autopsy reports and photographs of their loved ones. She decided to look at the photographs of Christopher. The pictures showed someone she didn't recognize at first. Jones's skin was badly shredded, and his features had been distorted by the impact with the ground. As gruesome as the photographs were, however, his mother was glad she had looked at them. The severity of his injuries convinced her he could not have suffered long. Nonetheless, after leaving the Pittsburgh meeting, she again began having trouble sleeping. She resumed her use of Ativan, the antianxiety medication, but took the pills only occasionally.

More than two years after the bombing, Georgia Nucci continued to believe that the relatives' organization's most tangible accomplishment was its emotional support of people who had nothing else to rely upon. She also recognized the value of the group's work in Washington. "Have we saved anybody's life? I don't know about that. But I know that the next time there's a plane crash, people won't have to wait for fifteen hours for verification from the State Department."

Occasionally she has been reminded of her son in surprising ways. One day, while cleaning out his gray herringbone coat, which she planned to give to a relative, she felt something sharp in the pocket. She pulled out her hand and saw that she was holding several plastic ants, the kind Christopher Jones liked to slip into drinks at bars.

MAJOR CHARLES McKee left behind more than secret army files and shirts with size seventeen collars. He also left his collection of sand roses, which had fascinated him so much.

Beulah McKee gave the sand roses to friends and relatives. McKee's furniture, kept in storage during his overseas assignments, was shipped to Pennsylvania and gradually distributed among his relatives. Mrs. McKee took her son's king-size bed. A nephew took a dining-room table and chairs. Another relative who was a body builder took some of his weights.

Months after the bombing, Scottish authorities sent Mrs. McKee some of her son's personal belongings that had been recovered from the wreckage of the 747. Included in the package was a solid gold cross, suspended from a gold necklace. A note accompanying the item said McKee had been wearing the necklace at the time of his death. Mrs. McKee wears it all the time now, even when she sleeps.

"That's my closeness to my son," she said.

She also received fourteen hundred dollars in currency McKee had been carrying, some clothing, a gym bag, and a number of his canceled checks. McKee's car, which had been parked in Washington, D.C., was driven to Pennsylvania by Lieutenant Colonel Scott Tolman, McKee's friend and former colleague. The family sold it. Most of the Christmas gifts the family had purchased for McKee were given to other relatives.

McKee's room at his mother's house in Trafford became a repository for the awards and mementos he had collected in his eighteen-year military career. Mrs. McKee bought a bookshelf to display some of them. On the top shelf she placed his Purple Heart, his Legion of Merit citation, and a photograph of him being promoted to major. On another shelf she placed the mugs he bought whenever he traveled abroad. In a cupboard she stored the green beret he wore as a member of the army's Special Forces.

Mrs. McKee was upset by the allegations in the Interfor report that suggested her son was working for the CIA while the intelligence agency had unknowingly helped the terrorists get the bomb on the plane. "I had this feeling when I attended the first meetings of the relatives' organization that these people looked at me out of the corner of their eye, as though Chuck had a role in getting the bomb on board," she said. "I had a very uneasy feeling, and I didn't appreciate having that feeling because I didn't see that he had any role in this at all. . . . It was awfully hard any time that I thought anything about it."

Her son's death has diminished her faith in the government. Never one to get excited about politics, Mrs. McKee found herself furious when President Bush began making overtures to Syrian President Assad, whose support was crucial to the coalition that waged war against Iraq. "When I saw him on the television, sitting next to Assad, I said to my daughter, 'That dirty S of a B. Here he is sitting with that guy who we know took more lives than were lost in the whole war.' They were grinning, just like they were having a great time. It angered and aggravated me." Her fear, she said, is that in their desire to forge a Middle East peace, leaders of the United States will backtrack on their efforts to find those who blew up her son's plane.

She has grown lonely in her old age, and McKee's death has added to her sense of isolation. Some days the only person she sees is her daughter Marjorie, with whom she still lives. "I accomplish nothing. I have no purpose it seems. There are days when it seems it doesn't matter that much whether I'm here or not. I'm not making much of an impact. My kids are all raised; they're off on their own. I get up in the morning, I do the regular household chores, but I don't participate too much in anything. . . . It just doesn't seem fair that Chuck should be gone, and I'm still here. Sometimes I think, *What am I living for?* It was great when my kids were all growing up, but that's long gone."

She continued to be thankful that her son decided to call home the night before his flight. She continued to wish she had not let him hang up so soon.

The philodendron McKee bought for his wife after the birth of their daughter sprouted more than a dozen healthy shoots and grew to about two feet tall. Mrs. McKee has never had much luck growing plants, but Chuck McKee's philodendron thrived in a wicker basket next to a window.

GEORDIE WILLIAMS left behind a lot of friends, and many of them made it a point to be with his parents as often as they could. His wake at a bar called the Horse You Came in On was so crowded the fire marshal showed up.

The summer after the funeral, the Williams and McIlmail families visited Scotland with Williams's friends Duane Tudahl and Bob DeFrank. The group went to Lockerbie to see where he had died.

During the trip Tudahl and DeFrank went into the property warehouse where authorities stored the unclaimed contents of the 747. Geordie's mom wanted to recover one of her son's jackets but could not bring herself to enter the room. As he walked in the door, DeFrank was struck by the room's odor. It was a powerful smell he could not describe, and for a moment he became so weakened he was unable to walk. For the first time he felt the death of all 270 victims, not just his friend's, and he thought about how many families had suffered after the bombing. As they walked through the aisles lined with belongings, Tudahl called out to DeFrank, who turned to see Tudahl standing motionless, staring at a pair of sneakers. There was no doubt that they were Geordie Williams's, red high-topped Keds, the ones they all had called Geordie's clown shoes. Tudahl had badly wanted to find something of his friend's, and now that he had succeeded, he wished he hadn't. He began to cry.

Williams's girlfriend in Germany, Lisa Moffatt, never knew any of his family or friends while he was alive. So no one told her of his death. After he had left her apartment on the morning of December 21, she assumed he had made it home to Maryland. She had heard about the crash of Flight 103 and panicked momentarily but quickly reassured herself that he was not on a flight to New York City. There were no lists of victims printed in any of the newspapers she saw in Germany. When she returned to her dormitory after New Year's, she found a postcard in her mailbox.

It was a picture of a plane taking off into the sunset at Frankfurt International Airport. At the bottom, Williams had drawn a tiny stick figure holding a bag in one arm and waving with the other toward the plane, yelling, "Hey, Wait!" On the back, he explained that he had arrived at the airport late and missed the flight. "That's my plane leaving me behind. You made me miss my plane. I got one out at 4:50 P.M. though. We could have laid in bed until 3:15." Moffatt laughed at his artwork, still not knowing which flight he had taken. She had been expecting him to call, and as the days passed and the call never came, she caught herself visualizing his name on Flight 103's passenger list. She called his phone number in Germany and listened to endless ringing. Finally, on Friday, January 13— more than three weeks after the bombing—she got up early, went to NATO headquarters in Heidelberg and asked if it had a list of Pan Am 103 passengers. She was rudely received, but finally a secretary produced a copy of an *Army Times* story headlined IT WAS NOT TO BE. Lisa Moffatt looked down and a grinning picture of Geordie Williams looked back. She kept her composure long enough to ask for a photocopy. She did not have any pictures of Williams.

About ten days later she began composing a letter to Williams's parents. She was nervous about making her first contact with them and rewrote the letter several times. She even sent it to her own parents to read before gathering up the nerve to mail it. In the letter she introduced herself and told Williams's parents about the kinds of things she and he had done in the fall of 1988.

Eventually Lisa Moffatt moved back to California and went to work as an airline reservations agent for Lufthansa. During the Gulf War she took a call from an Arabic-sounding man who threatened the airline. She also heard a tape of a second call in which a different man, who specifically mentioned Pan Am 103, threatened to blow up a plane. She found herself wishing Geordie Williams had died in a car crash or train wreck so she would not have to relive his death on the job.

She finally met his parents when they made a trip to the West Coast, joining them for dinner in San Diego. The night before, she worried so much about what to say that she hardly slept, but to her relief she found his parents were able to put her at ease. Mr. Williams rented a horse and buggy after dinner, and the three of them toured the old section of the city. Soon she felt comfortable enough to ask questions about Lockerbie and how Williams's body was found.

As they were saying good-bye in a parking lot, Williams's dad confessed to Lisa that he had secretly wished she had become pregnant with his son's child. She had not, and she really did not know what to say to this man whose only child was now dead, so she said good-bye and left. But she, too, had wondered after Williams's death if she had been carrying his child. She had even discussed the possibility with her closest friends. At twenty-two an unplanned pregnancy could have disrupted her life. She had no idea what she would have done, but over the months that followed she found herself thinking about it, a lot.

JASWANT BASUTA remained in London for five days after being turned away at the Flight 103 boarding gate. The day after Christmas he flew home on Pan Am. He had been so shaken up by the events of December 21 that he hadn't noticed, at Heathrow, that the Pan Am agent he spoke with before he was taken into police custody had booked him on another flight to New York for the following day. After he had not shown up for the December 22 flight, London police paid Basuta another visit. They left after questioning him briefly.

Basuta's experience at Heathrow Airport left him with invisible scars. Sometimes he woke up in the middle of the night and sat up for hours, unable to get back to sleep.

Several weeks after coming home, Basuta called Pan Am in New York

City to make a claim for his baggage. His two suitcases had been loaded with gifts, purchased both by him and by other relatives in England and intended for his family and friends. For his daughter he had been carrying two expensive bottles of perfume, a dozen Punjabi suits, several sweaters, and a twenty-four-karat gold birthday ring. For his son he was carrying home two three-piece suits, several dress shirts and sweaters, dress shoes, and a leather jacket. Basuta said the Pan Am agent he spoke with told him he had waited too long to file his claim, that he should have done it the day he arrived home. Basuta thought of hiring a lawyer to pursue his claim but decided that would be too expensive. Two years after the bombing of Flight 103, Basuta had received no compensation for his lost luggage.

On a Friday morning in February, about two months after the crash, Basuta and his family went to a Sikh temple in New York City. Just as she had promised when she looked at the image of the prophet on her kitchen wall clock, Surinder Basuta had arranged for a Sikh priest to perform a forty-eight-hour prayer ceremony. From 10:00 A.M. that day until 10:00 A.M. Sunday, the Basutas prayed together at the temple, thanking God for sparing Jaswant's life and praying for the souls of the 270 crash victims.

Sometimes when Surinder Basuta recalled how close her husband came to boarding the plane that night, her mind's eye conjured up the image of a plane door. On one side of the door was death; on the other, life. She imagined her husband walking toward the door, then stopping and turning around. "It's like someone pulled him back," she said.

BERT AMMERMAN told people the death of his brother and the subsequent struggle to reform aviation security changed his whole attitude toward life. He still valued his job as a high school principal, but his perspective of professional life took on a new focus. Nothing was as serious as it had once seemed. No matter how pressing an issue seemed at work, he realized it was not going to bring about the end of the world. When a meeting of his peers became so heated that people sounded as if the fate of the entire educational system hung in the balance, he would smile to himself and think, *You people don't know what tragedy is or what issues are.*

The passage of the Aviation Security Improvement Act, although it omitted some of the improvements he would have liked, helped restore his faith in a system that had turned him into a cynic. When he met with young people, the message he preached was that the structure of the U.S. government ultimately allows for reform even if those in power resist it as long as the reformers work hard enough.

"The biggest lesson I've learned from this is you as a citizen in this country can make a difference," he said. "If you have the persistence, if you have the commitment and the belief that something has to be corrected, you can make the difference."

During the struggle Ammerman's visibility had increased until his name became virtually synonymous with the relatives' movement. The irony of Bert's involvement was that it severed the bond with his brother's widow, Carolyn. As he assumed a higher and higher profile through the relatives' lobbying efforts, Carolyn Ammerman distanced herself from her brother-in-law's work. Once she got her brother to call Ammerman and ask him to end his involvement, apparently so the name Ammerman would not appear as a painful reminder in so many newspaper and television stories. Ammerman told her brother he respected her wishes, but he refused to stop.

"She has to respect the way I want to do it," he said. "I would never intrude on what she wants, and she should not intrude on what I want." Partly in deference to his sister-in-law, he never appeared in public with a picture of his brother pinned to his chest—a practice followed by many other relatives—and he never mentioned the names of his brother and other members of Tom's family unless he was asked about them.

When Ammerman returned to Lockerbie months after the bombing, townspeople told him to give their best to his sister-in-law. Carolyn Ammerman had traveled to Lockerbie with him in the wake of the bombing, and she had spent much of her time in a kitchen, working with the volunteers who prepared meals for the searchers. She put in long days, often working from 9:00 in the morning until about 8:00 or 9:00 P.M., and people in Lockerbie remembered her. Ammerman did not tell them he and his sister-in-law no longer spoke to each other.

More than two years after the bombing he still had no contact with her. "If I don't deal with her and don't see her, it doesn't bother me," Ammerman said. "We have never spoken, and I doubt very much we ever will."

KAREN HUNT'S family began to suspect something was wrong the moment her body came home from Lockerbie. The body was dressed in a scarf and wore a silver bracelet and a ring. Hunt never wore a scarf, and no one recognized the description of the jewelry. When her parents asked the county medical examiner's office in Rochester, New York, to look at the body, forensic experts quickly told Robert and Peggy Hunt their suspicions were justified. Authorities in Scotland had transposed name tags during the identification process and had sent the Hunts the wrong body.

The Hunts learned of the mistake on January 7, 1989, which would have been their daughter's twenty-first birthday. FBI agents frantically began searching for her body, suspecting it was about to be buried or cremated by another family. The next day, they found it. The family of Mary Alice Lincoln Johnson was within an hour of burying Karen Hunt's body at a cemetery in suburban Boston when two FBI agents showed up at their door. Johnson, a twenty-five-year-old graduate of Brown University, had been killed while coming home after more than a year of travel and teaching in the Far East. Johnson's body was the one that had been erroneously sent to the Hunts in Rochester.

In the weeks that followed Hunt's death her boyfriend, Mark Esposito, began painting a portrait of her. "It's my therapy," he said. He worked on the painting for months, returning to it after classes or between gymnastics practice.

Scottish authorities returned some of Hunt's belongings several months after the attack. A teapot she had bought for her mother as a Christmas present was intact, except for its lid. A Lockerbie woman who sorted out the passengers' belongings marveled at how something so fragile survived a fall of six miles. The delicate anklet Robyn Hunt had made for her at summer camp was returned to the family, too.

It was in pieces.

MARION ALDERMAN decided to keep Theodore, the cat that her daughter Paula had left in her care. "I couldn't part with him now," Mrs. Alderman said.

Paula and Glenn Bouckley were buried on a hillside in the village of Sowerby Bridge in England, near his parents' house. The cemetery is close to a field where the Bouckleys used to let their dog run. The burial service was performed by the same minister who had married the couple.

It took time for Marion Alderman to adjust to the absence of her daughter and son-in-law. Not long after the bombing, at a family gathering at another daughter's house in suburban Buffalo, Marion Alderman looked around the dinner table and could not get over the feeling that someone was missing. In the year preceding the Bouckleys' death, Mrs. Alderman's husband and mother-in-law had died, too.

"Well, now this is us. Times are changing," she finally said.

Marion Alderman found herself alone in a rambling house. One day during a trip to the local hair salon, she met a woman who was hosting a group of foreign exchange students from Europe. Mrs. Alderman thought of the four bedrooms in her house and got in touch with the program's administrators, who arranged to have two students from West Germany and Spain come to stay with her and to study in the local high school. Those two students were joined later by teenagers from Switzerland and Lockerbie. The Lockerbie youth, seventeen-year-old Peter Blumenthal, came to live with Mrs. Alderman after she had written to the U.S. State Department to ask if there were any youths from Lockerbie who wanted to study in the United States.

Blumenthal had been at home the night Flight 103 fell from the sky, and he had assisted in the recovery efforts. He and Mrs. Alderman rarely talked about the bombing. "I didn't bring him over here to tell me all about it," she said. "He's here to have a good time."

Mrs. Alderman did not forget about good times either. Before her daughter and son-in-law were killed, she had begun taking flying lessons. She stopped the lessons afterward but then resumed them after realizing they helped her forget her loneliness. About a year and a half after the destruction of Flight 103, Marion Alderman climbed into the cockpit of a Cessna airplane and took her first solo flight.

In October 1990, after visiting the graves of her daughter and son-in-law, Mrs. Alderman traveled to Lockerbie. There she and Ed Jablonski, a man from Rome, New York, whom she had met ten weeks before while taking a pair of shoes into a repair shop, were married by the Reverend Alan Neal at All Saints Church.

NAZIR JAAFAR told his wife she would have to unpack his son's luggage when Scottish authorities sent it home to Dearborn, Michigan. He lacked the strength to confront the belongings Khalid Jaafar had carried with him on the last day of his life.

All those killed in the Flight 103 bombing had been mourned by their relatives, but the death of Khalid Jaafar had been particularly painful for his family. News accounts repeatedly identified Khalid as a drug courier, or mule, who had unwittingly carried the bomb on board the flight, compounding the family's grief with anger.

"I feel I am being persecuted," Jaafar said. "Somebody killed my son, and somebody is trying to kill my family. There's a kind of political Mafia behind this story."

Several newspapers and a book reported that Khalid Jaafar's bag had contained the bomb that destroyed the flight. His father dismissed those reports, saying his son—a quiet, shy boy who had a strong sense of responsibility toward his family—had nothing to do with terrorists and bombs. Khalid was being singled out, he said, because he was of Lebanese descent. As evidence of his son's innocence, Nazir Jaafar pointed out that when Khalid left the United States, he carried his clothing and other belongings in two duffel bags. Both bags had been recovered intact from Lockerbie.

Still, the reports persisted. Interfor identified Jaafar as the bomb courier in its report to Pan Am's insurance carrier. And in late 1990 a former Drug Enforcement Administration informant named Lester K. Coleman III claimed he had met with Khalid Jaafar three times in Cyprus prior to the bombing. Jaafar, Coleman said, was helping the DEA infiltrate heroin trafficking from the Bekaa Valley into Detroit. Coleman claimed that terrorists who infiltrated the DEA operation apparently took advantage of the protected drug route to smuggle a bomb on board Flight 103.

The drug courier scenario attracted intense media attention after two American television networks had reported that the DEA was conducting an internal probe to determine if any undercover operations were connected to Flight 103. Later the government said its investigation showed there were no DEA operations involving Pan Am at the time of the bombing. Soon after those reports Scottish police publicly revealed that they had checked both of Jaafar's bags for traces of drugs and explosive damage and had found neither.

On the second anniversary of the attack on the flight Jaafar's father held a press conference in Dearborn, to defend his son's name. "I brought my family here to escape the violence in the Middle East," he said. "Now my son is still a victim of that violence, but they still want to count him with those that did this instead of the victims." Earlier he had said his anger at the reports linking his son to the bomb was surpassed only by his fury at those responsible for the murders. "I say hit him! Hit him. Wherever he is, hit him! It's the minimum reward for our sorrow, our loss."

In accordance with the Hindu religion, the bodies of three-year-old Suruchi Rattan, her two-year-old brother, Anmol, their mother, Garima, and Garima's parents, Om and Shanti Dixit, were cremated.

Several weeks after his wife and two children had been killed, Shachi Rattan took their ashes to Kankhal, a sacred spot in northern India. After performing a religious ritual, he scattered the ashes in the Ganges River. Relatives of Om and Shanti Dixit made a similar trip to the river to scatter their ashes.

Shachi Rattan moved to Dayton, Ohio, settling into private practice as an intensive care specialist. About a year after the Flight 103 bombing he remarried.

His brother-in-law Sudhakar Dixit decided to leave Cleveland and finish his physician's residency someplace else. In the spring of 1990 he enlisted in the U.S. Air Force and was commissioned as a captain. He and his wife, Sandhya, moved to Travis Air Force Base in California, where he became a resident at the base hospital.

Dixit hoped that by immersing himself in his work, he could forget about the attack, and to some extent he was successful. But on the first and second anniversaries of the bombing he was unable to think clearly at the hospital and decided to take time off. On both of those occasions he spent the day with family members.

Dixit never became active with either of the relatives' organizations, although he received their newsletters. "I support what the organization is doing, and I agree with what they are doing, but I haven't devoted my life to it, as some of the other members have," he said.

The terrorist attack on Flight 103 occurred when Dixit was twenty-six years old, and it left him the sole surviving member of what had once been a family of five. His older brother, Prabhakar, had been killed in 1974 by a tornado that destroyed the family's home in Xenia, Ohio. For many months he was filled with grief and sadness, but eventually those feelings left him. "As time goes on, you begin to filter them out and you're left with pleasant memories. . . . Time heals all, it really does." Fourteen months after the bombing, his wife gave birth to a son, Pranav. In March 1991 the couple had a second son, Anuj.

WITH THE passage of the Aviation Security Improvement Act of 1990, members of both relatives' groups began to see reduced roles for their organizations. Some leaders of Ammerman's group kept monitoring the investigation and vowed to make sure security reforms were implemented, but they also acknowledged a need to return their own lives to normality as best they could.

Paul Hudson also began to see an end to the work he and his wife had devoted themselves to for more than two years. He had poured most of his energies into the Washington lobbying effort, and his real estate business and personal life had suffered. In addition, Hudson realized he had put off some of the mourning he wanted to do for his daughter. "I feel there are a lot of things I should have done in 1989 or 1990 that I'm not going to be able to do until this year or even later," he said more than two years after the attack. "I took time away from my other children, which I would rather not have done, but they've bounced back pretty well."

When his relatives' organization was at its most active, Hudson spent thirty to sixty hours a week working on Flight 103 business. By the middle of 1991 he was devoting fewer than ten hours a week to the effort. His organization scaled back its meetings, gathering only two or three times a year and publishing newsletters only sporadically. As the major deadlines for compliance with provisions of the aviation security law were met, his time spent on Flight 103 matters dwindled even more.

The success of the relatives' lobbying effort did little to improve his faith in those who regulate air travel. "The system worked," Hudson said, "but we had to pull it uphill, and the wheels squeaked the whole way. If the only way to get significant changes is to kill hundreds of innocent people, obviously that is not a good way to operate. And people are dying all the time in terrorist acts, and basically, as I found out afterwards, no one is caring what happens to them and making sure it doesn't happen again."

Eleanor Hudson continued to struggle with her daughter's death, often on a daily basis. For close to two years she could not bring herself to look in the eye any young girl who was Melina's age. And she was unable to bring herself to respond to the letters she had received from Melina's best friend, who was growing into a young woman.

Slowly Mrs. Hudson made strides toward recovery. She had been a substitute teacher before Melina was killed, and two years after the attack she went back to the classroom for the first time. She also began to accompany her son Paul Joseph to Little League games.

Occasionally she asked herself when she and her husband would resume a normal social life. "We don't go out with other couples anymore; we just go to school functions," she said. At the suggestion of friends she tried getting help from a counselor, but she found the experience unsatisfying. "I felt like I was talking to a news reporter. Because truthfully, how many people have experienced the kind of trauma we've gone through?"

From time to time she continued to have difficulty explaining herself to strangers. When she and her husband took a vacation to the Bahamas late in 1990 with their two youngest sons, a flight attendant tried to guide them to four seats that were not adjacent. Eleanor Hudson told the attendant she wanted four seats together, so that if the plane crashed, she and her family would die side by side. "She looked at me kind of funny after that," Mrs. Hudson recalled. "I think she was kind of frightened. She didn't know what had happened to Melina, but I felt like saying, 'How dare you not know?' I finally told her the reason I was so concerned was because I had a daughter who died on a plane."

At other times Eleanor Hudson found herself overwhelmed by the kindness of strangers. Not long after the bombing a Scottish shepherd, Alistair Paterson, found in one of his pastures Melina's passport, which had blown miles away from her body. He turned it over to authorities and noted that her birthday was January 24. On that date—the day Melina Hudson would have turned seventeen—Paterson and his wife, Elizabeth, made a special trip to the town hall in Lockerbie, carrying a pot of snowdrops they had dug from the lawn of their farm seven miles east of the village. They left the flowers there in Melina's memory, then wrote to the Hudsons to let them know they had been thinking of their daughter.

Many of Melina Hudson's belongings eventually came home, including a button that said "I am 21," a thick study guide to the Scholastic Aptitude Test, the Billy Joel album friends had autographed at her going-away party, and the gold ring her parents had given her, the one with the name Melina inscribed on the inside of the band. The record album was shattered. And in the center of the SAT study guide, some violent force had punched a jagged hole.

The night before prosecutors in the United States and Great Britain announced charges against the two Libyans, Eleanor Hudson imagined herself looking at photographs of the two men accused of killing her daughter and felt a chill run down her back. "It's like seeing evil brought in front of you," she said. "What do you say when you're confronted by that kind of evil?" She mentioned the impending charges to her twelve-year-old son, Paul Joseph.

"They're going to know for sure who put the bomb on the plane," she said.

"What do you mean?" Paul Joseph said, turning to see his mother's face.

"The person who killed Melina."

The Hudsons continue to celebrate their daughter's birthday. Every year on January 24 they gather in the cold at a government plaza near their home and release sixteen helium-filled pink balloons into the air, one for every year of her life. Then they watch as the balloons float up and out of sight into the Albany sky. Each of the balloons contains a message, written by Melina's youngest brother, David.

"Today is Melina's birthday. She died on Pan Am 103. She was 16 years old. We love her very much."

THE VICTIMS OF PAN AMERICAN WORLD AIRWAYS FLIGHT 103

Cockpit Crew

CAPTAIN: JAMES BRUCE MACQUARRIE, 55, Kensington, New Hampshire, American
FIRST OFFICER: RAYMOND RONALD WAGNER, 52, Pennington, New Jersey, American
FLIGHT ENGINEER: JERRY DON AVRITT, 46, Westminster, California, American

Pursers

MARY GERALDINE MURPHY, 51, Middlesex, England, British
MILUTIN VELIMIROVICH, 35, Middlesex, England, American

Flight Attendants

ELISABETH NICHOLE AVOYNE, 44, Croissy-sur-Seine, France, French
NOELLE LYDIE BERTI, 40, Paris, France, American
SIV ULLA ENGSTROM, 51, Berkshire, England, Swedish
STACIE DENISE FRANKLIN, 20, San Diego, California, American
PAUL ISAAC GARRETT, 41, Napa, California, American
ELKE ETHA KUEHNE, 43, Hannover, West Germany, West German

MARÍA NIEVES LARRACOECHEA, 39, Madrid, Spain, Spanish
LILIBETH TOBILA MCALOLOOY, 27, Kelsterbach, West Germany, American
JOCELYN REINA, 26, Isleworth, England, American
MYRA JOSEPHINE ROYAL, 30, London, England, American
IRJA SYHNOVE SKABO, 38, Oslo, Norway, American

Passengers

JOHN MICHAEL GERARD AHERN, bond broker, 26, Rockville Centre, New York, American
SARAH MARGARET AICHER, playwright, 29, London, England, American
JOHN DAVID AKERSTROM, 34, Medina, Ohio, American
RONALD ELY ALEXANDER, businessman, 46, New York, New York, Swiss
THOMAS JOSEPH AMMERMAN, marketing manager, 36, Old Tappan, New Jersey, American
MARTIN LEWIS APFELBAUM, stamp dealer, 59, Philadelphia, Pennsylvania, American
RACHEL MARIE ASRELSKY, student, 21, New York, New York, American
JUDITH ELLEN ATKINSON, art historian and consultant, 37, London, England, American
WILLIAM GARRETSON ATKINSON III, engineer, 33, London, England, American
CLARE LOUISE BACCIOCHI, hair stylist, 19, Warwickshire, England, British
HARRY MICHAEL BAINBRIDGE, attorney, 34, Montrose, New York, American
STUART MURRAY BARCLAY, businessman, 29, Barnard, Vermont, Canadian
JEAN MARY BELL, 44, Berkshire, England, British
JULIAN MACBAIN BENELLO, student, 25, Brookline, Massachusetts, American
LAWRENCE RAY BENNETT, pharmaceutical chemist, 41, Chelsea, Michigan, American
PHILIP BERGSTROM, army sergeant, 22, Forest Lake, Minnesota, American
ALISTAIR DAVID BERKLEY, law professor, 29, London, England, American
MICHAEL STUART BERNSTEIN, lawyer, Justice Department, Office of Special Investigation, 36, Bethesda, Maryland, American
STEVEN RUSSELL BERRELL, student, 20, Fargo, North Dakota, American
SURINDER MOHAN BHATIA, businessman, 51, Los Angeles, California, American
KENNETH JOHN BISSETT, student, 21, Hartsdale, New York, American
DIANE ANNE BOATMAN-FULLER, playwright, 35, London, England, American
STEPHEN JOHN BOLAND, student, 20, Nashua, New Hampshire, American
GLENN JOHN BOUCKLEY, salesman, 27, Liverpool, New York, British

PAULA BOUCKLEY, cashier, 29, Liverpool, New York, American
NICOLE ELISE BOULANGER, student, 21, Shrewsbury, Massachusetts, American
FRANCIS BOYER, 43, Toulosane, France, French
NICHOLAS BRIGHT, businessman, 32, Brookline, Massachusetts, American
DANIEL SOLOMON BROWNER (BIER), 23, Parod, Israel, Israeli
COLLEEN RENEE BRUNNER, student, 20, Hamburg, New York, American
TIMOTHY GUY BURMAN, banker, 24, London, England, British
MICHAEL WARREN BUSER, advertising executive, 34, Ridgefield Park, New Jersey, American
WARREN MAX BUSER, civil engineer, 62, Glen Rock, New Jersey, American
STEVEN LEE BUTLER, teacher, 35, Denver, Colorado, American
WILLIAM MARTIN CADMAN, musician, 32, London, England, British
FABIANA CAFFARONE, 28, London, England, British
HERNAN CAFFARONE, 28, London, England, Argentinean
VALERIE CANADY, auditor, 25, Morgantown, West Virginia, American
GREGORY CAPASSO, student, 21, Brooklyn, New York, American
TIMOTHY MICHAEL CARDWELL, student, 21, Cresco, Pennsylvania, American
BERNT WILSON CARLSSON, diplomat, 50, New York, New York, Swedish
RICHARD ANTHONY CAWLEY, businessman, 43, New York, New York, American
FRANK CIULLA, banker, 45, Park Ridge, New Jersey, American
THEODORA EUGENIA COHEN, student, 20, Port Jervis, New York, American
ERIC MICHAEL COKER, student, 20, Mendham, New Jersey, American
JASON MICHAEL COKER, student, 20, Mendham, New Jersey, American
GARY LEONARD COLASANTI, student, 20, Melrose, Massachusetts, American
BRIDGET CONCANNON, 53, Oxfordshire, England, Irish
SEAN CONCANNON, 16, Oxfordshire, England, British
THOMAS CONCANNON, 51, Oxfordshire, England, Irish
TRACEY JANE CORNER, 17, Sheffield, England, British
SCOTT CORY, student, 20, Old Lyme, Connecticut, American
WILLIS LARRY COURSEY, army sergeant, 40, San Antonio, Texas, American
PATRICIA MARY COYLE, student, 20, Wallingford, Connecticut, American
JOHN BINNING CUMMOCK, 38, Coral Gables, Florida, American
JOSEPH PATRICK CURRY, army captain, 31, Fort Devens, Massachusetts, American
WILLIAM ALLAN DANIELS, research chemist, 40, Belle Mead, New Jersey, American
GRETCHEN JOYCE DATER, student, 20, Ramsey, New Jersey, American
SHANNON DAVIS, student, 19, Shelton, Connecticut, American
GABRIEL DELLA-RIPA, Pan Am employee, 46, Floral Park, New York, Italian

JOYCE CHRISTINE DIMAURO, marketing director, 32, New York, New York, American
GIANFRANCA DINARDO, 26, London, England, Italian
PETER THOMAS STANLEY DIX, management consultant, 35, London, England, Irish
OM DIXIT, college professor, 54, Fairborn, Ohio, Indian
SHANTI DIXIT, 54, Fairborn, Ohio, American
DAVID SCOTT DORNSTEIN, student, 25, Philadelphia, Pennsylvania, American
MICHAEL JOSEPH DOYLE, accountant, 30, Voorhees, New Jersey, American
EDGAR HOWARD EGGLESTON III, air force sergeant, 24, Glens Falls, New York, American
TURHAN ERGIN, student, 22, West Hartford, Connecticut, American
CHARLES THOMAS FISHER IV, banker, 34, London, England, American
CLAYTON LEE FLICK, businessman, 25, Coventry, England, British
JOHN PATRICK FLYNN, student, 21, Montville, New Jersey, American
ARTHUR FONDILER, attorney, 33, West Armonk, New York, American
ROBERT GERARD FORTUNE, insurance executive, 40, Jackson Heights, New York, American
PAUL MATTHEW STEPHEN FREEMAN, 25, London, England, Canadian
JAMES RALPH FULLER, corporate vice president, 50, Bloomfield Hills, Michigan, American
IBOLYA R. GABOR, 79, Budapest, Hungary, Hungarian
AMY BETH GALLAGHER, student, 22, Point Claire, Quebec, Canada, American
MATTHEW KEVIN GANNON, foreign service officer, 34, Los Angeles, California, American
KENNETH RAYMOND GARCZYNSKI, industrial engineer, 37, North Brunswick, New Jersey, American
KENNETH JAMES GIBSON, army specialist four, 20, Romulus, Michigan, American
WILLIAM DAVID GIEBLER, bond broker, 29, London, England, American
OLIVE LEONORA GORDON, 25, London, England, British
LINDA SUSAN GORDON-GORGACZ, 39, London, England, American
ANNE MADELENE GORGACZ, 76, New Castle, Pennsylvania, American
LORETTA ANNE GORGACZ, 47, New Castle, Pennsylvania, American
DAVID J. GOULD, college professor, 45, Pittsburgh, Pennsylvania, American
ANDRE NIKOLAI GUEVORGIAN, businessman, 32, Sea Cliff, New York, American
NICOLA JANE HALL, 23, Sandton, South Africa, South African
LORRAINE FRANCES HALSCH, special education teacher, 31, Fairport, New York, American
LYNNE CAROL HARTUNIAN, student, 21, Schenectady, New York, American

ANTHONY LACEY HAWKINS, businessman, 57, Brooklyn, New York, British

PAMELA ELAINE HERBERT, student, 19, Battle Creek, Michigan, American

RODNEY PETER HILBERT, 40, Newton, Pennsylvania, American

ALFRED HILL, 29, Sonthofen, West Germany, West German

KATHERINE AUGUSTA HOLLISTER, student, 20, Rego Park, New York, American

JOSEPHINE LISA HUDSON, nurse, 22, London, England, British

MELINA KRISTINA HUDSON, student, 16, Albany, New York, American

SOPHIE AILETTE MIRIAM HUDSON, 26, Paris, France, French

KAREN LEE HUNT, student, 20, Webster, New York, American

ROGER ELWOOD HURST, marketing manager, 38, Ringwood, New Jersey, American

ELIZABETH SOPHIE IVELL, dog handler, 19, East Sussex, England, British

KHALID NAZIR JAAFAR, student, 20, Dearborn, Michigan, American

ROBERT VAN HOUTEN JECK, 57, Mountain Lakes, New Jersey, American

PAUL AVRON JEFFREYS, musician, 36, Surrey, England, British

RACHEL JEFFREYS, advertising executive, 23, Surrey, England, British

KATHLEEN MARY JERMYN, student, 20, Staten Island, New York, American

BETH ANN JOHNSON, student, 21, Greensburg, Pennsylvania, American

MARY ALICE LINCOLN JOHNSON, 25, Wayland, Massachusetts, American

TIMOTHY BARON JOHNSON, student, 21, Neptune, New Jersey, American

CHRISTOPHER ANDREW JONES, student, 20, Claverack, New York, American

JULIANNE FRANCES KELLY, student, 20, Dedham, Massachusetts, American

JAY JOSEPH KINGHAM, pharmaceuticals executive, 44, Potomac, Maryland, American

PATRICIA ANN KLEIN, social worker, 35, Trenton, New Jersey, American

GREGORY KOSMOWSKI, marketing executive, 40, Milford, Michigan, American

MINAS CHRISTOPHER KULUKUNDIS, ship brokerage director, 38, London, England, British

RONALD ALBERT LARIVIERE, 33, Alexandria, Virginia, American

ROBERT MILTON LECKBURG, engineer, 30, Piscataway, New Jersey, American

WILLIAM CHASE LEYRER, businessman, 46, Bay Shore, New York, American

WENDY ANNE LINCOLN, student, 23, North Adams, Massachusetts, American

ALEXANDER SILAS LOWENSTEIN, student, 21, Morristown, New Jersey, American

LLOYD DAVID LUDLOW, army sergeant first class, 41, Macksville, Kansas, American

MARIA THERESIA LURBKE, 25, Balve Beckum, West Germany, West German

WILLIAM EDWARD MACK, puppeteer, 30, New York, New York, American

DOUGLAS EUGENE MALICOTE, army specialist four, 22, Lebanon, Ohio, American

WENDY GAY MALICOTE, 21, Lebanon, Ohio, American

ELIZABETH LILLIAN MAREK, actress and peace activist, 30, New York, New York, American

LOUIS ANTHONY MARENGO, marketing director, 33, Rochester, Michigan, American

NOEL GEORGE MARTIN, 27, Clapton, England, Jamaican

DIANE MARIE MASLOWSKI, currency trader, 30, New York, New York, American

WILLIAM JOHN MCALLISTER, 26, Middlesex, England, British

DANIEL EMMET MCCARTHY, banker, 31, Brooklyn, New York, American

ROBERT EUGENE MCCOLLUM, university professor, 61, Wayne, Pennsylvania, American

CHARLES DENNIS MCKEE, army major, 40, Arlington Hall Station, Virginia, American

BERNARD JOSEPH MCLAUGHLIN, marketing manager, 30, Cranston, Rhode Island, American

JANE SUSAN MELBER, musician and teacher, 27, Middlesex, England, American

JOHN MERRILL, seaman, 35, Hertfordshire, England, British

SUZANNE MARIE MIAZGA, student, 22, Marcy, New York, American

JOSEPH KENNETH MILLER, accounting firm executive, 56, Woodmere, New York, American

JEWEL COURTNEY MITCHELL, army second lieutenant, 32, Brooklyn, New York, American

RICHARD PAUL MONETTI, student, 20, Cherry Hill, New Jersey, American

JANE ANN MORGAN, attorney, 37, London, England, American

EVA INGEBORG MORSON, 48, New York, New York, American

HELGA RACHAEL MOSEY, student, 19, West Midlands, England, British

INGRID ELIZABETH MULROY, 25, Lund, Sweden, Swedish

JOHN MULROY, journalist, 59, East Northport, New York, American

SEAN KEVIN MULROY, 25, Lund, Sweden, American

KAREN ELIZABETH NOONAN, student, 20, Potomac, Maryland, American

DANIEL EMMETT O'CONNOR, U.S. Diplomatic Service, 31, Dorchester, Massachusetts, American

MARY DENICE O'NEILL, student, 21, Bronx, New York, American

ANNE LINDSEY OTENASEK, student, 21, Baltimore, Maryland, American

BRYONY ELISE OWEN, 18 months, Bristol, England, British
GWYNETH YVONNE MARGARET OWEN, student, 29, Bristol, England, British
LAURA ABIGAIL OWENS, 8, Cherry Hill, New Jersey, British
MARTHA OWENS, 44, Cherry Hill, New Jersey, American
ROBERT PLACK OWENS, 45, Cherry Hill, New Jersey, American
SARAH REBECCA OWENS, 14, Cherry Hill, New Jersey, American
ROBERT ITALO PAGNUCCO, attorney, 51, South Salem, New York, American
CHRISTOS M. PAPADOPOULOS, 45, North Lawrence, New York, American
PETER RAYMOND PEIRCE, architect and student, 40, Perrysburg, Ohio, American
MICHAEL PESCATORE, businessman, 33, Solon, Ohio, American
SARAH SUSANNAH BUCHANAN PHILIPPS, student, 20, Newtonville, Massachusetts, American
FREDERICK SANDFORD PHILLIPS, student, 27, Little Rock, Arkansas, American
JAMES ANDREW CAMPBELL PITT, student, 24, South Hadley, Massachusetts, American
DAVID PLATT, architect, 33, Staten Island, New York, American
WALTER LEONARD PORTER, musician, 35, Brooklyn, New York, American
PAMELA LYNN POSEN, student, 20, Harrison, New York, American
WILLIAM PUGH, businessman, 56, Margate, New Jersey, American
ESTRELLA CRISOSTOMO QUIGUYAN, hotel cashier, 43, London, England, Filipino
RAJESH TARSIS PRISKEL RAMSES, 35, Leicester, England, Indian
ANMOL RATTAN, 2, Warren, Michigan, American
GARIMA RATTAN, computer programmer, 29, Warren, Michigan, American
SURUCHI RATTAN, 3, Warren, Michigan, American
ANITA LYNN REEVES, 24, Laurel, Maryland, American
MARK ALAN REIN, businessman, 44, New York, New York, American
DIANE MARIE RENCEVICZ, student, 21, Burlington, New Jersey, American
LOUISE ANN ROGERS, student, 20, Olney, Maryland, American
EDINA ROLLER, 5, Hungary, Hungarian
JANOS GABOR ROLLER, 29, Hungary, Hungarian
ZSUZSANA ROLLER, 27, Hungary, Hungarian
HANNE MARIA ROOT, management consultant, 26, Toronto, Canada, Canadian
SAUL MARK ROSEN, businessman, 35, Morris Plains, New Jersey, American
ANDREA VICTORIA ROSENTHAL, student, 22, New York, New York, American
DANIEL PETER ROSENTHAL, student, 20, Staten Island, New York, American
ARNAUD DAVID RUBIN, 28, Waterloo, Belgium, Belgian
ELYSE JEANNE SARACENI, student, 20, East London, England, American

SCOTT CHRISTOPHER SAUNDERS, student, 21, Macungie, Pennsylvania, American

THERESA ELIZABETH JANE SAUNDERS, marketing, 28, Sunbury-on-Thames, England, British

JOHANNES OTTO SCHAUBLE, 41, West Germany, West German

ROBERT THOMAS SCHLAGETER, student, 20, Warwick, Rhode Island, American

THOMAS BRITTON SCHULTZ, student, 20, Ridgefield, Connecticut, American

SALLY ELIZABETH SCOTT, chef, 22, Huntington, New York, British

AMY ELIZABETH SHAPIRO, student, 21, Stamford, Connecticut, American

MRIDULA SHASTRI, 24, Oxford, England, Indian

JOAN SHEANSHANG, 46, New York, New York, American

IRVING STANLEY SIGAL, research biologist, 35, Pennington, New Jersey, American

MARTIN BERNARD CARRUTHERS SIMPSON, financier, 52, Brooklyn, New York, American

CYNTHIA JOAN SMITH, student, 21, Milton, Massachusetts, American

INGRID ANITA SMITH, chiropodist, 31, Berkshire, England, British

JAMES ALVIN SMITH, 55, New York, New York, American

MARY EDNA SMITH, army sergeant, 34, Kalamazoo, Michigan, American

GERALDINE ANNE STEVENSON, 37, Surrey, England, British

HANNAH LOUISE STEVENSON, 10, Surrey, England, British

JOHN CHARLES STEVENSON, 38, Surrey, England, British

RACHAEL STEVENSON, 8, Surrey, England, British

CHARLOTTE ANN STINNETT, 36, Duncanville, Texas, American

MICHAEL GARY STINNETT, army specialist, 26, Duncanville, Texas, American

STACEY LEANNE STINNETT, 9, Duncanville, Texas, American

JAMES RALPH STOW, 49, New York, New York, American

ELIA G. STRATIS, accountant, 43, Montvale, New Jersey, American

ANTHONY SELWYN SWAN, 29, Brooklyn, New York, Trinidadian

FLORA MARGARET SWIRE, medical student and researcher, 24, London, England, British

MARC ALEX TAGER, 22, London, England, British

HIDEKAZU TANAKA, 26, London, England, Japanese

ANDREW ALEXANDER TERAN, student, 20, New Haven, Connecticut, Bolivian

ARVA ANTHONY THOMAS, student, 17, Detroit, Michigan, American

JONATHAN RYAN THOMAS, 2 months, Southfield, Michigan, American

LAWANDA THOMAS, air force sergeant, 21, Southfield, Michigan, American

MARK LAWRENCE TOBIN, student, 21, North Hempstead, New York, American

DAVID WILLIAM TRIMMER-SMITH, publishing executive, 51, New York, New York, American

ALEXIA KATHRYN TSAIRIS, student, 20, Franklin Lakes, New Jersey, American

BARRY JOSEPH VALENTINO, exhibit designer, 28, San Francisco, California, American

TOMÁS FLORO VAN TIENHOVEN, 45, Buenos Aires, Argentina, Argentinean

ASAAD EIDI VEJDANY, 46, South Great Neck, New York, American

NICHOLAS ANDREAS VRENIOS, student, 20, Washington, D.C., American

PETER VULCU, stockbroker and student, 21, Alliance, Ohio, American

JANINA JOZEFA WAIDO, 61, Chicago, Illinois, American

THOMAS EDWIN WALKER, electronics specialist, 47, Quincy, Massachusetts, American

KESHA WEEDON, student, 20, Bronx, New York, American

JEROME LEE WESTON, engineer, 45, Baldwin, New York, American

JONATHAN WHITE, accountant, 33, North Hollywood, California, American

BONNIE LEIGH WILLIAMS, 21, Crown Point, New York, American

ERIC JON WILLIAMS, army sergeant, 24, Crown Point, New York, American

GEORGE WATTERSON WILLIAMS, army first lieutenant, 24, Joppa, Maryland, American

BRITTANY LEIGH WILLIAMS, 2 months, Crown Point, New York, American

STEPHANIE LEIGH WILLIAMS, 1, Crown Point, New York, American

MIRIAM LUBY WOLFE, student, 20, Severna Park, Maryland, American

CHELSEA MARIE WOODS, 10 months, Willingboro, New Jersey, American

DEDERA LYNN WOODS, air force sergeant, 27, Willingboro, New Jersey, American

JOE NATHAN WOODS, 28, Willingboro, New Jersey, American

JOE NATHAN WOODS, JR., 2, Willingboro, New Jersey, American

ANDREW CHRISTOPHER GILLIES WRIGHT, site agent, 24, Surrey, England, British

MARK JAMES ZWYNENBURG, investment banker, 29, West Nyack, New York, American

Lockerbie Residents

JOANNE FLANNIGAN, 10, 16 Sherwood Crescent

KATHLEEN MARY FLANNIGAN, 41, 16 Sherwood Crescent

THOMAS BROWN FLANNIGAN, 44, 16 Sherwood Crescent

DORA HENRIETTA HENRY, 56, 13 Sherwood Crescent

MAURICE PETER HENRY, 63, 13 Sherwood Crescent

MARY LANCASTER, 81, 11 Sherwood Crescent

JEAN AITKEN MURRAY, 82, 14 Sherwood Crescent

JACK SOMERVILLE, 40, 15 Sherwood Crescent

LYNSEY A. SOMERVILLE, 10, 15 Sherwood Crescent
PAUL SOMERVILLE, 12, 15 Sherwood Crescent
ROSALIND SOMERVILLE, 40, 15 Sherwood Crescent

Sources: Lockerbie police, Georgia Nucci of Victims of Pan Am Flight 103, and
    U.S. Justice Department

AVIATION BOMBINGS

The following is a chronology of bomb attacks against aircraft listed by date, airline and aircraft type, location of incident, totals of people killed and injured. It also includes a brief description of each attack:

October 31, 1933
United Airlines, Boeing Monoplane
Palm Springs, California
7 killed
A bomb destroyed the plane.

May 7, 1949
Philippine Airlines, DC-3
Philippines
13 killed
A man and woman hired two ex-convicts who placed a time bomb on board the plane, hoping to kill the man's wife. The plane crashed into the ocean.

September 9, 1949
Canadian Pacific Airlines, DC-3
Near Sault au Cochons, Quebec, Canada
23 killed
Someone placed a bomb in the number one forward baggage compartment. The plane exploded forty miles from Quebec City and crashed.

April 13, 1950
British European Airways
English Channel
1 injured
A bomb, hidden in a paper towel receptacle in the lavatory, exploded in flight. The plane landed.

September 24, 1952
Mexicana Airlines, DC-3
Near Mexico City
2 injured
A suitcase bomb in the forward baggage compartment exploded fifteen minutes after takeoff. The plane landed.

April 11, 1955
Air India, L-Constellation
South China Sea near Great Natuna Island
16 killed
A time bomb placed in the wheel well of the starboard wing root exploded, causing the plane to catch fire and crash.

November 1, 1955
United Airlines, DC-6
Longmont, Colorado
44 killed
A dynamite bomb exploded in the number four baggage compartment, destroying the plane and killing everyone on board.

March 4, 1956
Skyways Ltd.
Nicosia, Cyprus
No injuries
The plane was damaged while on the ground by an explosion in the forward freight compartment.

July 25, 1957
Western Airlines, CV-240
Daggett, California
1 killed
A passenger detonated dynamite while in the lavatory, perforating the skin of the fuselage. The plane landed.

December 19, 1957
Air France
Over central France
No injuries
A bomb exploded in the lavatory. The plane landed.

September 8, 1959
Mexicana Airlines, DC-3
Over central Mexico
1 killed, 8 injured
A passenger detonated a bomb that punched a hole in the fuselage at eleven thousand feet. The plane landed.

January 6, 1960
National Airlines, DC-6
North Carolina
34 killed
A bomb concealed beneath a passenger seat exploded at eighteen thousand feet. The pilot flew for sixteen miles before the plane broke apart.

April 28, 1960
Linaea Aeropostal Venezolana, DC-3
Near Calabozo, Venezuela
13 killed
An explosive device in the cockpit destroyed the aircraft in flight.

May 22, 1962
Continental Airlines, Boeing 707
Over Unionville, Missouri
45 killed
A dynamite bomb, hidden in a waste receptable in the right rear lavatory, exploded at thirty-nine thousand feet, killing everyone on board.

December 8, 1964
Aerolinaa Abaroa, DC-3
Near Milluni, Bolivia
15 killed
A dynamite bomb, apparently brought aboard by a heavily insured passenger, exploded in flight, causing the plane to crash.

July 8, 1965
Canadian Pacific Airlines, DC-6
British Columbia, Canada

52 killed
An explosive device inside the fuselage detonated, breaking off the tail section and causing the plane to crash.

November 22, 1966
Aden Airways, DC-3
150 miles east of Aden, South Yemen
8 killed
A bomb concealed in carry-on baggage exploded on the port side of the cabin, causing the plane to disintegrate in flight.

May 29, 1967
Aerocondor (Colombia)
Between Barranquilla and Bogotá, Colombia
No injuries
A time bomb concealed in the rear of the fuselage exploded, perforating the fuselage. The plane landed.

June 30, 1967
Aden Airways (South Yemen)
Aden, South Yemen
No injuries
While the plane was still on the ground and empty, a time bomb made from plastic explosive blew up in the forward compartment.

October 12, 1967
British European Airways, Comet 4
Mediterranean Sea off Rhodes Island
66 killed
A bomb hidden in the tourist-class section exploded while the plane, traveling from London to Athens, was at twenty-nine thousand feet. The plane crashed into the ocean.

November 12, 1967
American Airlines, Boeing 727
Alamosa, Colorado
No injuries
A crude, homemade bomb exploded in the rear baggage compartment about an hour into the flight. Nearly two hours later the plane landed.

November 19, 1968
Continental Airlines, Boeing 727
Gunnison, Colorado

No injuries
An explosion in the lavatory started a fire. The plane landed.

March 11, 1969
Ethiopian Airlines, Boeing 707
Frankfurt, West Germany
Several injured
Two explosions rocked the passenger compartment while the plane was on the ground. Several members of the cleaning crew were injured.

August 5, 1969
Philippine Airlines, IIS-748
Zamboanga, Philippines
1 killed, 4 injured
A passenger apparently detonated a bomb in the lavatory while the plane was in flight. The plane landed.

August 29, 1969
Trans World Airlines
Damascus, Syria
Several injured
While the plane was on the ground, a hijacker detonated a grenade and an explosive device in the cockpit. Passengers were hurt exiting the plane.

December 2, 1969
Air Vietnam
Near Nha Trang, South Vietnam
32 killed, many injured
An explosion in the lavatory damaged the braking system in flight. When the plane landed, it went off the end of the runway and struck a school.

February 21, 1970
Swiss Air Transport Co., CV-990
Würenlingen, Switzerland
47 killed
An explosion ripped through the aft compartment shortly after takeoff. The plane crashed in a forest. The Popular Front for the Liberation of Palestine—General Command claimed initial responsibility, then disavowed it.

February 21, 1970
Austrian Airlines, Caravelle
Near Frankfurt, West Germany
No injuries

An altitude-sensitive bomb placed in a mailbag exploded in the freight hold, perforating the fuselage. The plane landed. Two members of the Popular Front for the Liberation of Palestine—General Command were arrested.

March 14, 1970
United Arab Airlines, Autonov 24
Near Alexandria, Egypt
2 injured
An explosive device hidden in the landing gear well detonated, damaging the aircraft and injuring two of the ten passengers. The aircraft landed.

April 21, 1970
Philippine Airlines, HS-748
Seventy-five miles north of Manila
36 killed
A bomb in the lavatory exploded at 10,500 feet, tearing off the tail. The plane crashed.

May 10, 1970
Iberian Air Lines, DC-9
Geneva, Switzerland
No injuries
A bomb exploded in the baggage compartment while the plane was on the ground.

June 2, 1970
Philippine Airlines
Near Roxas, Philippines
1 killed, 12 injured
A hand grenade under a seat exploded in flight, tearing a hole in the plane's skin. The plane landed.

September 7, 1970
Pan American World Airways
Cairo, Egypt
Several injured
Hijackers blew up the plane on the ground. Passengers were injured while making an emergency exit.

September 12, 1970
Trans World Airlines
Dawson Field, Jordan
No injuries
Hijackers blew up the plane on the ground.

September 12, 1970
Swissair
Dawson Field, Jordan
No injuries
Hijackers blew up the plane on the ground.

September 12, 1970
British Overseas Airways
Dawson Field, Jordan
No injuries
Hijackers blew up the plane on the ground.

August 24, 1971
Royal Jordanian Airlines, Boeing 707
Madrid, Spain
No injuries
While the plane was on the ground, an explosion in an aft lavatory ripped a hole through the fuselage. The apparent target was King Hussein's mother.

November 20, 1971
China Airlines, Caravelle
Over South China Sea en route from Taipei to Hong Kong
25 killed
A midair explosion caused the aircraft to crash into the ocean.

December 29, 1971
Private aircraft
Elkhart, Illinois
Casualties unknown
A bomb placed on a cabin seat destroyed the aircraft while it was in a hangar.

January 26, 1972
Jugoslovenski Aero-transport, DC-9
Over České Kamenice, Czechoslovakia
27 killed, 1 injured
A homemade bomb blew up in the forward luggage compartment at high altitude. The plane, traveling from Stockholm to Belgrade, crashed. Croatian exiles are suspected in the attack.

March 8, 1972
Trans World Airlines
Las Vegas, Nevada
No injuries

An explosive device was detonated in the cockpit while the plane was on the ground. The bombing apparently was linked to a two-million-dollar extortion plot.

May 25, 1972
Lan-Chile
Caribbean Sea near Cuba
No injuries
A homemade pipe bomb exploded in flight. The plane landed safely.

June 14, 1972
Japan Air Lines, DC-8
Near New Delhi, India
87 killed, 2 injured
The Tokyo to London plane crashed after a stopover in New Delhi. Airline officials consider sabotage a possible cause.

June 15, 1972
Cathay Pacific Airways, CV-880
Near Pleiku, South Vietnam
81 killed
A suitcase bomb hidden beneath a passenger seat exploded. The plane crashed.

August 16, 1972
El Al
Rome, Italy
No injuries
A bomb hidden in a record player and given to two unsuspecting British passengers partially exploded in the luggage compartment. The plane landed. The Popular Front for the Liberation of Palestine—General Command has been linked to this attack.

September 16, 1972
Air Manila
Near Roxas, Philippines
No injuries
A hand grenade hidden in the cargo compartment exploded at eleven thousand feet. The plane landed.

December 8, 1972
Ethiopian Airlines
Near Addis Ababa, Ethiopia
6 killed, 11 wounded

A hijacker detonated a hand grenade in mid-flight, during a gun battle between seven hijackers and security guards. The plane landed.

March 19, 1973
Air Vietnam
Ban Me Thuot, South Vietnam
59 killed
An explosion in the cargo area caused the plane to crash as it was about to land.

April 24, 1973
Aeroflot
Near Leningrad, USSR
2 killed
A hijacker detonated a grenade in flight. The plane landed.

June 3, 1973
Aeroflot, TU-144
Goussainville, France
14 killed
A bomb exploded in flight.

June 20, 1973
Japan Air Lines
Over Germany; on airfield at Benghazi, Libya
1 killed, 1 wounded
Hijackers accidentally set off an explosive device in flight. After the plane landed, the hijackers blew up the aircraft.

September 21, 1973
Private aircraft
Crestwood, Illinois
Casualties unknown
Someone put an explosive device in the exhaust manifold of a private plane and detonated it while the plane was on the ground.

December 17, 1973
Pan American World Airways
Rome, Italy
30 killed, many injured
Terrorists threw grenades into the cabin area and fired guns as the plane was being boarded. The plane caught on fire.

February 20, 1974
Air Vietnam
Hue, South Vietnam
3 killed
A hijacker detonated an explosive device after the plane landed. The blast killed the hijacker and two passengers.

March 22, 1974
Air Inter
Bastia, Corsica
No injuries
A bomb hidden in the forward landing gear exploded while the plane was on the ground.

August 22, 1974
Trans World Airlines, Boeing 707
Rome, Italy
No injuries
A suitcase bomb malfunctioned; instead of exploding, it started a fire in the aft baggage compartment. The fire occurred after the plane landed following a flight from Athens.

September 8, 1974
Trans World Airlines, Boeing 707
Ionian Sea near Greece
88 killed
A bomb exploded in the aft cargo compartment as the plane was traveling from Tel Aviv to Rome, via Athens. The plane crashed into the ocean. Some sources blame the Popular Front for the Liberation of Palestine—General Command for the bombing. Others blame the Arab Nationalist Youth Organization for the Liberation of Palestine, an organization sponsored by Libya and Abu Nidal.

September 15, 1974
Air Vietnam, Boeing 707
Phan Rang, South Vietnam, 150 miles northeast of Saigon
70 killed
A hijacker detonated two hand grenades in the cockpit as the plane was about to land. The plane crashed.

February 3, 1975
Pan American World Airways
60 miles west of Rangoon, Burma
1 injured

A passenger used gasoline and a butane refill canister to create an explosion in a lavatory. The plane landed.

June 3, 1975
Philippine Airlines, BAC-111
200 miles southwest of Manila, Philippines
1 killed, 45 injured
A bomb placed in a rear lavatory exploded in flight. The plane landed.

July 5, 1975
Pakistan Airlines
Rawalpindi, Pakistan
No injuries
A bomb hidden under a passenger seat exploded while the plane was on the ground.

December 19, 1975
Private aircraft
Near Angels Camp, California
No injuries
Someone detonated blasting caps near the fuel tank of a plane while it was on the ground.

January 1, 1976
Middle East Airlines
Saudi Arabian desert between Saudi Arabia and Kuwait
82 killed
An explosive device in the forward baggage compartment detonated in flight. The plane crashed in the desert.

May 21, 1976
Philippine Airlines
Zamboanga, Philippines
13 killed, 14 injured
Hijackers exploded grenades while the plane was on the ground.

July 2, 1976
Eastern Airlines
Boston, Massachusetts
1 injured
An explosive device hidden between the strut and the landing gear was detonated while the plane was on the ground.

September 7, 1976
Air France
Ajaccio, Corsica
No injuries
Seven men used dynamite to destroy the plane on the ground.

October 6, 1976
Cubana Airlines, DC-8
Barbados, West Indies
73 killed
An in-flight explosion caused the plane to crash about five minutes after takeoff.
Two exiled Cubans living in Venezuela were blamed.

December 15, 1976
Egyptian Airlines
Baghdad, Iraq
40 killed, many wounded (estimate reports varied widely)
A suitcase bomb exploded as the plane was landing.

December 24, 1976
Egyptian Airlines, Boeing 707
North of Bangkok, Thailand
72 killed
A plane, already in flames, crashed into a factory, killing all forty-two people on board and thirty people working the factory night shift. Bombing is a possible cause.

January 13, 1977
Aeroflot Airlines, TU-104
Alma-Ata, USSR
90 killed
A bomb exploded on the plane in flight.

May 1, 1977
Private aircraft
Salinas, California
No injuries
Five helicopters were damaged by explosive devices that detonated while the helicopters were on the ground.

December 4, 1977
Malaysian Airlines, Boeing 737
Off the coast of Malaysia

100 killed
Hijackers shot and killed the pilots, then apparently used hand grenades to blow up the plane in flight.

May 24, 1978
Private aircraft
Nairobi, Kenya
4 killed
The plane either exploded in flight near Nairobi or blew up on the ground at Entebbe Airport. There are conflicting accounts.

August 18, 1978
Philippine Airlines
Over the Philippines
1 killed, 3 injured
A bomb exploded in the rear lavatory, perforating the fuselage.

September 7, 1978
Air Ceylon
Colombo, Sri Lanka
No injuries
An explosion destroyed the empty plane on the ground.

April 26, 1979
Indian Airlines
Over Madras, India
8 injured
A bomb exploded in the forward rest room during the flight, punching a hole in the fuselage.

November 15, 1979
American Airlines, Boeing 727
En route from Chicago to Washington, D.C.
12 injured
A mail bomb activated by an altimeter exploded in the cargo section, causing only slight damage. Some passengers required treatment for smoke inhalation.

September 9, 1980
United Airlines
Sacramento, California
2 injured
A bomb exploded in the cargo hold while passengers were disembarking the plane.

July 1, 1981
Eastern Airlines
Guatemala City, Guatemala
1 killed
A suitcase bomb exploded as it was being loaded onto a flight from Guatemala City to Miami. A baggage handler was killed.

August 31, 1981
Middle East Airlines
Beirut, Lebanon
No injuries
A dynamite bomb exploded inside an empty plane that was on the ground after completing a flight from Libya.

October 13, 1981
Air Malta
Cairo, Egypt
2 killed, 8 injured
Two bombs exploded fifteen minutes apart as luggage was being taken off a plane on the ground. The plane's baggage compartment was damaged.

December 12, 1981
Aeronica, Boeing 727
Mexico City, Mexico
5 injured
A bomb exploded shortly before takeoff, tearing a hole in the rear of the aircraft. The flight was nearly an hour behind schedule. Had it been on time, more than a hundred people may have died.

July 25, 1982
CAAC (China)
En route from Xian and Shanghai, China
No injuries
Hijackers detonated an explosive device inside the cabin, blowing a hole in the fuselage. The aircraft landed.

August 11, 1982
Pan American World Airways, Boeing 747
En route from Tokyo, Japan, to Honolulu, Hawaii
1 killed, 15 injured
A bomb hidden beneath a seat cushion exploded, tearing a hole in the floor. The plane, which carried 285 people, landed.

August 19, 1983
Syrian Airlines, Boeing 727
Rome, Italy
No injuries
An incendiary device hidden beneath a cabin seat started a fire shortly before takeoff.

September 23, 1983
Gulf Air, Boeing 737
Over United Arab Emirates
112 killed
A bomb hidden in the baggage compartment destroyed the plane, which was traveling from Pakistan to Abu Dhabi. The plane crashed about thirty miles from its destination.

January 18, 1984
Air France, Boeing 747
En route from Karachi, Pakistan, to Paris
No injuries
A bomb concealed in the cargo hold exploded in flight, blowing a hole in the fuselage. The plane, which carried 261 passengers, landed safely. The bomb had been placed in the bag of a UNESCO official.

March 10, 1984
Union des Transports Aériens (UTA), DC-8
N'Djamena, Chad
24 injured
A bomb exploded in the central baggage compartment while the plane was on the ground. If the explosion had occurred in flight, about a hundred people would have died.

July 31, 1984
Air France
Teheran, Iran
No injuries
Hijackers blew up the cockpit while the plane was on the ground.

August 2, 1984
Airline unknown
Madras, India

About 40 killed, 19 injured
A suitcase bomb blew up at Madras International Airport. The bag belonged to a passenger who bought a ticket from Madras to Sri Lanka but never boarded the plane.

January 23, 1985
Lloyd Aereo Boliviano, Boeing 727
En route from La Paz, Bolivia, to Miami
1 killed
A passenger carrying dynamite in his briefcase died in a forward lavatory when the explosive detonated. The plane landed in Santa Cruz, Bolivia.

March 3, 1985
Private aircraft
Bieber, California
No injuries
A bomb destroyed the twin-engine aircraft on the ground.

March 9, 1985
Royal Jordanian Airlines, Tristar airliner
Dubai, United Arab Emirates
No injuries
An eighteen-year-old Arab on a suicide mission placed a suitcase bomb on the plane, but the explosion occurred after the plane landed as the bags were being unloaded from the baggage compartment. The main portion of the bomb failed to detonate.

June 11, 1985
Royal Jordanian Airlines
Beirut, Lebanon
No injuries
Hijackers blew up the cockpit after the plane had landed.

June 23, 1985
Air India, Boeing 747
Off the coast of Ireland
329 killed
A bomb in the forward cargo hold destroyed the aircraft, which was traveling from Montreal to London. The plane crashed into the ocean. Less than an hour earlier a suitcase bomb killed two airport workers in Tokyo. The Tokyo bomb, probably concealed within a Sanyo Model FMT 611K radio, was headed for an Air India flight from Tokyo to Bombay, India. Investigators linked Sikh extremists to both attacks.

July 1, 1985
Alitalia
Rome, Italy
15 injured
A suitcase bomb exploded in the terminal of an airport in Rome, injuring fifteen baggage handlers. The suitcase was about to be loaded onto a flight to New Delhi.

October 30, 1985
American Airlines, Boeing 727
Dallas/Fort Worth Airport, Texas
No injuries
A bomb concealed in a tote bag that had been loaded into the forward baggage compartment exploded after the plane landed.

November 23, 1985
Egyptair
Valletta, Malta
60 killed, 35 injured
Hijackers detonated several hand grenades in the cabin during a battle on the ground with Egyptian troops.

December 12, 1985
Arrow Air (charter flight), DC-8
Gander, Newfoundland
256 killed
The plane, which carried U.S. troops from Egypt to the United States via Cologne, West Germany, and Gander, crashed after takeoff from Gander. A majority of the Canadian panel that probed the incident concluded the cause was ice on the wings, but a minority report found strong evidence of a bomb.

April 2, 1986
Trans World Airlines, Boeing 727
Near Athens, Greece
4 killed, 9 injured
A bomb exploded in the cabin as the plane was preparing to land at Athens. Four passengers, including an infant, were sucked out of the plane and fell to their deaths. The plane landed. A woman who occupied a window seat on an earlier leg of the flight is suspected of having planted the bomb. The American plastic explosive C-4 is believed to have been used in the attack.

May 3, 1986
Air Lanka, L-1011
Colombo, Sri Lanka

16 killed, 41 injured
A bomb exploded in the cargo hold as the plane, which was fifteen minutes behind schedule, was preparing for departure. The flight carried 126 people.

June 26, 1986
El Al
Madrid, Spain
12 injured
A suitcase bomb destined for an El Al flight exploded at Barajas Airport. The man who was unwittingly carrying the bomb thought he was smuggling drugs to Israel.

October 26, 1986
Thai Airways, A-300
En route from Bangkok, Thailand, to Manila, Philippines
62 injured
A bomb in a rear lavatory exploded. The plane landed.

December 25, 1986
Iraqi Air, Boeing 737
Saudi Arabia
65 killed
A grenade exploded in flight during a hijacking.

January 13, 1987
Private aircraft, Beechcraft
Osceola, Arkansas
No injuries
While the plane was on the ground, an explosion in the cabin destroyed the aircraft.

February 12, 1987
Private aircraft, Beechcraft
Osceola, Arkansas
No injuries
While the plane was on the ground, an explosion in the cabin destroyed the aircraft.

November 29, 1987
Korean Air Lines, Boeing 707
Off the coast of Burma
115 killed
A time bomb, made from plastic and liquid explosives and hidden in an overhead luggage bin, destroyed the aircraft in midair as it traveled from Abu Dhabi, United

Arab Emirates, to Bangkok, Thailand, en route to Seoul, South Korea. Two North Korean agents placed the device on board before leaving the plane during a stopover.

March 1, 1988
BOP Air (South Africa)
En route to Johannesburg
17 killed
A bomb in the cabin area detonated in flight, destroying the aircraft.

August 18, 1988
Pakistani military plane, C-180 Hercules
Over Pakistan
30 killed
A midair explosion destroyed a plane carrying Pakistan's president, the U.S. ambassador to Pakistan, and several key military figures. Sabotage remains a possible cause.

December 21, 1988
Pan American World Airways, Boeing 747
Lockerbie, Scotland
270 killed
A suitcase bomb exploded in the forward baggage compartment, destroying the plane at high altitude.

September 19, 1989
Union des Transports Aériens, DC-10
Niger
171 killed
A bomb made from plastic explosive destroyed the flight at high altitude.

November 27, 1989
Avianca Airlines, Boeing 727
Near Bogotá, Colombia
107 killed
A bomb hidden beneath a cabin seat exploded a few minutes after takeoff, destroying the plane.

Several sources were used to compile this list of aviation bombings.

The document that provided the most comprehensive listing was the May 15, 1990, Report to the President by the President's Commission on Aviation Security and Terrorism.

Other useful sources included an unpublished Rand Corporation document,

"Attacks Against Aircraft, Including Attempted Sabotage, 1968–1988,"; an article in the *American Journal of Forensic Medicine and Pathology,* "The Lockerbie Disaster and Other Aircraft Breakups in Midair," by William G. Eckert, M.D., vol. 11, no. 2 (1990); a transcript of the Hearing Before the Committee of Foreign Affairs, House of Representatives, 101st Congress, First Session, February 9, 1989; the 1976 book *Destination Disaster, from the Tri-Motor to the DC-10: The Risk of Flying,* by Paul Eddy, Elaine Potter, and Bruce Page (New York: Quadrangle/New York Times Book Co.); a statement submitted for the record to the President's Commission on Aviation Security and Terrorism on November 17, 1989, by Billie H. Vincent, former head of the Federal Aviation Administration's Office of Civil Aviation Security; and an unpublished list compiled by Bernard Adamzcewski, a retired terrorism authority living in London.

Supplemental information from newspaper accounts, government investigative reports, and interviews has been included.

SOURCES

The authors began their research within minutes of the bombing of Pan Am Flight 103 as reporters for the *Post-Standard* in Syracuse, New York. Their newspaper devoted extensive resources to its coverage because of the extraordinary impact the disaster had on the central New York region, where forty of the victims lived or attended college. The authors spent more than two years conducting hundreds of interviews with sources from the United States, Scotland, England, Germany, Sweden, Malta, Israel, Iran, India, and Canada. They also reviewed more than thirty thousand pages of documents related to the bombing. Such primary sources account for the bulk of the material in this book. Background information drawn from secondary sources or sections that otherwise warrant specific attribution or explanation are outlined below:

Information concerning flaws in Pam Am Flight 103's departure security was based on the working papers of the President's Commission on Aviation Security and Terrorism. Information on the travels of Khalid Jaafar in Chapter 1 came from interviews conducted by reporter Stephanie Gibbs of the *Post-Standard* and the May 1989 issue of the German publication *Quick*. Information on Jaafar's being detained by customs was reported in the *Chicago Tribune* on May 5, 1989. The authors' interviews with Eleanor Hudson and Sudhakar Dixit were supplemented with information from interviews conducted by Stephanie Gibbs. The description of Jaswant Basuta's experiences at Heathrow came from the authors' interviews and from the reports of FAA investigators' interviews with Pan American and Alert Management Systems, Inc. employees.

In Chapter 2, information on the activity on board the USS *Vincennes* was taken from the July 28, 1988, report *Formal Investigation into the Circumstances Surrounding the Downing of a Commercial Airliner by the USS Vincennes (CG 49) on 3 July 1988,* prepared by the U.S. Navy's Office of the Judge Advocate General, and from the transcript of hearings, *Iran Air Flight 655 Compensation,* conducted August 3 and 4, September 9, and October 6, 1988, by the Defense Policy Panel of the House Committee on the Armed Services. Accounts of the funerals of the Iran

223

Air Flight 655 victims came from the July 8, 1988, edition of the *New York Times*. July 1988 statements by Iranian and U.S. government leaders also came from the *New York Times*. Information regarding fund transfers between Iran and the PFLP—GC was reported by the Public Broadcasting Service's documentary program "Frontline." Some background information on Dalkamouni and Khreesat came from the BBC's documentary program "Panorama." The *Sunday Times* of London reported on September 30, 1990, that Marwan Khreesat had arrived in Germany in October 1988 with two copper-colored Samsonite suitcases. The newspaper also reported other information about Khreesat's and Dalkamouni's activities in West Germany, as well as the comments by Judge Christian Rinne. Some details of the German police raids against the PFLP—GC came from the U.S. State Department, "Panorama," and German media reports, including stories by *Die Welt* and *Frankfurter Allgemeine Zeitung* on October 29, 1988, *Stern* in May 1989, and *Stuttgarter Nachrichten*, December 24, 1988.

Details on the construction of the bomb seized during the October 1988 raids in West Germany came from a knowledgeable source in Europe who was given the information by German forensic authorities who examined the device. The quote about the bomb from the BKA report was taken from the *Sunday Times* of London, September 30, 1990. Some information regarding the Semtex factory came from a February 14, 1990, report by the British *Daily Telegraph* and a British television report broadcast on June 28, 1990, by the Thames Television program "This Week."

In Chapter 3 information on Charles McKee came from interviews the authors conducted with his mother, Beulah McKee; interviews conducted by Stephanie Gibbs; and sixty-one pages of McKee's army personnel file, released by the army under the Freedom of Information Act.

The comments of former Alert president Fred Ford in Chapter 4 were made on the ABC news magazine program "Prime Time Live." Some details on the radio-cassette player warnings came from the March 29, 1989, edition of *Der Spiegel*; the November 2, 1989, edition of the *Times* of London; and the December 22, 1989, edition of *Die Zeit*. Information on the distribution at the U.S. Embassy in Moscow of the Helsinki threat warning came from notes of interviews conducted by Susan Malone, an investigator with the President's Commission on Aviation Security and Terrorism. Pan Am's procedures in screening passengers following the Helsinki warning were outlined in aviation security hearings before the U.S. Senate Committee on Appropriations on March 14, 1989. Details on Ulrich Weber's background were first reported by *USA Today*. Details on the travels of Karen Noonan and Patricia Coyle came from interviews conducted by staff investigators of the president's commission.

Details on the preflight baggage handling procedures outlined in Chapter 5, and the descriptions of activities at Frankfurt and Heathrow airports on December 21, 1988, came from interviews by Federal Aviation Administration investigators with Pan Am and Alert employees. Details on the breakup of the Boeing 747 came from a February 1990 report by the British Department of Transport's Air Accidents Investigation Branch. Not all aerospace medicine experts are in agreement on how long the passengers lived after disintegration of the aircraft. The authors consulted Dr. Anthony Busuttil, who headed the team of physicians conducting autopsies at Lockerbie; Dr. Stanley Mohler, director of aerospace medicine at Wright State University in Dayton, Ohio; Dr. William G. Eckert of Wichita, Kansas, who reported on the disaster in the *American Journal of Forensic Medicine and Pathology*; and a fourth physician specializing in aerospace medicine who asked that his name not be used.

The account of the crash in Lockerbie was compiled from extensive interviews of eyewitnesses conducted during two visits in Lockerbie, subsequent telephone interviews, and testimony at the Fatal Accident Inquiry conducted in Dumfries, Scotland. Supplemental reporting was provided by Maurice Smith, of the British Broadcasting Corporation, and Frank Ryan, a Scottish free-lance journalist who has covered extensively the disaster and its aftermath. Details of the crash from the perspective of the train station were taken from a first-person account published by reporter Jane Anderson in the *Annandale Herald*. Details of the emergency response came from a November 1989 report on the disaster prepared by the Dumfries and Galloway Regional Council. Other details on the fire-fighting effort were published by the Dumfries and Galloway firemaster, J. Barry Stiff, in the May 1989 edition of *Fire Chief* magazine.

The information on the activities of Federal Aviation Administration employees Bill Bumpus and Bob Mosca in Chapter 7 came from a Department of Transportation publication. The activity of Inspector George Stobbs prior to the disaster was reported by Steven Billmyer in the June 25, 1989, edition of the *Syracuse Herald-American*. The conversation between Oliver Koch and Ulrich Weber was outlined in a court document related to a civil suit brought against Pan Am by relatives of the victims. Information on the ownership of suitcases comes from testimony by Detective Constable Derek Henderson of the Lothian and Borders Police to the Fatal Accident Inquiry in Scotland, November 12, 1990. The angry reaction customs official William von Raab had to not knowing about the Helsinki threat was drawn from information in the files of the president's commission. Details about police procedures used to determine the model of radio-cassette player and the type of explosive, as well as some other information about the work of the forensic team, came from the December 17, 1989, and September 30, 1990, editions of the *Sunday Times* of London.

In Chapter 8 the information about the two canceled meetings between investigators and Jordanian government officials comes from the *Sunday Times* of London, September 30, 1990. A U.S. government official said agents of the United States interviewed Marwan Khreesat in Jordan. The comment from Hashem Abassi was aired on "Panorama." Some details involving the German handling of bombs found in April 1989, as well as the comment from Helmut Bauer, came from the May 8, 1989, edition of *Der Spiegel*. The *Sunday Times* of London, on

December 17, 1989, and September 30, 1990, reported details on the late arrival of the baggage loading list at Lockerbie, as well as some of the information on both the unaccompanied Air Malta bag and the clothing traced to Malta. Information regarding Abu Talb was taken from Swedish police reports. The source for the Israeli counterterrorism official's discrediting of Juval Aviv is investigative notes of the president's commission.

The observations of Edward Smith on the divisions among the relatives in Chapter 9 were reported in December 1989 by Stephanie Gibbs in the *Post-Standard*. The information on "Ed's Party" was reported by Frank Ryan and supplemented by a report that appeared in the *Washington Post*. Information regarding the background of Representative James A. Traficant, Jr., was reported by the Knight-Ridder news service on November 4, 1989. The Germans' threat to file kidnapping charges following the attempt to deliver the two Pan Am baggage handlers to Scotland Yard was revealed in a telegram from the Bonn embassy to the State Department in Washington. Roland O'Neill's experience in London was described by his attorney, Mary Gräfin Praschma.

The account in Chapter 10 of Marion Alderman's opening her home to foreign exchange students was reported by Sean Kirst in the *Post-Standard* on April 30, 1990. The details of her wedding were reported by Frank Ryan in Scotland and by Dan McGuire in the *Syracuse Herald-American* on October 7, 1990. Details on the allegations against the Libyans came from the indictment filed in the United States District Court for the District of Columbia on November 13, 1991. Details on the action of the Libyan agents were first published in the October 4, 1990, issue of *L'Express*. Other details were drawn from reports in the *New York Times*, by George Lardner, Jr., in the *Washington Post*, by Robin Wright and Ronald J. Ostrow in the *Los Angeles Times*, and by B. J. Cutler of the Scripps Howard news service. Information on the background of DEA informant Lester Coleman III comes from interviews by the authors, and from federal court files. The information about Mohammed Abu Talb's connections to Libya were reported by Jan-Olof Bengtsson in the Swedish newspaper *iDAG* on October 12, 1990. Bonnie O'Connor's comment about the U.S. government's exoneration of Syria appeared in *Newsday* on November 15, 1991.

INDEX